the
seamy
side
of
democracy

the seamy side of democracy

☆

repression in America

Second Edition

Alan Wolfe

Longman

New York and London

THE SEAMY SIDE OF DEMOCRACY
Repression in America

*Longman Inc., New York
Associated companies, branches, and representatives
throughout the world.*

*Developmental Editor: Edward Artinian
Editorial and Design Supervisor: Linda Salmonson
Interior Design: Angela Foote
Cover Design: Lawrence Ratzkin
Manufacturing and Production Supervisor: Louis Gaber
Composition: American Book–Stratford Press, Inc.
Printing and Binding: Fairfield Graphics*

Library of Congress Cataloging in Publication Data

Wolfe, Alan, 1942–
    The seamy side of democracy.

    Includes bibliographical references and index.
    1. Civil rights—United States. 2. Violence—
United States. I. Title.
JC599.U5W64 1978   301.5'92   78–9410
ISBN 0–582–28052–4

Manufactured in the United States of America

To the memories of
Brenda and Bonnie Wolfe.

preface to the
second edition

The Seamy Side of Democracy was written in what sometimes seems a more innocent era—before Watergate, before the Church Committee investigation of domestic political intelligence, before the publicity about the illegal activities of the FBI—in the days when it was shocking to believe that our government did not always act fairly. Now the tide has swung the other way: by the spring of 1975, 68 percent of the American people expressed the belief that their government regularly lies to them.[1] Today's Americans apparently are unwilling to accept a statement as true merely because their political leaders pronounce it so.

One obvious cause of this loss of innocence is the vast amount that has been learned about the illegal activities of government. Statistics, like official statements from presidents, carry with them a built-in distrust;

nonetheless, the facts revealed in the past few years about domestic spying and other nefarious activities are a bit overwhelming. Consider these agencies of government in the light of what we now know about them:

The FBI. At one time the Federal Bureau of Investigation had as "clean" an image as any organ of state can ever expect to have. G-Men were "on our side"; they swept up criminals and communists and kept the unsightly garbage of society out of our sight.[2] Then came the Nixon Administration and Watergate, during the course of which L. Patrick Gray, acting director of the FBI, admitted that he had personally destroyed evidence. A stunned silence echoed throughout the land. Richard Nixon, it appeared, was using the FBI for his own purposes. Defending himself, Nixon made the outlandish claim that he was doing nothing new. The official media scoffed. But Nixon, for once, was telling the truth. Subsequent documentation revealed that every single president since Franklin Roosevelt was not above using the FBI for political purposes.[3]

The Nixon men had commissioned William Sullivan, once the deputy director of the bureau, to write a memo on the domestic political uses of the FBI. Sullivan concluded that the worst offenders were FDR and LBJ.[4] Roosevelt had turned over to J. Edgar Hoover the names of people who had opposed his policies asking that they be investigated. Johnson had asked the FBI for "dirt" about his political opponents, including senators in his own party. Showing total disregard for the sanctity of the nominating process, Johnson also had ordered the FBI to keep key members of the 1964 Democratic convention under surveillance, in order to ensure the smoothness of his coronation. He also had FBI men follow and report on possible political opponents during the 1968 election. But if Roosevelt and Johnson were the worst offenders, others were not blameless. Truman regularly received confidential memos from Hoover, as did Eisenhower. John F. Kennedy ordered wiretaps and bugs against political opponents, including staff members of Congress. Directly anticipating a page from Nixon's book, Kennedy also ordered the phones of newspaper reporters tapped in order to discover the source of "leaks" he did not like.

Revelations of this sort did not help the image of the FBI, even though much of the early information derogatory to the bureau was rumor. But, on July 14, 1975, Clarence Kelley, the FBI director, held a press conference in which it was officially announced that the FBI had broken the law repeatedly.[5] Yes, Kelley admitted, the FBI had broken into and entered offices and homes in search of information. But, like a reformed drinker, he also proudly announced that this practice had stopped by 1966. The public seemed relieved; but addictive habits are not so easily broken. When John F. Malone, head of the New York office of the FBI, retired, his files indicated that breaking and entering had continued after 1966.[6] On July 7, 1976, ten years later, FBI agent Timothy Redfearn entered the headquarters of the Denver branch of the Socialist Worker's party.[7] The FBI was lying again.

What is the total extent of the illegal actions of the FBI? We do not know. A raid on the Media, Pennsylvania, headquarters of the bureau turned up statistics that indicated somewhat the FBI proclivity toward illegal acts.[8] New York City figures showed that the local office of the Socialist Worker's party had been broken into 92 times between 1960 and 1966 and that over 10,000 documents had been photographed.[9] Testifying before the Church Committee investigation into political espionage, Attorney General Levi in November 1975 offered some figures.[10] He said that since 1966, the year when illegal acts were supposed to have stopped, hidden microphones and wiretaps had been planted by the bureau as follows:

	Micro-phones	Wiretaps		Micro-phones	Wiretaps
1966	10	174	1971	16	101
1967	0	113	1972	32	108
1968	9	82	1973	40	123
1969	14	123	1974	42	190
1970	19	102	1975	24	121

In addition, Levi offered some information about the total number of micophones installed and wiretaps placed since the days of the New Deal:

Administration	Microphones Installed	Wiretaps Placed
Roosevelt	510	1,369
Truman	692	2,984
Eisenhower	616	1,574
Kennedy	268	582
Johnson	192	862
Nixon	163	747
Ford	24	121

"Dirty tricks" played by the Federal Bureau of Investigation have been an everyday aspect of political life for over thirty years.

The CIA. Unlike the FBI, the purpose of the Central Intelligence Agency was to carry out illegal actions, or so many Americans felt. There is no legal basis to this sensibility. Illegal acts by the CIA have been defended on thin grounds; the National Security Act of 1947, which created the agency, does not explicitly give it the right to carry out illegal actions. Nonetheless, few Americans were surprised to learn that in one country or another the CIA had been plotting in ways that violated any sense of fair play. As the Hoover Commission stated early on:

> If the U.S. is to survive, longstanding American concepts of "fair play" must be reconsidered. We must develop effective espionage and counterespionage services and must learn to subvert, sabotage, and destroy our enemies by more clever, more sophisticated, and more effective methods than those used against us. It may become necessary that the American people be made acquainted with, understand and support this fundamentally repugnant philosophy.[11]

In the spirit of the Hoover Commission, the CIA extended itself, searching out every kind of dirty trick in the black bag of the professional spy. The Church Committee was shocked to learn that the CIA had established a regular program for political assassinations, and had carried some of them out.[12] The public was taken aback when it was revealed that, in its zeal to assassinate Fidel Castro, the CIA had entered into an alliance with the Mafia. Both the Rockefeller Commission and the Church Committee discovered that the CIA experiments with drugs, uses and abuses foreign universities, forments opposition from both the right and left indiscriminately, and makes its presence felt in every corner of the world. There is no official tally, but the Pike Committee of the House of Representatives did come up with some fascinating figures of CIA activities. Between 1965 and 1975, this committee reported, of the projects approved by the so-called 40 Committee, 32 percent were devoted to influencing foreign elections (including a total $65 million in Italy alone over a twenty-year period, extending the story related in chapter 7 of this book); 29 percent were oriented to media and propaganda campaigns; and 23 percent called for violence and military intervention.[13]

For all its actions overseas, the CIA managed to escape hostile public opinion within the United States. Such acts were part of what I call the export of repression, and Americans have never been overly concerned with the moral implications of what they export. But revelations about the CIA did not end overseas. In total violation not only of its charter but also public expectations about the agency, the CIA, both the Rockefeller Commission and the Church and Pike committees found, was quite active at home. This was serious business. The Rockefeller report spoke of something called Operation CHAOS, begun under Lyndon Johnson and continued under Richard Nixon. CHAOS kept close tabs on the antiwar movement, eventually collecting computerized indices on over 300,000 persons and organizations within the United States.[14] The vice-president and his colleagues also learned that the CIA had been reading our mail for over twenty years, opening 215,820 letters in New York City alone before resealing them and sending them on to their destinations.[15] Other revelations indicated that the agency had followed and photographed American citizens, had carried out break-ins at home, had wiretapped and bugged, and had obtained citizens' tax records from the Internal Revenue Service.[16] The CIA was as willing to put aside notions of fair play at home as it was abroad. Publicity about its domestic acts was bound to cause upset.

Even more surprising than the CIA's actions were its attitudes about those actions. Richard Helms, former director of the agency, seemed willing to stretch the truth while under oath, for which he escaped the consequences. (A "plea bargaining" arrangement with the Carter administration left Helms a free man.) James Angleton, head of covert operations for the agency, expressed his contempt for democracy as follows: "It's inconceivable that a secret intelligence arm of the government has to comply with all the overt orders of the government."[17] Henry Kissinger expressed the amoralism of America's political elite perfectly. Justifying the role of the CIA in overthrowing a duly chosen president of Chile, Kissinger said in passing: "I don't see why we need to stand by and watch a country go Communist due to the irresponsibility of its own people."[18] Much could be justified in the name of anticommunism, but not everything. Operating at a time when the public was concerned about violence and lawlessness, the CIA came to be seen by ordinary Americans as more a problem than a solution.

Other intelligence services. Though they capture the lion's share of the publicity, the FBI and CIA are not the only intelligence services our country has produced. Like small competitors operating in the interstices of a monopolistic economy, other intelligence agencies occasionally break into the market. Each military service has its own intelligence outfit. During the height of the Vietnam war, army intelligence sent out 1,500 spies to watch and infiltrate domestic political organizations. Data on over 100,000 Americans were collected by the army alone. The army infiltrated the 1963 March on Washington, the 1966 freedom march of James Meredith, the civil rights movement's major organizations, the Americans for Democratic Action, the American Civil Liberties Union, the 1968 Poor People's March on Washington, the 1968 Democratic convention (where agents posed as reporters to gather information), the 1969 moratoria against the Vietnam war, and other political organizations and events. In spite of reforms passed in 1971, military intelligence continues to flourish; eight examples of covert surveillance by the military intelligence services between 1971 and 1975 were noted by the Senate Intelligence Committee.[19]

The National Security Agency has programs for the regular collection of data on American citizens. Its files contain huge numbers of dossiers collected by illegal means.[20] Private corporations constitute another source of intelligence gathering. American companies—especially including banks and insurance companies—keep extensive files, and these files often wind up in the hands of one repressive agency or another. Nor are private companies choosy about how they obtain their information, relying on dubious investigative outfits against whose excesses people have little recourse. Nor has our survey yet included the repressive agencies of state and local governments, many of which—like New York City's Bureau of Special Services—keep illegal tabs on political dissidents. New York's bureau was a source for some of the lawbreakers close to the Nixon Administration.[21] Finally, the Internal Revenue Service has its own data-gathering operations. The Special Services Staff of the IRS compiled 11,458 files on 8,585 persons and 2,873 organizations; by 1975, the Intelligence Gathering and Retreival System had indexed a total of 465,442 persons.[22] America has as many varieties of snoopers as it has laundry detergents.

In revising this book I have been struck by the extent to which events have overtaken some parts while other parts remain fresh. Much of my energy in the 1969–72 period, when the first edition of this book was written, went into attacking the myth of a neutral and fair government dispensing rewards and punishments without bias. Like the muckrackers of an earlier time, I was determined to expose what I thought were drastic untruths about the American government. These parts of the book have held up least—not because I was wrong, but because I was too right. There was no way I could have demystified American politics as Richard Nixon was able to do. Through his contempt for public opinion and his ruthless self-serving beliefs, Nixon unintentionally became the greatest muckraker of them all. More than any book could hope to achieve, the inglorious end of his regime showed Americans what unchecked political power can do. Even as we congratulate the system for bringing Nixon down, we are aghast at what he managed to do before the dénouement came.

What stands up in this book is the once daring hypothesis that repression is—continues to be—an everyday aspect of American politics. I am not sure whether to feel proud that I raised the repression issue before it was popular or to feel chagrined that I managed to underestimate its extent. Surely there can no longer be any doubt that in America, the state can be used for ends that are in no way implied by the theory of representative government. But understanding why this is the case is much more important. In the remainder of this preface I want to add to what I said in 1973 about the causes and consequences of repression in liberal democracies.

The first edition of this book made the point that the ultimate cause of political repression lay in the existence of a society stratified by class. I argued that a structure of power existed, through which some obtained a disproportionate amount of wealth and power; in this context, repression was a mechanism through which those who obtained benefits perpetuated the society that was good to them. Today this seems not so much true as obvious. The point is not to document the fact that American capitalism is inegalitarian and therefore repressive. More emphasis should be placed on developing some theoretical notions about the nature of politics in advanced capitalist societies, for we must understand the nature of the state if we are to grasp the dynamics of repression.

In the years since *The Seamy Side of Democracy* was written, a number of analysts have begun to concern themselves with the nature of the capitalist state.[23] Of the various approaches in the process of being developed, the most powerful to me is one that locates the state in a capitalist society as being caught between contrasting imperatives.[24] Capitalism is, first and foremost, a mode of production in which the dominant choices made about the accumulation of wealth and commodities are made privately. The major decisions about how a society's productive resources are to be used are *not* made democratically through a collective process of discussion. In the twentieth century, this system of private accumulation has been buttressed by an extensive public network. Through its macro-economic policies, its monetary policy, its patent system, its court decisions, and in numerous other ways, the state involves itself in a system of accumulation oriented toward the needs of the most powerful monopolistic corporations. In this context repression serves a useful ideological manipulation, it is difficult to see why people would accept a system that continuously shortchanges them. In other words, if the focus were on accumulation pure and simple, very little would need to be added to the analysis of repression contained in the first edition of this book.

But the focus does not stop with accumulation pure and simple. To do so would be to have an analysis that was incapable of recognizing the contradictions of contemporary politics, because it would seek to reduce all phenomena to one explanation. This would be ironic for a Marxist approach, for in its analysis of economics the Marxist tradition is acutely sensitive to all the contradictions of capitalist economies. One way to avoid this reductionism is to view the capitalist state, particularly the United States, as existing within a liberal democratic structure that imposes restraints, however small, on the accumulation process. Any ruling class must seek more than the maximization of its privileges; it must seek to legitimate itself as well. Thus, essential to understanding the way the state operates in America is seeing it as having certain legitimation tasks that can, and sometimes do, contradict its tasks in the accumulation process.[25]

Legitimation involves those activities through which a ruling class tries to win support for its policies. Welfare, education, reforms in health care—all these things help ruling groups to legitimate their rule. But there is more to legitimation than this. The term must refer also to those victories that popular struggles have obtained through the democratic process. When the working class fights for, and wins, political participation; when a dissident group, through struggle, obtains the freedom to organize and speak; when social pariahs prove to people the basis for their dignity—these real victories transform the dynamics by which politics take place. Given a focus on legitimation, in short, one can avoid the trap in which the ruling class always wins. Such an emphasis allows for a dynamic approach, which sees the state as a battleground where contending forces organize for their own benefit. To be sure, one side generally wins; superior organization and historic control over the state affect the outcome. But the other side has numbers and the force of a popular ideology, which means that it is not totally powerless.

Legitimation, in many ways, acts as a check on repression. To the extent that a working class, broadly defined, is able to organize and make its demands on the state, to that extent repression against it will be minimized. One reason why some of the historical examples cited in this book are so telling is that they took place before the working class was organized. One reason why contemporary examples of repression are so fascinating is because they constitute attempts to *dis*organize classes that are capable of challenging the present order.[26] In other words, if dominant classes attempt to maintain their control over the accumulation process through repression, dominated classes can resist repression and struggle for their legitimate demands through the process of legitimation. The key to understanding the capitalist state is that it must, at some level, be responsive to both these demands; yet attempts to satisfy the one continuously contradict the other and vice versa.

Perhaps the emphasis in the first edition on the ubiquity of repression in America, while necessary to counterbalance the claim that the United States had become the good life in operation, contributed to a misplaced emphasis. It is clear that the dialectical and contradictory nature of the repressive process needs to be brought out sufficiently. What I have tried to provide in this edition is a recognition of the dynamics of the larger economic system within which repression takes place and an accompanying understanding of the contradictory nature of that larger system.

In revising *The Seamy Side of Democracy*, I have made numerous changes in the text. First, insofar as it was possible to do so without distorting the original analysis, I have added clarifying words that I hope will incorporate some of the more theoretical material contained in this preface. Second, where appropriate I have added new material based on recent revelations. These examples continue through the first year of the Carter Administration and should render the book more useful to a new generation of readers. Third, I have used this opportunity to clarify some passages that were ambiguous in the first edition of the book. In undertaking these tasks, I would like to thank Edward Artinian for the faith he has shown in my work and for encouraging the publication of a new edition. I would also like to thank the many readers who, sometimes politely and sometimes not, discussed the strengths and the weaknesses of the book with me. I have learned from them, and my hope is that they will learn from me.

notes

1. *Cambridge Report* 3 (Spring 1975): 118. See also Arthur H. Miller et al., "Political Issues and Trust in Government," *American Political Science Review* 68 (September 1974): 953; and James S. House and William M. Mason, "Political Alienation in America, 1952–1968," *American Sociological Review* 40 (April 1975): 123–47.

2. A recently published and well-written history of the bureau is Sanford J. Unger, *FBI* (Boston: Little, Brown, 1975).

3. For documentation of this point, see Barton J. Bernstein, "The Road to Watergate and Beyond: The Growth and Abuse of Executive Authority Since 1940," *Law and Contemporary Problems* 40 (Spring 1976): 58–86.

4. Details of the Sullivan memo are contained in David Wise, *The American Police State* (New York: Random House, 1976), 285–86.

5. *New York Times*, 15 July 1975, p. 1. See also Wise, *American Police State*, pp. 142–43.

6. Wise, *American Police State*, p. 144.

7. *New York Times*, 1 August 1976, p. 1.

8. Paul Cowan et al., *State Secrets* (New York: Holt, Rinehart & Winston, 1974); see also Pat Watters and Stephen Gillers, *Investigating the FBI* (Garden City, N.Y.: Doubleday, 1973), especially the chapter by John T. Elliff.

9. Wise, *American Police State*, p. 398.

10. *Final Report of the Select Committee to Study Governmental Regulations with Respect to Intelligence Activities, 94th Cong., 1st sess. bk. 3. Supplementary Detailed Staff Reports on National Security and the Rights of Americans* (Washington, D.C.: Government Printing Office, 1976), pp. 273–351.

11. Quoted in Morton Halperin et al., *The Lawless State* (New York: Penguin, 1976), 34.

12. *Final Report*, bk. 4, pp. 121–42; bk. 5, *The Investigation of the Assassination of President John F. Kennedy* (Washington, D.C.: Government Printing Office, 1976), p. 11.

13. *Hearings of the Select Committee on Intelligence, House of Representatives, 94th Cong., 1st sess.* Portions reprinted in *The Village Voice*, 16 and 23 February 1976.

14. *Report to the President by the Commission on CIA Activities within the United States* (Washington, D.C.: Government Printing Office, 1975), pp. 130–50.

15. Ibid., pp. 101–15.

16. Wise, *American Police State*, p. 184; Halperin, *Lawless State*, pp. 135–54.

17. Quoted in Wise, *American Police State*, p. 208.

18. Quoted in Halperin, *Lawless State*, pp. 17–18.

19. Ibid., pp. 155–70.

20. Ibid., pp. 171–86.

21. Both John Caulfield and Anthony Ulasewicz came from BOSS.

22. Wise, *American Police State*, pp. 326, 348; Halperin, *Lawless State*, pp. 187–208.

23. For a review of this literature, see David Gold, Clarence Lo, and Erik Olin Wright, "Marxist Theories of the Capitalist State," *Monthly Review*, October and November 1975.

24. Jurgen Habermas, *Legitimation Crisis* (Boston: Beacon, 1975); Claus Offe, "The Theory of the Capitalist State and the Problem of Policy Formation," in Leon Lindberg et al., *Stress and Contradiction in Modern Capitalism* (Lexington, Mass.: D. C. Heath, 1975); and James O'Connor, *The Fiscal Crisis of the State* (New York: St. Martin's, 1973).

25. This problem is explored at greater length in Alan Wolfe, *The Limits of Legitimacy* (New York: Free Press, 1977).

26. Nicos Poulantzas, *Political Power and Social Classes* (London: New Left Books, 1973), pp. 190–91.

preface to the
first edition

*There is a whorehouse for
the blind, and the prostitutes
are blind too. Must write a
story about that.*

THE DIARY OF ANAÏS NIN

*The civilization and justice of
bourgeois order comes out in
its lurid light whenever the
slaves and drudges of that
order rise against their mas-
ters.*

Karl Marx, THE CIVIL WAR IN
FRANCE

"How can you write a book on repression?" I was frequently asked
when I told friends what I was doing. "Don't you get depressed?" The
answer is yes. Researching and thinking the material that went into this
book did lead to periodic bouts with depression. But, in good dialectical
fashion, the low points produced their antitheses, for also out of the same
work came the commitment to a politics that allows people to take their
lives into their own hands and thereby realize true freedom for perhaps
the first time. Somehow, then, the book turned out to be an optimistic
one, in spite of its subject matter.

Research on the book began in 1969 during the height of a repressive
period. In fact, the outline was developed the day after the opening of

the Chicago Eight trial, and that trial was the direct inspiration for the book. But since then I have learned that in capitalist society repression means not only dramatic trials and police spies but also everyday life. While I have tried to discuss both these things, it was the former that first struck my attention and the emphasis lies there (especially since studies of the role of force in liberal democratic societies were rare). If I were to start now, I am sure that the focus on everyday life would be stronger, but perhaps that will have to await another book.

It took four years to come up with a finished product in this venture, and during that time the Nixon Administration solidified its hold on the machinery of the American capitalist state. While the first four years of the Nixon Administration were marked by a *decrease* in the amount of violent repression (for reasons argued in the text), there is also evidence that the Nixon Administration is the most repressive (in the more general sense of the term) ever to hold power in America. So this book comes out at the start of Nixon's second term in office, an appropriate thing since repression in its many forms seems clearly to be the leitmotif of the next four years.

Numerous individuals gave me aid and comfort during this project. It was begun while I taught at the Old Westbury campus of the State University of New York. Donald Bluestone of that school was particularly helpful in those early days. The remainder of the book was written while I worked at Richmond College of the City University of New York, where various people took an interest, including Larry Nachman, Gerry Sider, Leonard Quart, Rima Blair, Paul Rabinow, and Albert Auster. But the strongest intellectual backing I received was from two study groups. One, centered around the magazine *Social Policy*, enabled me to benefit from the wisdom of the following people: Bertram Gross, Frances Piven, S. M. Miller, Colin Greer, Stanley Aronowitz, Sumner Rosen, Frank Reissman, and Robert Greenberg. The other group included invaluable advice from Ira Katznelson, Kay Trimberger, Veronica Beechey, Roz Petchesky, David Gold, Lawrence Tharp, Nanette Funk, Larry Spiro, and Mike Merrill. In addition to these groups, individuals who read parts of the manuscript and gave me advice and encouragement include Mike Hirsch, Ike Balbus, and Harry Braverman. A special word of thanks, for both criticism and comfort, goes to Allis Wolfe, who during much of this project was my wife but who has since become one of my closest friends. For typing the manuscript, I wish to thank Sharon Geise, Lorelie Migenes, and Judith Lichtenberg.

I do not believe that the study of society is the result of individual scholars proceeding in individualistic ways. Knowledge is a social product, and in that sense this book is not just my own work but the product of a

social movement out of which it grew. I recognize my debt to that movement which was responsible for my developing a critical faculty; at the
same time, I also recognize that errors of fact and interpretation are mine
alone to bear.

contents

part two: the dynamics of repression

part three: the future of repression

part one ☆ the back-ground of repression

chapter
one ☆
the sociology
of
repression

Americans from a wide variety of backgrounds are increasingly discovering the seamier aspects of their country's history. "Civilizing" the West is now seen as genocide practiced on the native population. Slavery is understood as but one aspect of a virulent racism that has not abated and that may in fact have become stronger over time. Industrialization, once considered the strength of the country, is interpreted as a panorama of oppression and exploitation. Even war—that most sacred of all American institutions—is being seen in a new light. Younger historians argue that the Spanish-American War was gross imperialism, an early version of Vietnam, and recent theorists advance the idea that it was the intransigence of the United States, and not of the Soviet Union, that led to the cold war.

In a sense, this book is part of that reevaluation of the American past. But unlike the others that have preceded it, it is not primarily a work of history, written about a single period, by a historian. It is a work of political sociology, that is, an attempt to understand a political phenomenon by placing it into a social context and trying to think about it theoretically. The purpose is not to relate a story but to understand a concept, using history, to be sure, but using it not as an end in itself but as a place that might provide the examples needed to test out the ideas advanced.

The specific political phenomenon under investigation is repression, one of those seamier aspects of the American experience currently being reexamined. Conventional wisdom for years maintained that repression was alien to America; the country prided itself on being a refuge of freedom, of free thought, free expression, free communication, free worship. Other countries might see their governments harassing dissidents and trying to drive them out of existence, but America—it was said—tolerated diversity as much as possible. Since ideas like these were simply untrue, once the blinders were lifted, the structure fell. Suddenly, numbers of people discovered that, in many ways, the history of the United States is a history of repression. The U.S. government has hassled workers, Indians, blacks, women, left-wingers, right-wingers, immigrants. In this century alone there have been two Red scares, concentration camps, guilt by association, deportations, preventive detention, political espionage—all carried out by a government supposedly dedicated to freedom. Given the myth and the actuality, clearly more needs to be said about this subject.

One thing should be made clear at the beginning, however: this book is not devoted to proving how repressive American society has been. That a substantial amount of repression has always existed is taken for granted, an assumption easily verified by anyone who would choose to understand American history. What is needed is not breast-beating about how awful we have been, but an analysis that makes sense out of the phenomenon. What is repression? How many forms does it take? Under what conditions does it take different forms? Is the democratic state more or less repressive than other types? Who benefits from repression? Do people who are being repressed know that they are being repressed? How much repression produces fascism? Can repression be exported overseas? What role do civil liberties play? How can repression be eliminated? Is repression inevitable wherever there is government? These are the kinds of questions that need answers, even tentative ones. It is obviously impossible to work effectively toward the elimination of a phenomenon until one understands it. This book is directed toward that understanding.

Defining Repression

Our first task is to know what we are talking about, which in this case is not easy. The problem stems from the fact that repression is a value-laden word. Few people wish to be called repressive, and even fewer societies would admit to engaging periodically in repression. Most social scientists have traditionally regarded repression as something that took place somewhere else. After World War II, for example, American social scientists developed the concept of totalitarianism, which they applied to Germany, Italy, and Russia.[1] Numerous studies appeared documenting the role that the governments of those countries played in quelling dissent, and various theories were developed to explain why events happened as they did. Meanwhile, in the country where these books were being written, the government was also attempting to remove dissidents forcibly; but these incidents were often ignored. Few wrote about domestic repression, with the exception of some who were being repressed.[2] In addition, most books that dealt with repression were either exposés or case studies;[3] few serious analyses of the nature of repression have yet been put forward.

A look at all these attempts to handle dissent by suppressing it brings us to a first element in a definition of repression: it is an act performed by people who have political power, that is, people who control the means of repression. In most countries this will mean that repression is governmental activity, a responsibility of the state. But this need not always be the case. In the United States, for example, nineteenth-century repression was often carried out by private detective agencies that were hired by corporation leaders to break strikes and infiltrate labor organizations. Although the government was not performing these acts of repression, people in power were, for the emerging corporate leaders of the time constituted a ruling class that determined the nature of the political system.

As those in power were the acting agents of the repression, a second element in the definition can be added: repression is practiced against those who challenge the existing powerholders. Since anyone who does not hold power may at any time by his mere existence constitute a threat to those who do, the number of people who could potentially be repressed is very high, and it includes nearly all the people who live in a given society. When any of these people set themselves up in an organization that threatens the government, or when they develop a set of ideas contrary to the ruling ideas of the society, they face the threat of repression. In the United States, the repressive mechanisms of the state have been used most heavily against such groups as the Industrial Workers of the World (IWW), the Communist party, and the Black Panther party, groups which had both an ideological and an organizational opposition to the way things were being run in the country at the time they existed.

We can now advance a formal definition of repression, and then go on to examine its weaknesses. *Repression is a process by which those in power try to keep themselves in power by consciously attempting to destroy or render harmless organizations and ideologies that threaten their power.* Repression can best be understood as a reproductive mechanism. In order to continue to exist, a society needs certain methods of ensuring that existing power relationships will be reproduced from generation to generation, as well as from day to day.[4] Repression is a process, one among many, that serves this function in the United States.

The concept of reproductive mechanisms focuses on the question of why those in power are allowed to remain in power, which is also a way of asking why those who are powerless accept that state of affairs. The powerless may do so because they believe that society can exist in no other way; they may wish to challenge their powerlessness but are afraid to do so because of possible reprisals; or they may actually have tried to change things but failed. In each case, what happens is that a situation in which some have power at the expense of others is reproduced continually. The means by which this process of reproduction takes place are the means of repression.

The process of repression can be illustrated by an example. In 1919, in the United States, dissatisfaction with the way things were taking place was concentrated in three organizations: the IWW, the Socialist party, and a group that was eventually to form the Communist party (actually, two Communist parties were formed at first).[5] The resulting structure contained a ruling group, organized in the presidency and other institutions of power, and containing an ideology that justified its rule; and a series of challenging groups, each with its own organization, and each containing its ideology challenging that rule. To clarify, such a situation might look like the diagram on the facing page.

In this example, the process of repression would constitute the various attempts by the group at the top to contain the influence of the group at the bottom. For example, leaders of the IWW were continually arrested and brought to trial on the basis of vague and unsubstantiated charges. Offices of the organization were periodically raided (in ways to be described in the next chapter).[6] Members of the Socialist party, duly elected to legislatures, were refused seats. Infiltrators were sent to join the Communist parties, and a secret unity meeting of the various groups was raided by the Justice Department. All these attempts to destroy the organizations that were seen as a threat were directly repressive.

But repression is not practiced solely against organizations. Once the

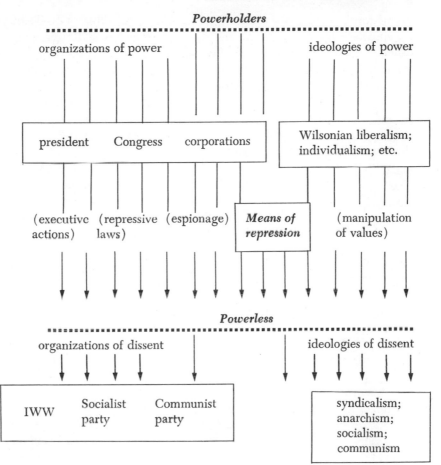

Powerholders

organizations of power | ideologies of power

| president | Congress | corporations | | Wilsonian liberalism; individualism; etc. |

(executive actions)   (repressive laws)   (espionage)   **Means of repression**   (manipulation of values)

Powerless

organizations of dissent | ideologies of dissent

| IWW | Socialist party | Communist party | | syndicalism; anarchism; socialism; communism |

dissidents existed, the government tried to destroy them by using force in the form of raids, trials, and infiltrators. From the point of view of the government, however, a better procedure existed, and that was to repress the ideology of the dissenting organizations. If the government could convince the overwhelming majority of the people in the United States that left-wing ideologies were evil, then the dissenting groups could gain no adherents and would die out. The result was the creation of a Committee on Public Information, which set out systematically to discredit the dissenters, not by destroying their organization, but by using propaganda to discredit their ideas.[7] Few can see which of the government tactics, proceeding against the organization or discrediting the ideology, was more successful in repressing these groups. Certainly both tactics played a major role.

This example illustrates the fact that repression in America takes two broad forms. One is the use of *state violence,* the attempt to destroy an *organization* by using the means that the state has at its disposal. The other is *ideological repression,* the attempt to manipulate people's *consciousness* so that they accept the ruling ideology, and distrust and refuse to be moved by competing ideologies. The two forms proceed together; it is really impossible to talk about one without the other. Those in power generally prefer to use ideological repression, since the use of violence indicates political instability and may win sympathy for the group being destroyed. But violent repression will be used when the ideological form does not work, so in order to understand the one we have to deal with the other.

The one major problem with this definition of repression is that it may cover too much. If we are interested in all the ways by which those in power attempt to keep themselves in power, we are interested in all governing, and we will have defined repression in such a way that no act could ever *not* be repressive.[8] For example, a government builds a highway from town A to town B. Surely that would not be repression, yet one might argue that a latent effect of such a law is to convince people that the existing government really serves their interests by building roads for them, so that the law does contribute to maintaining present power relationships and is in that sense repressive. In other words, in order to avoid the problem of having everything seen as repression, we need a way of differentiating road building from calling out the National Guard.

Two things can help here. One is the use of the word *conscious* in the definition of repression. There must be a specific consciousness on the part of those engaging in an act that its purpose is to repress. This is often difficult to establish, but when Congress passes a law providing for the registration of members of the Communist party, one can presume, with justice, that the conscious purpose of the act is to repress the CP, not to give jobs to registrars. Other examples are not so easy. Is a law that regulates the use of loudspeakers a form of harassment against dissident speakers or is it necessary for the maintenance of public order? Here there can be no answer with respect to the passage of the law, but a judgment can be made when we look at how such laws are enforced. If they are consciously enforced against socialists or John Birch Society members, but not against the American Legion, then there are grounds for concluding that they are repressive.

In addition, an act will not be seen as repressive if its repressive effect is latent, rather than manifest. Professional football, for example, is an activity with many political consequences. It reinforces respect for authority, teaches the value of competitiveness, and stresses achievement.[9] In that sense, it could be argued that professional football is a form of ideological repression because it is designed to win respect for the ruling ideas of society and to discredit competing notions. Much of this is true about football; nevertheless, it could be argued that these are latent consequences of this activity. Football was *not* originally designed to be explicitly political, and it still has other manifest purposes (recreation, distraction, sublimation). So long as its political consequences are not primary, we would not include football as a repressive mechanism, although we would recognize that a part of its activity operates in that way. The distinction is a hazardous one, expecially now that football is becoming more explicitly connected with patriotism and repressive politicians. But for purposes of limiting this book to a manageable size, and in order to give logical coherence to the concept under discussion, we will examine here only those kinds of practices that are directly repressive in function.

Repression and Liberalism

We are concerned here with repression only in America, although the phenomenon exists throughout the world. Given that some repression is always ideological, and that the ruling ideology of the United States since its founding has been one type or another of liberalism, some words on the relationship between liberalism and repression are obviously in order.

This is particularly the case because liberalism has a highly ambiguous attitude toward the question of repression. Unlike many ruling ideologies that existed in the past, liberalism seeks to preserve individual rights against the government. In America, these rights are recognized in the Bill of Rights, which grants certain political freedoms, such as the rights to speak and to organize, which appear from the language to be absolute. If this is true, then it means that the power of the government to engage in repression is highly limited, for theoretically it could take no repressive action that interfered with people's right to say whatever they wanted. Yet the essence of repression is to deny people that very right. Clearly, if the ideas of the Bill of Rights were enforced, little or no repression could take place in America.

The problem arises from the fact that the same Constitution that provides for individual freedom also grants the state the right to engage in repression. At one point, the Constitution gives Congress the power "to provide for calling forth the Militia to execute the Laws of the Union, *suppress Insurrections* and repel Invasions" (Art. I, sect. 8; italics added). The key words are emphasized, for it is one thing for a state to have the right to ward off invaders, but a totally different thing constitutionally to justify challenges to its rule from within the society itself. The same idea of providing a means for the government to protect itself from domestic challenge is also suggested in another clause of the Constitution: "The United States shall guarantee to every State in the Union a republican form of government, and shall protect each of them against invasion; and on the application of the legislature, or the executive (when the legislature cannot be convened), against *domestic violence*" (Art. IV, sect. 5; italics added).

The ambiguity of liberalism is that it wants to protect both the rights of the individual and the rights of the state, and these are frequently bound to conflict. When they do, the state is much more likely to win, since it has the power to enforce its claims, whereas most individuals do not. In this sense, most theorists of liberal democracy eventually conclude by justifying repression, a point that can be emphasized through a brief summary of some of the key liberal thinkers.

Modern democratic theory is generally seen as having its origins in the problems faced by thinkers trying to make sense out of seventeenth-century events. From these problems arose Thomas Hobbes and John Locke, the one stressing the need for authority and the other focusing more on the individual and his freedom. To those who like to think the universe of discourse takes place within the limits of contemporary liberalism and conservatism, there is often an attempt to read this "end of ideology" back into the seventeenth century. Hobbes and Locke are seen as expressing two ends of the continuum, two traditions within which a prolonged debate on the nature of authority vs. liberty has taken place. Such a view is misleading, for it minimizes the commonality of thought between the two men. For one thing, as C. B. MacPherson has shown (well enough so that the points need only summarization here), both were united in their commitment to the model of a possessive market society.[10] The assumptions, the analyses, and the conclusions of both men were compatible with and shaped by the needs of an emerging bourgeois order. Both were agreed that ". . . freedom is a function of possession."[11] In addition, *both writers were attempting to justify the existence of a state*, which means that both were trying to justify repression. In Hobbes' case the state was to be more absolutist than in Locke's, but in neither case was there anything resembling an antistate bias. This point of agreement is crucial, because the thoughts of either man can at some point be used to justify the actions of those who control the state, regardless of how they obtained that control.

Hobbes viewed the state, described as the sovereign, in almost religious terms. What has been called the "state of nature" is really not natural (or historical) at all but is simply what would exist if there were no state. Since the stateless situation is so reprehensible, tending constantly toward civil war and death, any alternative is to be preferred. The state is created by men so that they might "live peaceable amongst themselves, and be protected against other men."[12] In this way, Hobbes certainly recognizes the tendency of men to conflict with one another; he is hardly a philosopher of a harmony of interests. But he does not see any benefits in conflict. Since the creation of a sovereign power is the only way to channel conflict and preserve peace, any actions taken by the state to further that function are justified. Therefore, following out his assumptions, Hobbes recognizes that the state will be engaged in the business of repression, and he viewed that as its necessary business:

> . . . to the Sovereign is committed the Power of Rewarding with
> riches, or honour; and of Punishing with corporall, or pecuniary
> punishment, or with ignominy every Subject according to the Law
> he hath formerly made; or if there be no Law made, according as
> he shall judge most to conduce to the encouraging of men to serve the
> Common-wealth, or deterring of them from doing dis-service
> to the same.[13]

The differences with Locke are more of emphasis than anything else. There is not the same dark view of human nature that one finds in Hobbes, but a state of war is still a condition to be avoided through the creation of civil society.[14] But the major difference between Hobbes and Locke is generally seen in the question of authority, Locke being much more willing than Hobbes to view authority as limited. After all, it is said that we owe to Locke the idea of a right to rebel, hardly a notion associated with an authoritarian. This view misreads the nature of the civil society Locke was describing. It is not hard to show, as MacPherson has done, that this society was limited to a propertied class: "The reason why Men enter into Society," Locke repeats a few times, "is the preservation of their Property."[15] In the hierarchy of values he creates, property is the highest. Therefore, the interests of property must be continually protected. If the right to property came into conflict with the right to rebel, the former would be considered more important. If, on the other hand, the right to rebel was concomitant with the right to property, it could be justified. Thus the right to rebel is not an absolute right but only one to be used in very special circumstances.

In an often overlooked passage, Locke goes so far as to suggest that the right to rebel is essential because its purpose will be to prevent rebellion:

> . . . this Doctrine of a Power in the People of providing for their
> safety anew by a new Legislative, when their Legislators have acted
> contrary to their trust, by invading their Property, is the best fence
> against Rebellion, and the problest means to hinder it.[16]

In the section from which this quotation is taken, Locke goes to great lengths to answer arguments from his more authority-minded critics. He continually insists that nothing in his doctrine is radical and he asserts strongly that rebels against bourgeois order, those who would attack the legislature that created peaceful laws for the maintenance of property, are outside the scope of his doctrine. They "bring back again the state of War, and are properly Rebels." Having been labeled as such, what should be done to them?

> Whosoever uses force without Right, as every one does in Society, who does it without Law, puts himself into a state of War with those, against whom he so uses it, and in that state all former Ties are cancelled, and all other Rights cease, and every one has a Right to defend himself and to resist the Aggressor.[17]

This sentence is easily misread. Locke is not arguing here that a political leader who uses force illegitimately can be legitimately deposed. The "whosoever" he is referring to are those who challenge the existing order in a revolutionary fashion. When they do so without laws, i.e., remain true to their revolutionary tenets, they can be repressed, since all former ties have been canceled. Thus, when the property rights of those who control civil society are threatened illegitimately, all decorum comes to an end and the property holders are free to take any repressive actions they choose against the rebels.

If Hobbes and Locke represent the foundation of democratic theory, it is a rather contradictory foundation. Although both writers made substantial contributions to the ideology of freedom, both were also committed to the emerging bourgeois order. Freedom came to mean freedom within the confines of that order. Preservation of that order was so important that those who challenged it could not participate in it. Both writers, in short, were aware of the phenomenon we now call repression, and both were sympathetic to it as long as it took the form of preserving civil society. Any other alternative meant a return to the state of nature, which was synonymous with the destruction of the emerging capitalist order, and which therefore could not be allowed to happen.

Those democratic theorists who wrote at a later period, one would think, would be more likely to address the problem of repression in a critical way, since they had more of a history of capitalism on which to base their speculations. Such is not the case. Writers such as John Stuart Mill, whose concern for liberty is self-evident, could never escape from the same paradox that was basic to the theories of Hobbes and Locke. Mill's desire to show the importance of political liberty continually conflicts with his belief that only bourgeois society can provide that liberty, leading him to strive constantly to find a balance between state sovereignty and individual liberty. Since the former was grounded in power and the latter in theory, this often meant that expressions of the importance of liberty were statements of what *ought* to be the case. Little time was devoted to the question of how that state of affairs could be brought about. The idea that it would never be brought about—that what prevented liberty was the granting of liberty without a recognition of power—was alien to Mill's writings. In other words, Mill did not recognize that liberty as a general principle meant that those who could control the state would use libertarian arguments to further their own interests but would turn the balance around and use the importance of authority to spurn the interests of others.[18]

This failure of Mill explains why "On Liberty" can be read as a statement of the need *for* state action against individual liberty. First there is the commitment to balance: "Everyone who receives the protection of society owes a return for the benefit, and the fact of living in society renders it indispensable that each should be bound to observe a certain line of conduct toward the rest."[19] Thus, even though the social contract is rejected, there is still a duty on the part of the citizen to obey the sovereign. Specifically, the citizen is asked not to injure the rights of others and is required to participate in defending the society. Since among the rights contained in a democratic government is the right to property, citizens are obliged to recognize the property rights of others. Furthermore, by the second condition, they are obliged to defend those rights from attack outside the system. What we have here is an argument that, in the name of liberty, urges deference on the part of the powerless to the powerful.

There is more to the problem than balance. Mill makes explicit that no tyranny over opinions is justified, including a tyranny of the majority. The rights of the minority must be guaranteed against abuse.[20] It is with minority rights that the failure of Mill to deal with the power context of democratic societies becomes particularly harmful. Certainly minority opinion must be protected; in the essays by Mill are the most eloquent statements of the need for freedom that one could hope to find. But eloquence is not enough. In order to exercise its freedom, any group in a democratic society needs power. The only group guaranteed power is that minority which owns extensive property. Thus, the protection of minority rights in general becomes protection of their rights in particular. The limits on majority tyranny come to mean that the majority of the propertyless are told—in the name of liberty—that they cannot restrict the rights of that minority which holds the property. At the same time, state action that violates the right of powerless minorities, particularly those who dissent from the bourgeois order, is taken. There may be protests from libertarians, but these protests do not stop the action from being taken. Mill's liberalism is unique for its ability to be eloquent in defeat. (Justices Holmes and Brandeis made their brilliant statements on the importance of free speech in dissent, and in some cases, in support of repressive action by the state.)[21] If Mill had been more concerned about who held power in his society, he would have realized the connection between the granting of minority rights to the propertied class and the repression of other minorities who challenge those rights.

The major change in liberal theory from Mill to the present is the replacement of the notion that the state should interfere as little as possible with the economy with the concept of a positive state entering the market to provide stability and more equality. At the same time, the idea of individual freedom has undergone a change. Previously it meant that businessmen could be free to do whatever they pleased, implying that nobody else could. In the twentieth century, civil liberties for most of the population are recognized as a principle by the courts, and for the first time, the government's power to repress is challenged, however meekly.[22] Yet neither of these developments, each in its own way progressive, has solved the contradiction in democratic theory between liberty and repression.

For one thing, contemporary liberalism gives much more power to the state than classical liberalism does and therefore will have to justify more state activity. Thus, the welfare state, supposedly working to benefit the majority of the people, has its own repressive mechanisms, which are much more extensive than those of any previous society for the simple reason that the activities of the state itself are so much more extensive.[23] In addition, those who act as justifiers of the new liberalism wish to protect their government as much as anyone else, and this means that some form of repression will exist. In an important statement of the principles of twentieth-century liberalism, written in 1948, Arthur Schlesinger, Jr., attacks the repressive policies of previous years, particularly the raids against radicals after World War I. But then he proceeds to allow further similar acts by endorsing the constitutional principles used to justify repression in that period, when he asserts that actions which constitute a "clear and present danger" to the security of the United States should not be allowed. When Schlesinger states that ". . . a democracy has the obligation to protect itself against hostile acts— against 'substantive evils,' whether espionage, violence, or incitement, and against the individuals who contrive these evils,"[24] he is giving the government full power to engage in repression against anyone it considers a threat to its power. Liberalism may have changed, but repression has not.

In sum, then, democratic theory was at one time both revolutionary and reactionary in its implications: revolutionary because it sought—through the concept of political freedom—to provide for rapid change in the societies that existed in the eighteenth century; reactionary because at the same time it sought an ordered society so that those who could obtain freedom would have a stable atmosphere in which to use it. Since that time, popular movements of masses of people have attempted to broaden the concept of liberty to provide for their own liberty, while those who controlled the society sought to emphasize the repressive aspects of liberalism in order to solidify their rule. As a result, the basic contradiction of liberalism has not been resolved, even at the present time. But since the more powerful group has the means to put its reading of liberalism into day-to-day practice, in most cases liberalism becomes a theory of repression, not one directed against it. Liberalism protects people against repression only in those relatively rare times when the Supreme Court has a majority that is disposed to do that. Otherwise, a liberal democracy such as the United States can be as repressive as any other kind of society, if it wants to be.

This is an important point to emphasize, because the notion has frequently been put forward that liberal democracy is not a repressive system and that when repression occurs under it, the occurrence is accidental. On the contrary, as this discussion has tried to show, *repression is an integral part of the theory of liberalism.* The existence of repression in practice flows from the fact that liberalism promises people power over their lives, but capitalism (economic liberalism) takes it away. The theory of liberalism continually allows for repression to take place. In the United States, repression has occurred too frequently to be considered accidental any longer. It is as much a part of liberal theory as the Bill of Rights.

Rediscovering the State

The nonexistence of a sociology of repression stems from a general ignorance about how the state operates in democratic societies. For years, political scientists described the formal organization of government without attempting to uncover the underlying dynamics of why the government acted as it did in different situations. Even in recent years, when the study of politics has been infused with sociological content, a problem remains, for political sociology has been more directed to the study of the powerless than the powerful.[25] We have had multitudinous studies of voting, of mass movements, of apathy, but few systematic attempts to examine the behavior of those who control societies and the means they have developed for doing so.

The one tradition that has focused on the powerful is the Marxist tradition, and it is within that tradition that one can begin to make sense out of repression. But Marxist theory provides only a beginning; a huge amount of work remains to be done if we are to comprehend adequately the dynamics of political power in liberal democratic societies.

To Marx and Engels, the state is almost synonymous with repression. As long as society was organized in a situation of scarcity in which all shared together, there was no state, no power that set itself above the social process of sharing. But the end of scarcity, the introduction of an economic surplus, produces differences among people, and when that happens, the need for a state is inevitable. The state

> is a product of society at a particular stage of development, it is the admission that this society has involved itself in insoluble self-contradiction and is cleft into irreconcilable antagonisms which it is powerless to exorcise.[26]

Instead of the prestate situation being anarchistic and the state rational, as in Hobbes and Locke, the exact opposite is the case. The mere existence of the state is prima facie evidence of the existence of conflict. Conflict has arisen because some have more than others. The purpose of the state is to preserve that maldistribution. The existence of the state, then, testifies to the existence of repression. The stronger the state, the more repressive it will be.

The state comes to be defined as the organized domination of one class by another. This is a helpful place to begin to analyze the phenomenon of repression, for domination is certainly a crucial aspect of that phenomenon. The problem arises from the fact that no major Marxist thinker has ever applied this insight to liberal democratic societies, at least until recently.[27]

It is true that Marxist writers have emphasized the two major aspects of repression, its violent and its ideological side. Lenin, for example, was preoccupied by the former. In his major book on the question, he continually refers to the state as holding the police and military power of the society.[28] Undoubtedly shaped by experiences in Tsarist Russia, where police activity constituted the major activity of the state, Lenin did not have much to say on the operations of the democratic state, except the fairly sophisticated notion that because it may give the appearance of fairness, the democratic state may be the most repressive of all, as far as the workers are concerned.[29]

The idea that a major form of repression could be ideological rather than physical has its major expositor in the Italian Marxist Antonio Gramsci.[30] Those in power, according to Gramsci, keep themselves there not only forcibly, but also by developing a certain cultural style that makes their rule seem inevitable. Gramsci used the word *hegemony* to describe this process, and the concept has been incisively summarized by Gwyn Williams as follows:

> . . . an order in which a certain way of life and thought is dominant, in which one concept of reality is diffused throughout society in all its institutional and private manifestations, informing with its spirit all taste, morality, customs, religious and political principles, and all social relations, particularly in their intellectual and moral connotations.[31]

After a while, the struggle against hegemony becomes as important as the physical struggle of the working class, and an important part of the process of revolution is the development of new forms of culture and ideology, just as it is one of developing new forms of power.

But neither Lenin nor Gramsci had to deal with the kind of state that exists in the United States and other advanced capitalist countries in the 1970s. Realizing this, a number of Marxist writers have in the last few years become fascinated with the state and the way it operates in capitalist societies. Responding to pluralistic liberals, who see the state as a neutral force dispensing its rewards fairly to those who ask for them, Ralph Miliband has published an important work that tries to show how the democratic state still operates as Marx said it would, as an instrument of domination.[32] A powerful response to pluralism, Miliband's book has the disadvantage of being essentially descriptive, and of not moving the Marxist theory of the state far beyond where it already is.[33]

In France, a major rediscovery of the state is taking place among Marxist writers. Unlike Miliband's work, this undertaking has been highly theoretical, seeking to isolate certain notions that will explain the workings of the state under capitalism. The problem here is that theory is pursued to the point where description is almost forgotten. Louis Althusser, an intellectual leader of much of this ferment, has written a fascinating essay on the ideological repression of the capitalist state without any specific examples of how this takes place in practice. In fact, the French writers seem overly fascinated with ideological repression, giving the use of force by capitalist states a minor role.[34] This does not seem sufficient when force, particularly in the United States but certainly in France as well, is on the upsurge; violent repression in both countries is as much a reality now as it ever was.

Paradoxically, although the Marxist theory of the state is incomplete, one Marxist writer has had a good deal to say about repression, although his insights come as much from Freud as Marx. That is Herbert Marcuse, who has pointed out that repression, in both its psychological and political aspects, is an essential feature of advanced, industrial society, affecting its every aspect, including language.[35] Marcuse's contribution to an understanding of repression is too monumental to be summarized here, but his focus on surplus repression is an important notion that can provide a theoretical backdrop for the material in this book. In its early stages, when it is still a society based on scarcity, capitalism keeps itself functioning by relying on the work ethic and its associated puritanical ideology. When conditions of scarcity no longer hold, energy is available that is not fulfilled through work. Providing outlets for that libidinal energy by utilizing the repressive potential of industrial society becomes one of the tasks of a ruling class.

Marcuse has been criticized for developing a concept of repression so broad that it includes everything, a danger warned against in an earlier part of this chapter. Without entering the controversy about the usefulness of his theory, it is enough to say that the focus of this book is specifically on *political* repression, which, if one is a Marcuse follower, could be viewed as a subcategory of a larger repressive apparatus. Marcuse's contribution to the narrower notion of political repression is, first, his recognition of its relationship to everyday life, and, second, his notion of preventive repression—the idea that policy makers may take steps to prevent hostile ideas and organizations from forming as an alternative to repressing them politically once they have already formed.[36] The development of preventive repression marks a major shift in the nature of repression from nineteenth-century capitalism to the corporate liberalism of our own times.

This book attempts to avoid some of the difficulties faced by previous writers. Although the book is about political repression, this phenomenon cannot be understood out of context. Part of the operations of the state, repression in liberal democracies must be seen as part of a theory of the state. Therefore, the attention must shift back and forth from a general analysis of the state in capitalist society to a specific discussion of one aspect of the state's activity: repression. This may seem confusing, and it probably is, but the procedure is necessary in order to avoid the twin dangers of too much description or too much theory. A book about the state alone would be insufficient because it would not say much about everyday operations of a specific type of state behavior. A book only about repression would likewise be incomplete because it would be talking about a phenomenon in a vacuum. In short, the confusion would be made greater by trying to separate the study of the state and of repression than it is by combining them.

This dual concern is reflected in the organization of much of what follows. Part 1 is concerned essentially with the theory of the state. It attempts, particularly in chapter 2, to understand the dynamics of the way the state operates in contemporary liberal societies. Through a discussion of a few representative examples, the question of why the state gives support to some groups yet tries to repress others is addressed. Chapter 3 deals with the question of domination. If it is true that the interests of the more powerful are still protected by the democratic state, who are those powerful and what is the basis of their power? Questions such as these need answers before an analysis of repression can take place, for without them, the discussion of repression is not rooted in any specific context.

The actual dynamics by which repression is practiced are the subject of part 2. One chapter analyzes state violence, discussing the means by which it is used and the problems it creates, both for those in power and for the dissenters, when it is used. Chapters 5 and 6 look at ideological repression to see how similar it is to violent repression, when its use is preferred, and what problems are associated with it. Finally, a remaining chapter argues that many of the repressive mechanisms of the American state are used in other countries, making a discussion of the exporting of repression essential.

The final section of the book raises questions about whether repression is an inevitable phenomenon. It views repression as an aspect of liberal capitalism by dealing with the proposition, advanced by quite a few Marxists and non-Marxists alike, that the United States is moving toward fascism. The idea is advanced that it is possible to build a non-repressive society once the causes of repression are understood and the conditions for their disappearance made clear.

Repression in the United States is not a "nice" thing both because it contradicts the rhetoric of the society and because it leads to intellectual stultification of masses of people, let alone physical harm and even death to some of the most perceptive and sensitive members of the society. Acts of repression generate protests, demonstrations, marches, defense committees, and even, on the part of some groups, armed self-defense. But an essential aspect in defending oneself against repression is understanding the mind of the repressor, discovering why repression is taking place. Insofar as this book attempts to do that, it is a form of political protest just like the marches and demonstrations. It is one person's way of saying that repression has gone too far, that a repressive society is not one to pass on to another generation, that the people of the United States have the means to put a stop to repression by changing, through a revolution if you wish, the kind of system they live under and replacing it with one that serves their needs. Writing this book has been a political act; whether its partisanship helps or hinders an objective understanding of a phenomenon most political scientists and sociologists have ignored cannot be answered until its assertions about the way the democratic state operates can be seen as compatible with reality. But the mere fact that the traditional social sciences have ignored the problem, as part of their presumed objectivity, indicates that a more accurate assessment of this phenomenon can come only through a commitment to substantial political change.

chapter
two ☆
the bias
of the
democratic state

Above all, repression involves domination, the attempt by one group in the population to destroy or stymie the growth of other groups. Any discussion of such domination inevitably involves a discussion of the state, for in the modern world, as Max Weber recognized, the state is ultimately the major force for domination.[1] This is as true for the democratic state as it is for any other, but the uniqueness of the democratic state requires that some words be addressed to the way it functions before repression in America can be properly understood.

According to pluralist writers, the democratic state is essentially neutral, dispensing its rewards (and its punishments) without bias. Marxists, on the other hand, view the democratic state, like any capitalist state, as the systematic oppression of the working classes by the ruling class. As the previous chapter indicated, neither idea is sufficient in itself for understanding the complexities of the democratic state, but the Marxist proposition at least provides a place to begin. This chapter examines the Marxist proposition more carefully, using examples in order to revise it so that it can account more for the actual operations of the state in America. The important insight provided by the Marxist theory is that a bias exists in the operations of the democratic state, that when the state confronts powerless groups, its *tendency* is to repress them, and that when it deals with the powerful, its *tendency* is to support them. Repression, in other words, has a class basis that must be understood if repression in America is to make sense.

The Basic Proposition

The Marxist definition of the state can be viewed as a basic proposition, true in some cases but in need of elaboration and revision in others. In its most elementary form, this proposition can be stated as follows: *other things being equal, in any conflict between privileged groups and those challenging those privileges, the state will support the former.*

The one experience in American history that comes closest to supporting the basic proposition is the experience of the Industrial Workers of the World (IWW). Its relationship to the government of the United States can be reviewed, not to prove that Marx was right, but to illustrate how, in certain circumstances, the state did operate the way that the Marxists expected it to do.

The IWW is a most interesting organization in this regard. It has a reputation for being hell-bent on violence, but, contrasting that legend with the facts uncovered by his meticulous analysis, Melvyn Dubofsky, the most comprehensive historian of the IWW, concluded with this:

> With the I.W.W., as with other radical organizations that have been
> romanticized and mythologized, the legend is several removes
> from reality. Wobblies did not carry bombs, nor burn harvest fields,
> nor destroy timber, nor depend upon the machine that works
> with a trigger. Instead they tried in their own ways to comprehend
> the nature and dynamics of capitalist society, and through
> increased knowledge, as well as through revolutionary activism, to
> develop a better system for the organization and function of the
> American economy.[2]

To be sure, the IWW's interests conflicted with those who held power in America (exactly what we are discussing at the moment). But its consistent advocacy of nonviolence make its repression all the more interesting as an example of the role of the state in protecting the dominant class from any group it perceives as threatening.

The IWW grew out of the Western Federation of Miners, and many repressive actions taken against that group would later be used against the IWW as well. When the WFM struck at Cripple Creek, Colorado, in September 1903, the governor responded to the pleas of the mine owners with the immediate dispatch of troops to the area. Announcing "to hell with the Constitution, we are not going by the Constitution," and appealing to a "military necessity which recognizes no laws, either civil or social,"[3] the leaders of the troops tried their best (unsuccessfully) to break the strike by arresting its leaders, illegally if need be. Two years later, when the IWW was formed, the same practice of state, as opposed to federal, intervention on the side of employers would become commonplace.

Between 1905 and the outbreak of World War I, such state action against the IWW occurred wherever its activities took place. In Pennsylvania, the state police, which had been originally created by reformers "anxious to abolish the use of private police forces during industrial conflicts"[4] constantly worked for the employers, not for the strikers. In San Diego, Washington State, and Arizona, vigilante mobs (encouraged in their action by local corporate officials) took direct repressive action against the IWW. Contacts between the mobs and leading state figures made such actions official government policy, even though they were ostensibly carried out by "private" groups. Vigilante action, however, was frowned upon by some state officials who felt that there were "cleaner" ways to repress the organization. A public safety committee in Minnesota, a council of defense in Washington State, and a Commission on Immigration and Housing in California became official bodies seeking official solutions for the elimination of the IWW. Leaders of these bodies felt that only through federal repression could the IWW successfully be dealt with, and they urged a multifaceted program upon the Wilson Administration. William Preston has described the reasoning of many such people:

> Nothing so infuriated and dismayed certain business men and
> law enforcement officials as their inability to prosecute labor agitators.
> Lacking any evidence of criminal activity and unable to indict men
> simply because they refused to work, threatened strikes or joined
> organizations hostile to capitalism, the exponents of repression
> envisioned the federal government as a *deus ex machina* for their
> difficulties with radicals. Until World War I, however, Washington
> was equally embarrassed by the lack of laws suitable for the
> prosecution of dissident members of the community.[5]

The reason, in other words, why the Wilson Administration had difficulty proceeding against the IWW was that it had broken very few laws. The Bureau of Immigration conducted a thorough investigation of the IWW, and it was forced against its will to conclude that IWW writings "contain nothing in direct advocacy of anarchism, active opposition to organized government, or the destruction of property, private or public."[6] To reinforce the point, a rising young official in the bureau, J. Edgar Hoover, commented bluntly that "I believe that the allegation that this organization is anarchistic can neither be substantiated in point of law or fact."[7] Nonetheless, whatever laws the federal government could find, it was willing to use. This was especially true of deportation proceedings under naturalization laws.

Deportation proceedings had been defined by the Supreme Court as not punitive but administrative;[8] therefore, no due process need be applied, and certainly none was. Many judges interpreted IWW membership as explicitly a sign of disloyalty or bad character, and alien radicals were expelled from the country promptly. Individual judicial discretion was not policy, however, so Congress passed, over President Wilson's veto (Wilson had other ways of repressing the IWW in mind) a new naturalization law in February 1917 which declared that:

> Any alien who at any time after entry shall be found advocating
> or teaching the unlawful destruction of property, or advocating or
> teaching anarchy or the overthrow by force or violence of the
> Government of the United States or of all forms of law or
> the assassination of public officials . . . shall, upon the warrant of
> the Secretary of Labor, be taken into custody and deported.[9]

Deportation provided no access to nonalien radicals who were not breaking any laws. In order to suppress them, the obvious strategies were either to create new laws or to proceed as if the IWW had broken laws, taking advantage of public sentiment against it, a sentiment that had been consciously exploited by such corporate bodies as the National Civic Federation and zealous government officials such as George Creel. The latter strategy was adopted, exclusive of naturalization and espionage legislation. The scholarly historian of the Supreme Court Charles Warren, then serving as an assistant attorney general, wrote a memorandum recommending, in Dubofsky's words, that "an extraordinary effort be undertaken to ascertain the future plans of all Wobblies, as well as the names, descriptions, and history of the IWW's leaders, the sources of its income, the nature of its expenses, copies of all IWW publications, and any data that might possibly incriminate the Wobblies."[10] Three months later, after the IWW had offered to open all its books and papers to the government, the offices of the IWW were raided, with the government removing what the organization needed to defend itself.[11] "From 1917 to

1919 the legal prosecution of radicals now characterized their suppression."[12]

Continuing a pattern that is one of the most pronounced in American history, Chicago was chosen as the city in which IWW leaders would be tried on a charge of conspiracy, this time a conspiracy against industrial production and the carrying out of certain laws, including the draft law.[13] Legal trials were urged on the Wilson Administration by lumber interests in the Northwest. They needed a strategy that would break the IWW but at the same time not win it very many adherents among skilled lumberjacks, who were difficult to find at that time because of the war.[14] The lumber manufacturers had come to realize what a later historian of this period also saw:

> The law had clearly proved to be an effective instrument of repression.
> When vigilantes had deported miners from Bisbee or had lynched
> [Frank] Little in Butte, the American conscience had been troubled.
> But when the Justice Department arrested suspected criminals,
> indicted them before impartial judges and randomly selected petit
> juries—that is, when the formal requirements of due process of law
> were observed—the American conscience rested easier.[15]

There is no question that the strategy worked. The jury, deliberating less than an hour, found more than a hundred defendants guilty on approximately four counts each; more than four hundred verdicts, approximately eight decisions per minute of deliberating time. The Chicago verdict then spurred more trials to completion throughout the country of less prominent IWW members.

Legal repression, however, is not the last step of the tale, for there was no guarantee that trials, propaganda, deportations, and vigilante mobs—all taken together—would permanently destroy the IWW. Something more was needed, and that something was provided by liberals such as Felix Frankfurter, conservative unionists such as Samuel Gompers, and so-called enlightened businessmen such as Ralph Easley of the National Civic Federation. They suggested that, along with other forms of repression, the government should convince employers to recognize "legitimate" union activity. Lieutenant Colonel Brice P. Disque convinced lumber manufacturers that ". . . granting workers the shadow of industrial democracy without the substance kept them contented and productive."[16] So instrumental was Frankfurter, then a young Harvard law professor, in urging such an approach on the Wilson Administration that he, as much as anyone, can be credited with the final destruction of the IWW as a meaningful force in American life.[17] The carrot and the stick had been combined, and never again would the IWW threaten the security of any dominant interest in the United States.

Few examples conform as closely as this one to the basic proposition. Here the bias of the democratic state is total. No pretense, no rhetoric of fairness was present—the state acted directly in the interests of the corporations and focused all its attention on the destruction of a radical organization affiliated with a powerless group. As time passed, however, the state in America rarely acted in as blatant a fashion as it did here. Its relationship to the powerful and powerless underwent changes, not major ones—for it still basically acted in the interests of the former and against the interests of the latter—but ones important to review nonetheless. It would be best, in examining these changes, to proceed logically for the moment. The basic proposition assumes circumstances in which a group from the ruling class is confronting a group from outside it. Two kinds of exceptions are therefore possible. In one case, the same circumstance would hold, but the empirical conditions would not lead to the same conclusion. In the other case, a different set of circumstances would be present.

If the circumstances are the same as they are in the basic proposition—one group from the ruling class confronting one group outside it—two possible situations can nullify the proposition. One is that the state can intervene against the powerful group; the other is that it can support the powerless group. Since some have argued that the democratic state has done both of these things, further refinement of the basic proposition is necessary for the Marxist definition of the state to have any validity.

The State Confronts the Powerful

The first alternative proposition can be stated in this fashion: *in those situations where the state intervenes against a group from the dominant class, it can be established as a general principle that such intervention will be the result of popular pressures that are too strong to ignore, that the intervention will be as symbolic as possible, and that the sanctions involved may even be beneficial to those interests over a period of time.* Many examples of this process could be provided, but with antitrust legislation there is a continuous historical process that brings out all these points, thereby illustrating the proposition well.

After the American Civil War, antitrust policy was almost nonexistent because industrial concentration was not yet a major characteristic of the economy. The only existing policies grew out of the English common law, a tradition that, to one historian of antitrust legislation, presents "a picture of great confusion and intermingling of ideas."[18] Contracts that restrained trade were vaguely illegal, but so many qualifications and different interpretations existed that the result was:

to make the common law an insufficient device in the conscious
effort to maintain a workable degree of competition and safeguard a
fair opportunity for the newcomer—gradually becoming an
American policy—in an era increasingly characterized by mass
production and big business.[19]

Farmers, workers, and others hurt by the increasing monopolization
of industry knew nothing of common law traditions. Their only aim was
to get relief from the effects of concentration. In order to do so they
turned first to their state governments, many of which responded by
passing Granger laws and similar, moderate attempts at regulation. Although these laws were upheld by the Supreme Court,[20] when concentration became national in scope, it was obvious that some federal action
was necessary. As any review of magazines of the period will show,
popular sentiment for regulation was strong. There is some disagreement
over the amount of public opposition to industrial concentration, but
considering the difficulty of expressing hostile opinions to as powerful an
agency as big business, popular pressure designed to stop monopolization
was indeed significant. As the most dispassionate account of these events
suggests:

> . . . it would seem that public concern, as conditioned by
> developments in the economic, social, constitutional, and political
> fields, at the end of the 1880's had become serious enough to
> make federal action against the trusts a clear desideratum, if not an
> absolute necessity.[21]

The response to that concern was the Sherman Antitrust Act of 1890.
Its language is familiar enough, but to repeat:

> Section 1. Every contract, combination in the form of trust or
> otherwise, or conspiracy in restraint of trade or commerce among the
> several states, or with foreign nations, is hereby declared
> to be illegal. . . .

> Section 2. Every person who shall monopolize, or attempt to
> monopolize, or combine and conspire with any other person or persons
> to monopolize any part of the trade or commerce among the several
> states, or with foreign nations, shall be deemed guilty of a
> misdemeanor. . . .

> Section 8. . . . the word "person" or "persons" whenever used in
> this act shall be deemed to include corporations and
> associations. . . .[22]

The language seemed clear enough, and farmers and workers were relatively happy with it. Clearly, they felt, the act made illegal the large
trusts that were destroying their livelihood. But some doubts began to

arise. Senator Sherman had argued that the act was no new policy but only a reiteration of common law doctrine. Such an interpretation would make the size of the enterprise irrelevant to the question of whether it was in restraint of trade, for the common law did not recognize any causal relationship between those factors. Then the courts, particularly in the *Knight* decision,[23] made the act impotent as a weapon with which to regulate the trusts, declaring that a firm which did over 90 percent of the business in its area was not in restraint of trade. Conditions seemed similar to those that existed before the act was passed.

But it is incorrect to see that similarity. In actual fact, concentration increased rather drastically after the passage of the Sherman Act. The greatest wave of industrial consolidation was between 1897 and 1904. During those years new corporate assets increased by a factor of over 600 percent when compared to the previous six years. Furthermore, 57 percent of industrial output came to be controlled by 4 percent of American firms.[24] The conclusion of the historian who cites these figures that "By any standard of measurement, large corporations had come to dominate the American economy by 1904"[25] is unchallengeable.

There have been additions to antitrust legislation since the Sherman Act, but they have not significantly altered the pattern described so far. Most of the reforms of the basic act were not designed to make it more effective against trusts but instead were aimed at rationalizing the economy to create industrial order. The last thing leading industrialists wanted was competition, and they were adept at using the rhetoric of antitrust in order to further their goals. The Clayton Act of 1914, called by one historian "all things to all men,"[26] was hardly the "Magna Carta" for labor that Samuel Gompers proclaimed. The exclusion of labor unions from the Sherman Act simply indicated that Congress was not as baldly pro-business as the Supreme Court, which in a series of cases had applied the Sherman Act against prominent labor unions while denying its validity against trusts.[27] Nor did the Federal Trade Commission Act of 1914, with its powers to compel industry to "cease and desist" from unfair practices, change much. The FTC was supported by sophisticated corporate leaders who were threatened by their more reactionary colleagues in small and newer business firms. The same National Civic Federation that was instrumental in devising a "liberal" approach to the repression of the IWW now paved the way for a "liberal" approach to government regulation of the economy. In 1917 Jeremiah W. Jenks of NCF declared his pleasure that the FTC "has apparently been carrying on its work with the purpose of securing the confidence of well intentioned business men, members of the great corporations as well as others."[28]

Given this background, it is no wonder that state action against industrial consolidation consistently has proved futile in stopping it. It was never meant to do so. That this is still the policy of the American government becomes clear from some recent figures on industrial concentration. In 1969 three firms controlled 100 percent of the aluminum industry; three firms, 95 percent of automobile manufacture; four firms, 95 percent of synthetic fibers; four firms, 95 percent of flat glass; three firms, 90 percent of electric bulbs; one firm, 90 percent of telephone equipment; four firms, 90 percent of copper; two firms, 90 percent of cereal foods; one firm, 85 percent of electric tubing; and so on through gypsum, cigarettes, typewriters, salt, rubber tires, soap-detergents, and steel ingots, all of them industries in which four or fewer firms control 80 percent or more of the industry.[29] Between 1967 and 1969, firms as large as Beech-Nut, Jones and Laughlin Steel, Schenley Industries, Youngstown Sheet and Tube, Container Corporation of America, Sinclair Oil, Hartford Fire Insurance, and Mack Trucks (total assets of all eight: $5.99 billion) were *bought* by other industrial firms.[30] Far from consolidation either tapering off or decreasing, it has increased to such an extent that the former counsel of the Senate Antitrust Subcommittee interprets it this way:

> What this means is that the presidents of a hundred companies—a group sufficiently small to be seated comfortably in the reading room of the Union League in Philadelphia—represent almost as much wealth and control as large a share of the nation's economic activity as the next largest 300,000 manufacturers—a group that would completely fill four Yankee Stadiums.[31]

Obviously, size is still not a relevant characteristic in determining whether a company is in restraint of trade.

It would be incorrect to conclude that antitrust legislation has never been used against corporations. It has, and the results of such attempts are uniformly interesting. Theordore Roosevelt, for example, proceeded against corporations he did not like (it was almost that simple), those he felt were uncooperative, and gave "responsible" corporate leaders a bad name. His application of that principle accomplished little. It gave the symbol of aggressive federal action when the opposite was consistently the case.[32] And even when the courts took action against "bad" trusts (under the Supreme Court's common-law-based "rule of reason," which declared that the Sherman Act prohibited only "unreasonable" restraints of trade),[33] the general result was either administrative decentralization or a publicized "breakup" that replaced one mammoth trust with three or four huge ones. But a more fascinating example of antitrust in action is a much more recent one.

The 1960 price-fixing case against executives of twenty-nine electrical corporations is the largest antitrust action ever taken by the American government. There was not much else the government could do. A private reporter, working in conjunction with officials of the Tennessee Valley Administration, publicized the fact that the TVA received sealed bids for electrical equipment that were identical to the last decimal point.[34] The corporations involved in price-fixing had not even bothered to hide what they were doing, so sure were they that their conspiracies, though obviously illegal, would not result in meaningful prosecution. Companies such as General Electric and Westinghouse had faced anti-trust action before (many times, in fact) and each time they had paid a small fine as a sort of tax on their activities. This case, however, was different. Similar prices did not come out of haphazard consultation but through scheming in secret places, code words, and elaborate plans. In addition to identical bids, for example, the companies used what was called a "phase of the moon" formula, described in the indictment as follows:

> Through cyclic rotating positioning inherent in the formula, one defendant manufacturer would quote the low price, others would quote intermediate prices, and another would quote the high price; these positions would be periodically rotated among the manufacturers. This formula was so calculated that in submitting prices to these customers, the price spread between defendant manufacturers' quotations would be sufficiently narrow so as to eliminate actual price competition among them, but sufficiently wide so as to give an appearance of competition.[35]

A more ingenious formula for dividing the pie could hardly be devised.

The conspiring in restraint of trade that was uncovered in the course of this case was nothing new or surprising to those familiar with corporate operations. Witnesses traced such practices back to the 1930s, although GE had been involved in antitrust action since 1911. Furthermore, the individuals convicted were among the highest-ranking officers of their companies. Although the chairman and president of GE both announced vigorously that they knew nothing about such practices, there is evidence that the president did, and most commentators are certain that practices so integral to a company are obviously known to its leadership. The chairman's stock answer to questions concerning his knowledge was to stress his distribution of a memo calling on employees not to violate the Sherman Act, as if that testified to his innocence. Finally, such practices continue to the present. Committees of Congress have discovered administered prices in just about every industry where there is concentration.[36] Some of these agreements are the result, not of conscious conspiracy, but of price imitation, but the effect is the same. There is reason to believe that corporations cannot exist without administered prices for the same reason that they desire state action to rationalize the economy: without fixed prices, chaos would result and the economy might not be able to rectify it. Administered prices, industrial concentration, and government regulation of the economy are all aspects of the same forces.

The fact that twenty-nine companies and forty-five individuals were convicted (of misdemeanors) under the Sherman Act is proof that *the state can intervene against privileged groups. But the conditions attached to that are legion:*

1. The offense must be so blatant that further inaction would be as bad for the company as it would for the administration in power.

2. The state action must consider only individual "wrongdoers"; the investigation is confined to that, no questions asked about the system that produced the conspiracy. In the price-fixing case, remarkably little attention was paid to who knew about the agreements, how they dealt with it, and whether anything could be done about it.

3. Attempts must not be made by the state to follow up the action in order to make sure that nothing will happen again. Things return to normal quickly.

One other difference is worth noting separately:

4. The punishment given will be token. Compare the following two cases. In the IWW federal trials, no illegal acts could be found, the defendants showed their total faith in the judicial system that was trying them, and the defendants offered to open all their books to the government. In the GE-Westinghouse price-fixing case, guilt was clearly established, continuous and overt guilt; the defendants, particularly those from the Big 2 companies, were uncooperative until the last moment; much of the actual evidence was shrouded in secrecy; and the sentences imposed were the highest ever given to corporations in an antitrust case.[37] The sentences received by the defendants in the two trials were:

IWW	GE/WESTINGHOUSE
5: release or indefinite postponement	7: 30 days in jail
2: 10 days in county jail	5: suspended sentences
10: year and a day in federal prison	33: fines
35: 5 years in prison	
33: 10 years in prison	
15: 20 years in prison	

In addition, all the GE defendants were convicted of misdemeanors, hence they lost no political rights. The IWW defendants, of course, had no such luxury. The only favorable comparison is that all IWW prisoners had their sentences commuted within five years, while all the corporation executives served five days less than their terms for good behavior. Even taking into account the time difference, such distinctions are obviously the result of a class bias in the democratic state.

If the democratic state had been as successful in its intervention in antitrust policy as it had been in its antiradical policy, justification for viewing the state as a neutral element might be present. But it never was. Antitrust legislation indicates that the democratic state will move against the powerful, but only with kid gloves. The nature of its movement is what reveals the bias of the democratic state, not the assumption that it does not move. For the state to view antitrust irregularities as a crime in the same way it viewed the (more legal) actions of the IWW as a crime, the whole nature of the society would have to be reversed, for antitrust violations are needed to keep capitalism working. As one individual in the price-fixing case said:

> No one attending the gatherings was so stupid that he didn't know the meetings were in violation of the law. But it is the only way a business can be run. It is free enterprise.[38]

If violation of the Sherman Act is an integral part of business enterprise, then why have the Sherman Act at all? If business calls the tune, why doesn't it tune out legislation like that? The answer has been provided by the strongly anti-Marxist writer Thurman Arnold:

> The actual result of the anti-trust laws was to promote the growth of great industrial organizations by deflecting the attack of them into purely moral and ceremonial channels. . . . The anti-trust laws remained as a most important symbol. Whenever anyone demanded practical regulation, they formed an effective moral obstacle, since all the liberals would answer with a demand that the anti-trust laws be enforced.[39]

The ironic thing is that Arnold, after he wrote this, became chief of the Antitrust Division of the Justice Department and vigorously pursued a policy designed to win compliance with a law which, intellectually, he must have known was unenforceable. In doing so, he aided his own enemies; by seeming to produce strenuous federal activity, industrial consolidation could proceed with less attention focused upon it.

The State and the Powerless

The basic proposition could also be nullified in another way when its circumstances are correct, and that is if the state were to aid a powerless group instead of repressing it. When that happens, another alternative proposition can be advanced: *aid given by the state to groups outside the ruling class will be given only so long as the privileges of the ruling class are not significantly threatened; indeed, such aid will be given when the provision of no aid at all would more significantly hurt the dominant groups.*

Is it possible that the democratic state could intervene in favor of labor unions without damaging the privileges of the corporate order, in fact, actually furthering those privileges? That is the question that must be asked in reviewing governmental recognition of labor unions during the New Deal, the area most often pointed to in order to show that the democratic state is neutral, but an area that can also be used to illustrate this alternative proposition. Most commentary on the Wagner Act (which provided that recognition) sees it as a direct contradiction to Marx's predictions about increasing class polarization and the dependency of the state on the more powerful of those classes. Although Marx recognized that ruling groups would seek amelioration of social conditions in order to make their rule stronger,[40] he probably underestimated the degree to which labor could become a conservative force within capitalist society. That does not, however, violate the Marxist analysis of the state, for the price labor paid for its economic gains was the recognition of its own political weakness; that is, organized labor agreed to leave the democratic state in the hands of the capitalists in return for recognition and more economic benefits. Expressed in one sentence, that is essentially what happened during the New Deal.

Section 7a of the National Industrial Recovery Act, later declared unconstitutional by the Supreme Court,[41] recognized the right of unions to engage in collective bargaining. But the remaining provisions of the act established a system designed by corporate leaders such as Henry Harriman and Gerard Swope of General Electric to use the state for the ends of corporate capital. It was "industrial self-government," to its director General Johnson: "NRA is exactly what industry organized in trade associations makes it."[42] Before the act was declared null and void, it had gone a long way toward showing that any partnership between business and labor would exist only as long as labor accepted its role as a junior partner. The actual effect of state recognition of collective bargaining under NRA was to encourage the formation of company unions.

The Wagner Act is generally seen as a more radical piece of legislation, which finally and convincingly established labor as a major force in American society. Introduced in the Senate over the strenuous objections of President Roosevelt and Secretary of Labor Frances Perkins[43] the Wagner Act guaranteed the right of workers to form a union. It ensured meaningful collective bargaining by legislating the principle that a majority of workers could establish themselves as a bargaining agent for all workers within a unit. All this was to be enforced through the National Labor Relations Board composed of representatives of labor, business, and the public.[44] The act was indeed far-reaching and under it organized labor flourished. The percentage of union members in the work force was 6.8 percent in 1930 and 6.7 percent in 1935. Under the Wagner Act it jumped to 15.8 percent in 1939, 22.4 percent in 1949, and 24.1 percent in 1959. Both the number of unions and the aggregate number of union members increased drastically.[45] By any such statistical indicators, labor had indeed "made it" under the Wagner Act.

Only if we conceive of society in the form of what mathematicians call a zero-sum game do these gains mean they were made at the expense of the dominant groups. A zero-sum game is like poker: winnings and losses at any point in time add up to zero. If one side wins, the other side must lose. This was decidedly not the case with labor-management relations. Even though the unions were greatly strengthened, this did not take place at the expense of management. Those accustomed to controlling the state were not unhappy to see labor organized. They had supported the NRA and were perfectly willing to support the Wagner Act as well, with recognized exceptions such as Sewell Avery of Montgomery Ward, who would have to be carried out of his executive office for his refusal to recognize a union. The Wagner Act assured corporate leaders two invaluable things. First, it took the sting out of the revolutionary potential that existed in the society. Second, it regularized and made more predictable the entire economy at no real economic cost to the corporations.

One cannot overemphasize the fact that recognition of labor by the state was done as a conscious alternative to what nonrecognition might have produced. One of Roosevelt's key advisers on the NRA, Donald Richberg, considered the most favorable to labor, expressed a general fear in these words:

> Let me warn those who desire to preserve the existing order but
> intend to do nothing to reform it that if this depression continues
> much longer the unemployed will be organized and action of a
> revolutionary nature will be demanded.[46]

The obvious solution was to bring into the corporate order those among organized labor who were "responsible," that is, those who would not drastically challenge the existence of that order. Finding such people was not difficult at all, for many labor leaders were perfectly happy to join up, regardless of the effect that might have on the unorganized or even on those unions not considered respectable. Rarely was this motive expressed as candidly as by Machinist Union President A. O. Wharton in April 1937 to his affiliates:

> Since the Supreme Court decision upholding the Wagner Act many
> employers now realize that it is the Law of our Country and they are
> prepared to deal with labor organizations. These employers have

expressed a preference to deal with A.F. of L. organizations, rather than Lewis, Hillman, Dubinsky, Howard and their gang of sluggers, communists, radicals and soap-box artists, professional bums, expelled members of other labor unions, outright scabs and the Jewish organizations with all their red affiliates.[47]

Wharton's strategy is called the "backdoor" ploy, in which a union purposely undercuts others perceived as more militant by demonstrating its own conservatism to the employers. The only trouble with it was that Wharton was incorrect. Lewis, Hillman, and the others were just as willing to become partners with corporate capital as he. Hillman, for example, was a strong advocate of the NRA, even when other labor leaders came to realize how much it was benefiting the corporations.[48] John L. Lewis was the most manipulative union leader of the period, using Communists to organize difficult industries and then dumping them from his union when they were no longer needed.[49] Dubinsky resigned from the Socialist party one year before Wharton's letter was written to campaign for Roosevelt and declare his loyalty to the principles of capitalism: ". . . socialism, certainly of the orthodox variety, will never work. Trade unionism needs capitalism like a fish needs water. Democracy is possible only in a society of free enterprise, and trade unionism can only live in a democracy."[50] Most ironic of all was that the final man named by Wharton, Charles P. Howard, outlined the exact same strategy in 1935:

> Now let me say to you that the workers of this country are going to organize, and if they are not permitted to organize under the American Federation of Labor they are going to organize under some other leadership or are going to organize without leadership. . . . I don't know . . . how many workers have been organized into independent unions, company unions and associations that may have some affiliation with subversive influences during the past few years. However, I am inclined to believe that the number in those classes of organization is far greater than any one of us would grant.[51]

The existence of a corporate ideology among key labor leaders did not mean that no revolutionary situation existed. The CIO was making dramatic gains, and agreements with its leaders were the best way of isolating the radicals among its rank and file. Furthermore, there were signs of what Arthur Schlesinger, Jr., called "upheaval" coming from outside the ranks of organized labor.[52] Huey Long promised to share the wealth, and other populist-type leaders were making their disrespect for Roosevelt and the New Deal well known. From the perspective of that time, with depression all around and no way out in sight, it is remarkable that the democratic state survived with as few concessions as it did. In fact, a good case can be made that state capitalism triumphed during a depression that an incomplete state capitalism had brought to the society. It is now accepted that the New Deal was a conservative event, but the extent of that conservatism, given the crisis, is impressive. As Barton Bernstein concluded about the New Deal: "There was no significant redistribution of power in American society, only limited recognition of other organized groups, seldom of unorganized people."[53]

Corporate leaders had other things to gain from legislation such as the Wagner Act besides the preservation of the existing system. Collective bargaining stabilized labor relations. Paying higher wages was no problem, for the added expense could be, and was, passed on to the consumer. Thus, inflation ate up the dramatic wage increases but had little effect on profits. But beyond that, if it is true that the democratic state exists to benefit powerful groups, then any collective bargaining under state sponsorship would nearly always benefit the corporations more than it would the unions, while appearing to represent each equally. There was a foreshadowing of this during World War II when the War Labor Board, composed of four members each from labor, business, and the public, handed down decisions that kept wages down, in spite of worker resentment during the war.[54] After the war was over, similar events began to occur. NLRB procedures became so cumbersome that they were rendered ineffective. It would take a union years, after appeals and corporate due process, to get the NLRB to act against an employer. The result was that old-fashioned strikes had to be resorted to.[55] In the years after the war, no attempts were made to "roll back" the gains by labor, but any attempts to further those gains were met with resistance by the state.

In many cases that resistance was expressed directly in policy. Taft-Hartley and Landrum-Griffin were acts of Congress passed with a hostile attitude toward labor in mind. Any doubt that labor and business were on an equal plane was thereby demolished, for both laws established restrictions against labor that did not exist against business. Senator McClelland's investigations into labor corruption furthered the trend. Corruption there undoubtedly was, but the fact that only labor unions were under investigation gave the impression that the state did not care as much to regulate corruption in industry. We have already seen the slight punishment given to leaders of GE and Westinghouse. When compared to the stiff sentences handed out by federal courts to Dave Beck, James Hoffa, and other labor union leaders whose conduct was similar, the secondary position of labor once again becomes apparent. In other words, in spite of real gains made during the depression, when that period was over, conditions returned pretty much to normal. Injunctions are still used against labor unions, but the existence of similar injunctions against corporate leaders is rare. The army can be called out to speed delivery of the mail during a strike, but it is rarely called out to run a corporation. (The one time it was—during the Korean war—the Supreme Court called it unconstitutional.)[56] Finally, labor's organizing drive seemed directly affected by this activity. Although, as we have seen, the percentage of the work force that was unionized increased drastically from 1930 to 1959, it declined between 1959 and 1966, from 24.1 percent to 22.7 percent.[57] During the same period in time, the number of work stoppages increased, from 3,708 involving 1,330,000 workers to 4,405 involving 1,960,000,[58] indicating that organized labor has found the state machinery established under the New Deal unsatisfactory for resolving disputes and has been forced to return to action outside the state.

At the present time, in spite of talk about a military-industrial-labor complex, labor is hardly any kind of important partner running the affairs of state. Talk of the power of labor is usually centered around its economic ability to hurt the economy. That it has such potential power is unquestioned, but that is the antithesis of sharing state power. The "complex" also refers to those "new men of power," those few labor leaders who are consulted on the making of important decisions.[59] In some cases labor leaders involved in the making of policy are indistinguishable in attitude from other policy makers, the price they have paid for entry into the halls of power. This is especially true in foreign policy, where, as Ronald Radosh has pointed out,[60] labor leaders can be even more reactionary than their corporate counterparts. In other cases, labor leaders will be consulted on matters of policy, but this is done simply to gain legitimacy for a decision by having it appear that labor was part of the process. Finally, labor does have some influence over local politics in a number of cities and within the Democratic party.[61] Here the influence is within institutions that do not make the major policy decisions in the society but have some control over lesser matters. All things considered, organized labor has been given a place in American society where its complaints will be minimal, but so will its power. It is a difficult balance, but it seems to have been accomplished.

To summarize the argument to this point, we have seen that the basic Marxist proposition, by itself, is unable to explain the manifold relationships between the state, the powerful groups, and the powerless groups. But the basic proposition is an excellent starting point, for, with some refinement, it can be used to explain most of the biases of the democratic state. It is not so much that the state acts mechanistically, always moving to support one group and repress the other, as it is that a regularized bias exists in the operations of the democratic state that tends to support the interests of the powerful against those who challenge them.

Conflicts Among the Powerless

The alternative propositions used so far in this chapter all assume a situation in which a group from the ruling class is confronting one that is relatively powerless. But there is another sense in which the basic proposition about the state must be modified: when this assumption does not hold. For example, it is possible that state intervention would occur to adjudicate between two groups, neither of which was powerful. On the other hand, situations of disagreement might exist between two or more groups within the ruling class. Each of these cases requires a modification of the basic proposition.

When the state intervenes between two groups neither of which is in the dominant class, such intervention is designed to favor the group that those in power would like favored; the unfavored group, if it mounts a challenge to this policy, will be repressed. Such a modification helps explain the policy of the state toward nonwhites, which, in the last twenty years, has been a combination of state aid to some and a healthy dose of repression to others.

In the 1950s the official segments of American society began to discover that there was a race problem in the United States. They were even moved to do something about it, primarily because segregation had caused embarrassment on the diplomatic front. In his address on the situation in Little Rock in September 1957, the president of the United States said:

> At a time when we face grave situations abroad because of
> the hatred that communism bears toward a system of government
> based on human rights, it would be difficult to exaggerate the
> harm that is being done to the prestige and influence, and indeed to
> the safety, of our nation and the world.
> Our enemies are gloating over this incident and using it
> everywhere to misrepresent our whole nation.[62]

Eisenhower was not the only one to use such rhetoric. President Kennedy was willing to tie the struggle against segregation in the South to the struggle to contain communism overseas. His address to the nation, designed to counter Governor Wallace's stand in the school doorway at the University of Alabama, pointed out that "today we are committed to a world wide struggle to promote and protect the rights of all who wish to be free. And when Americans are sent to Vietnam or West Berlin we do not ask for whites only."[63] They certainly did not.

Once the decision was made finally to combat segregation—not, by the way, to eliminate inequality or racism, just to combat segregation—another motive began to develop. The civil rights movement, it was discovered, was hardly incompatible with capitalist growth; in fact, the South in general and the northern ghettos in particular were the last places within the borders of the United States where capitalism had not fully developed. In the South cheap labor was available for new factories, but a tense racial situation could make things uncomfortable for branches of national industries. Furthermore, major developments in "service" industries, particularly civil service, were locating in the South. Cities like Huntsville, Alabama, and Houston, Texas, found millions of dollars sent their way to become veritable civil service colonies of the Defense Department. The federal government's own prestige required at least token integration in those areas. In the northern cities consumerism in the ghetto—while far above what it should have been, given per capita income—was nevertheless lower than it might have been, given a more rational economy. No wonder that powerful groups, politicians, and corporate leaders could adopt civil rights rhetoric, at least for areas outside their ken.

These tendencies were enhanced when rebellions broke out in the cities. It seemed for a while that the entire political system might fall apart. In his charge to the National Advisory Commission on Civil Disorders, President Johnson spoke of attacking slum conditions "because there is simply no other way to achieve a decent and orderly society in America."[64] An orderly society has always meant one in which corporations could pursue their goals without continual unnerving interruptions, as riots are wont to be. The Commission's report itself, by calling attention to white racism as the cause of civil disorder, naturally ignored making distinctions about racism, as if the racism of a working-class white plumber could be compared to the institutional racism of Chase Manhattan Bank. Intelligent businessmen came to realize that the dangers posed by civil disorder could be great. One of them—the vice-president of Sheraton Corp.—expressed it this way:

> Since the Detroit and Newark riots in 1967, a closer identity has
> sprung up between the needs of the ghetto economy and the needs
> of the normal economy. The riots now reach beyond the black or
> "grey" areas of the cities and threaten the entire American economy.
> Curfews and enforced closings of businesses undermine downtown
> real estate values. Riots now mean massive losses of profits, millions
> in forfeited wages, and cancelled conventions for entire cities.[65]

Rhetoric is one thing; action another. The difficulties facing the state in its attempt to do something about poverty and racism were revealed in the war on poverty program. Had this been another piece of New Deal legislation—in which the government paternalistically distributes money to agencies that spent it on welfare-type activities—it could be considered as simply another attempt to keep money in the ghettos. But the law explictly encouraged the "maximum feasible participation of the poor," a term associated with advisers to the late President Kennedy.[66] The idea was a powerful one, and it had the effect of encouraging people to believe that, this time, something really was going to be done. In any case, it was an interesting choice of words, for it exposes an important dilemma: the problems that result when the democratic state tries to do what it cannot. The words led naive ghetto residents to believe that they could participate, and when that occurred, the phrase went out of the law as fast as they went out of their programs. Congress became the institution forced to bury the notion:

> When Congress realized what had been wrought or at least might
> be wrought in the name of maximum feasible participation, it moved
> to vest in local government the authority for deciding on the
> form of a CAP (Community Action Project). It also required that the
> board, whether under government or corporate auspices, would
> consist of no more than one-third poor people, with the
> remaining places equally divided between government officials and
> representatives of community groups.[67]

What was or might have been wrought? Implicit in the participatory notion was the foil of the democratic state, a place where people might be allowed to deal with their own lives as they saw fit. That was killed, not only because it was a threat to local political "machines," as was publicized, but because it was a threat to the entire concept of the democratic state as it exists in practice. The state, and the institutions that support it, depend on a passive citizenry for their existence, and they made sure that no challenge to passivity would emerge from the war on poverty.

So far the picture that has been drawn is similar to that of labor, in that the state was willing to give the appearance of aid to a powerless group for political reasons. There was always the danger that no action by the state to combat segregation would encourage the development of a revolutionary perspective on the part of blacks who were building a political consciousness. But the government could not take action that violated the vested interests of those who had power, and therefore its support for the fight against racism has two qualifying amendments: (1) it urged a moderate approach, but (2) it also meant that the state would seek allies among black groups who accepted the legitimacy of the present order and would work within it. Under the antipoverty and related programs, a new nonwhite elite was created which was nonrevolutionary and which was based on ideas of cultural nationalism, black capitalism, or bureaucratic power, none of which were great threats to the system.

But unlike the situation involving labor in the 1930s, one other element was present here, and that was the systematic attempt by the government to repress a more militant group that did not accept the legitimacy of the capitalist order, the Black Panther party. The repression of the Panthers was part of the same policy that put a former director of the Congress on Racial Equality on the president's staff. This was not a contradiction at all, but an attempt to make clear that the state would "play ball" with "responsible" leaders (those who presented no challenge) but would try to drive out of existence those who did not accept the rules. Here the state attempted to do two things simultaneously, and neither can be understood without the other.

Interestingly enough, while the state's policy of cooptation was only partly successful, its policy of repression was very successful. An extraordinary campaign against the Panthers was unleashed, rivaling (but not matching) the one against the IWW earlier in the century. It is impossible at this point to analyze the documents involved in the preparation of this policy, as one can do for the IWW, but the size, seriousness, and coordination of the campaign can be gleaned from some figures collected by the Panthers, which can be rearranged and categorized to illustrate what repression meant in this case.[68] Between May 2, 1967 (when a group of Black Panthers legally visited the California state capitol carrying guns), and the end of 1969, 768 arrests of Black Panthers were made; for the literal minded, that is an average of more than one per day over a two-year span. Total bail for all those arrested was $4,890,580 (roughly equal to the total receipts from corporate income taxes in Iowa in 1962). Data on the resolution of the arrests exist for 427 of the cases. They show that 201 were still pending in early 1970, which means that approximately half that number were in jail, unable to afford bail. Another 136 charges were dismissed, indicating the extent to which members of the organization are periodically arrested under insubstantial charges and later released. Of the remaining 90 cases, 5 pleaded guilty and 85 not guilty. Of the 85, 75 were convicted and 10 found innocent, a conviction rate of 88 percent. These arrests took place in communities as diverse as Oakland; San Francisco; Berkeley; Seattle; Indianapolis; Victoria, B.C.; New York; Brooklyn; Newark; Detroit; Baltimore; Omaha; Milwaukee; Denver; Jersey City; Chicago; Des Moines; Los Angeles; Boston; Harrisburg; Peeksill, New York; Champaign-Urbana; Eugene; Kansas City; New Haven; Sausalito; Salt Lake City; Philadelphia; Albany; San Diego; White Plains, New York; Queens; the Bronx; and Richmond, California.

A breakdown of the various charges under which the 768 Panthers were arrested reveals a total of 1,003, divided as follows:

Various charges of weapons possession	178
Disorderly conduct and disturbing the peace	96
Attempted murder, suspicion of murder, conspiracy to murder	92
Theft, robbery, and burglary	62
Resisting arrest, threatening an officer, interference	48
Assault; felonious assault	42
Attempted robbery	40
Possession of drugs	38
Conspiring to bomb	38
Leafletting and selling newspapers	36
Traffic, obstructing traffic, and jay-walking	33
Auto theft	26
Aggravated battery	22
Haboring a fugitive	19
Profanity and obscenity	16
Riot or inciting to riot	16
Unlawful flight	16
Kidnaping	15
Trespassing	14
Failure to disperse	12
Arson or conspiring to arson	12
Unlawful assembly	11
Defrauding an innkeeper	11
Loitering	10
Receiving stolen goods	9
No ID	8
Murder	8
Conspiracy (unspecified)	8
Induction offenses	7
Obstruction of government administration	5
Harassment	5
Bench warrants	5
Failure to give account	4
Curfew violations	3
Conspiracy to assassinate	3
Parole and probation offenses	3
Threat to commit a felony	3
Conspiracy to purchase machine guns	3
Forgery	2
Grand larceny	2
Hitchhiking	2
Using a sound device	2
Failure to appear in court	2
Aiding and abetting attempted murder	2
Spitting on sidewalk	2

Prowling	1
Machine-gunning police headquarters	1
Pimping and pandering	1
Purse snatching	1
Desertion from army	1
Suspected larceny	1
Malicious behavior	1
Conspiracy to overthrow the government	1
Defacing a public monument	1
Being a runaway	1
Setting up an unlawful table	1
Threatening the life of the president	1
	1,003

The imaginativeness of some of the charges indicates the wide options open to the democratic state when it chooses a policy of legal repression. (For more on this see chapter 4.)

In addition to arrests, the same two-year period saw fifty-seven separate incidents of police or vigilante harassment taken against the Panthers. These can be broken down as follows:

Individual harassment of BPP members	21
Police raids on office	18
Office bombings	5
Gunfights	3
Refusals of entry to foreign country	3
Deportations	3
Disruptions of meetings	2
Raids at home	1
Rent evictions	1
	57

As with the arrests, harassment was not confined to a few cities but existed throughout the United States. The irony of this situation was that the Panthers were in the process of becoming more peaceful just when the government was encouraging violence.

These figures raise all kinds of questions about repression and democracy, many of which will be examined toward the end of this book. For the moment, they indicate how sustained government action can be when repression of a serious challenge is the goal. State aid to *help* blacks ran into all kinds of difficulty: noncooperation by local elites, congressional obstruction, bureaucratic inefficiency. The result was that it was haphazard and never achieved what it said it would. But when *repression* was the goal, local officials cooperated and even went out of their way to help; Congress refused to interfere; and the Justice Department found itself mobilized on a policy involving blacks for the first time. The only ones who tried to stop repression, interestingly enough, were ordinary people: on juries, they found many of the Panther leaders not guilty. But while their acts were courageous and sincere, the existence of a "not guilty" verdict hardly removes any indictment from the state for its actions, for the government's goal was to break up any threat that the Panthers might have mounted. It would be difficult to evaluate the effects of the government's campaign, since the Panthers are still alive and well in Oakland, California. But the impact was nonetheless there. The recent return of Panther leader Huey Newton from Cuba should indicate to what extent the government will change its policy of violence against this group.

State Cooperation with the Powerful

The last possibility envisioned in the typology of relationships being explored here is the one that occurs when the state is a party to conflict among groups, all of whom belong to the dominant class. In those situations, the following can be established as the alternative proposition: *the goal of state intervention is to favor neither group (assuming relatively equal power) but to bring the groups together around a compromise before this conflict has any effect on less powerful groups that might be able to take advantage of a major rupture.*

Selective Service presents a situation in which real conflicts did exist between powerful groups. When the law came up for revision in 1967, these conflicts became apparent. The military, which expected from Selective Service a ready supply of draftees who would accept military discipline and serve around the world without complaint, decided that their best method of achieving that goal was to support Selective Service as it previously existed, making only minor reforms. Business, which relied on Selective Service because of its "channeling" function, its ability to establish manpower criteria with more authority than any other aspect of domestic policy, wanted a change in the law that would have centralized the draft boards around criteria of a national sort and would have integrated the system with the manpower divisions of the Department of Labor. Finally, universities, which had since the end of World War II become powerful institutions in many respects, were embarrassed by repeated student antiwar and antidraft demonstrations. They wanted any rational reforms that would remove the draft as an issue on campus; for example, a lottery system or the elimination of student deferments. Since there were obvious contradictions between the desire to keep the law as it was and the desires to change it drastically, something had to give when the state was called upon to make policy.

Not only were there conflicts between groups, but some also existed within each category. The "military" refers to General Hershey, General Mark Clark, and others who were instrumental in blocking reform. There were also, however, other generals, such as David Shoup and James Gavin, who found themselves in opposition to that position, and they eventually received support from Defense Secretary McNamara and his staff when McNamara found himself calling for major draft-law revisions in a Montreal speech.[69] A similar situation existed at the university level. Kingman Brewster, president of Yale, spoke for a number of liberal college presidents when he attacked the draft in these terms:

> Selective Service in order to staff a two million man force from a two
> hundred million population has invited a cops and robbers view
> of national obligation. National morality has been left exposed
> to collective self-corruption by the persistent refusal of the national
> administration to take the lead in the design of a national manpower
> policy which would rationally relate individual privilege and
> national duty.[70]

Despite Brewster's insight that an irrational law works to destroy the legitimacy of all other repressive institutions, much of the educational "establishment" did not follow him. The American Council for Education, the most powerful lobbying voice for the industry, representing universities, professional associations, and other educational institutions, tended to support the idea of educational deferments.[71] Within the business community, some businessmen did not support such men as Thomas S. Gates, chairman of Morgan Guaranty Trust, who wanted reform of the draft. They were either unconcerned or did not wish to appear at odds with the military.

Finally, another item that contributed to the confusion was that the governmental apparatus had no clear position on Selective Service reform. Congress, led by a few southerners close to the military, was determined to prevent reform. Most of the president's staff favored reform of deferments and decentralization and pushed them hard. President Johnson, torn by his desires to lead the nation but also unwilling to antagonize his good friends in the Senate and House, came out formally for reform but refused to make it a major issue.

In the face of all these pressures and counterpressures, is it possible to conclude that there was a role of the state at all? Isn't this example proof that the Marxist hypothesis on the state is too simplified and monocausal to account for the complexities that arise in a situation such as this? It is only if one misreads the Marxist hypothesis, for the purpose of that hypothesis is not to deny the existence of complexity but to make sense out of it. Keeping that in mind, the alternative proposition (that is, that the role of the state when there is conflict among the dominant groups is one of conflict resolution) does make sense out of the draft-reform controversy of 1967–70. A more specific examination should show how this is the case.

As the deadline for reform of the draft came closer, some action had to be taken by Congress or else the law would simply expire. Because of his desire to stop antidraft demonstrations on the campus, President Johnson in July 1966 employed an old symbolic stratagem: he created a commission to study the Selective Service System. The composition of the commission reflects the conflicts discussed above, but also indicates that business and the universities were to predominate.[72] The chairman was Burke Marshall, former assistant attorney general for civil rights, but more significantly the then vice-president and general counsel of International Business Machines Corporation. Other corporate representatives included the following: Thomas Gates, not only chairman of the incredibly powerful Morgan Bank, but also a former secretary of defense; Oveta Culp Hobby, former secretary of HEW and publisher of the *Houston Post;* and Warren G. Woodward, vice-president, American Airlines. A number of smaller businesses were also represented. Educational leaders included Kingman Brewster; theology professor John Courtney Murray, S.J.; the former surgeon general of the United States, now a vice-president of the University of Pennsylvania; a professor of surgery; a professor of human relations; and the president of President Johnson's alma mater, a man who would later be forced to resign when it was proved that he plagiarized his thesis. Also on the panel were two labor union leaders, one judge, one antipoverty official, one project director for the Southern Regional Council, and former Marine Corps Commandant General David Shoup. This was obviously a pro-reform commission; the only disagreements within it were likely to be over the scope of the reforms.

The composition of the panel was so biased that congressional leaders who were opposed to any reforms at all decided to create their own commission to study selective service. A more vivid contrast to the Marshall Commission could hardly be found.[73] The chairman was General Mark Clark, president emeritus of the Citadel, a military academy in South Carolina. General Clark was known to be close to Chairman L. Mendel Rivers of South Carolina and the House Armed Services Committee, the most powerful man in Congress on Selective Service policy. His panel included the chairman of Avco Corporation, a fast-growing conglomerate that built planes and houses and owned movie theaters and movies (e.g., *Midnight Cowboy*). The fact that this man, Colonel Earl Blaik, also had been a popular and successful football coach at West Point made sure that his views would be close to those of Clark. Other members included the presidents of Hampton Institute and Purdue University, former diplomat and author Robert Murphy, the former chairman of the Religion Department at Catholic University who was also a vice-admiral, and an official of the investment house of Goldman, Sachs, and Co. While some attempt was made to give the appearance of religious, social, and institutional diversity, it was clear to all that this commission would favor the Selective Service law in its present form as much as the Marshall Commission would seek to change it. Neither commission gave even token representation to those most affected by the draft.

Outside the commissions, public pressure to change the law was intense. Demonstrations on campus continued, but not only antiwar protestors wished to see the draft altered. People in the highest reaches of power in the United States were anxious to join them. For example, the Ford Foundation sponsored a major conference on the draft, which was held at the University of Chicago. Present were a wide diversity of individuals, including students, scholars, generals, manpower specialists, intellectuals, judges, government officials, and representatives of business.[74] This conference found itself being carried away by proposals that would reject the draft in its present form—a volunteer army or some form of national service. After some brilliant papers from Milton Friedman and Walter Y. Oi showed the feasibility of a volunteer army,[75] a majority of the participants voted in a straw poll to endorse the idea.[76]

What was so convincing about those papers? Oi showed the hidden costs of the draft and how a volunteer army would actually be cheaper. Friedman rejected the idea that such a system would be racially unbalanced or lead to an elite corps. Instead he showed how it would maximize individual freedom, yet at the same time, "Industry and government would benefit from being able to hire young men on their merits, not their deferments."[77] Although a volunteer army would eliminate the national manpower planning ("channeling") function of Selective Service, that function could be supplied elsewhere where it should be, as in the labor department or, in Friedman's vision, by the free market. National Service was advocated by some at the conference, particularly Margaret Mead and the then associate director of the Peace Corps, Harris Wofford. Secretary McNamara had endorsed the idea that all might be asked to serve in some capacity or another—army, VISTA, Peace Corps, etc.—and, although he backed down from that position, the idea had strong academic support. Such service would eliminate some of the absurd inequities and at the same time would give the appearance of equality.

The Chicago conference indicated the difficulty of balancing the needs of business, the military, and the universities. Both alternative plans were fully compatible with the interests of colleges and industry, but the military was aware that it might not be able to recruit men to fight under either plan. While the conference was being held, the army was having personnel problems. For example, reenlistment in 1969 was the lowest since 1960. Enrollment in ROTC programs was in the process of falling to an astounding 26.6 percent. The navy was unable to reenlist enough men to the point of danger. Salaries were so low that a minimum of 100,000 army families were on welfare.[78] The outlook was becoming so dim that key military officials were strongly against any tampering with the draft. In the face of that, any recommendations along the lines of those coming out of the Chicago conference would have to be put off for some time.

Shortly after the conference ended, each of the two commissions reported as expected. The Marshall Commission, in its own words, "saw as its overriding obligation the necessity to search for a method of manpower procurement which would assure the armed forces' ability to acquire the men they need, under any circumstances, to protect the nation's security and meet its commitments; and at the same time function as uniformly and equitably as possible with due regard for the problems and the rights of individuals into whose lives it must intrude."[79] In other words, the Marshall Commission became the body entrusted with carrying out the role of the state. Its job was to reconcile the need for men with the nation's security, at the same time removing irrational inequities that were undermining the legitimacy of the entire procedure. To that end, it proposed a number of recommendations, the most important of which were as follows: continuation of the idea of Selective Service (extremely important in the face of alternatives being discussed), centralization of the draft boards around uniform policies, the draft of young men first (to make careers more predictable), a random order of call, and the end of student or occupational deferments. Something was promised for all, whether they be military officers (continuation of the draft), business planners (centralized boards, young men first), university officials (no student deferments), and lucky potential draftees (random selection).

By contrast, the Clark Commission, which had no staff and little time to work, thus relying on the personnel and research of the House Armed Services Committee, had few recommendations.[80] Outside of changing the name of the law, it did propose selected graduate deferments for fields in the national interest and a procedure for circumventing the Supreme Court's liberalization of conscientious objector policy. Otherwise, its recommendations would leave the law alone except for minor administrative reorganizations.

The law that eventually passed the Congress in 1967 was disappointing to the reformers. The name of the act was indeed changed but very little else was. The president's recommendation of a lottery system was explicitly rejected, and in its place Congress denied the president the power to implement a lottery until a new law could be passed. Student deferments were continued while graduate student deferments were to be permitted in fields defined as part of the national interest. The clerk of the local board became the executive secretary, and a retirement age of seventy-five was set. An attempt was made to counter the Supreme Court on conscientious objectors, and that was about it. The Marshall Commission, the Chicago conference, and Senator Kennedy's hearing on manpower and labor—a last-minute try to provide a new platform for reform proposals—were all ignored and the Clark Commission's recommendations became policy. In other words, although the role of the state was to bring all groups together around reform, the law that was passed indicated that they were defeated in this objective.

The defeat was only a partial one. The new law was severely criticized by many, including an impressive array of educators and educational organizations.[81] With the Nixon presidency, further charges seemed imminent. By an executive order of May 13, 1969, President Nixon implemented one key reform proposal. Announcing that "it is . . . important that we encourage a consistent administration of draft procedures by the more than 4,000 local boards around the country," a new policy was to be worked out "to limit geographic inequities and enhance the equity of the entire system."[82] The first steps toward rationalization through central administration were being taken. The same message called for a lottery system, and Congress responded by repealing the section of the 1967 law that did not allow the president to create one. Shortly thereafter a lottery was held. Then, Nixon's own commission on the draft recommended the creation of a volunteer army. Chaired by Thomas Gates of the Marshall Commission and the Morgan Guaranty Bank, and composed of the usual plethora of industrialists, former officers, and educators, even one student, this commission said:

> A return to an all-volunteer force will strength our freedoms,
> remove an inequity now imposed on the expression of patriotism that
> has never been lacking among our youth, promote efficiency in
> our armed forces, and enhance their dignity.[83]

Martin Anderson, a special assistant to the president and strong believer in a volunteer army, was assigned to study the Gates proposals and win support for them. What he found was that Congress was not ready for it yet. Although Senator Stennis and Congressman Rivers had promised draft reformers a comprehensive study of the draft in 1970 in exchange for passage of the 1967 law,[84] the military was still fighting for no change. Secretary of Defense Laird, General Westmoreland, the National Guard Association, Stennis, Rivers, and other military spokesmen all called a volunteer army an interesting idea, but one that was not feasible while a war in Southeast Asia was continuing.[85] Once again reform was postponed but its time was obviously drawing nearer.

Meanwhile, Nixon took actions in Vietnam which affected the draft. By changing the nature of the war from one involving troops to one based on bombing, he enabled draft calls to be lowered, thereby removing much of the popular pressure for draft reform. The conflicts still existed, however. In 1971 the situation was at a stalemate, and an unprecedented event occurred, as Congress allowed the draft law to expire while it wrestled with its dilemmas. Eventually reform was postponed again, the urgency for it having diminished. Nonetheless, even though the state was not successful in bringing all the conflicting points of view together around a common program, it did make the attempt, and its efforts were not entirely unrewarded. Conflict over the draft did not break out into open warfare, splitting the ruling class and revealing its weaknesses. The abolition of the draft under Nixon and Carter's refusal (to this point) to reinstate it testify to the ability of public pressure to force changes in certain kinds of repressive policies.

chapter three ☆
who benefits from repression?

Despite some variations, when the state acts in a liberal democratic society such as that of the United States, it acts in a biased fashion, as the previous chapter tried to show. It is partial to the dominant interests, hostile to those whose power is minimal. By nearly all of its actions, it reproduces a society in which some have power at the expense of others, and it moves to support the "others" only when their protests are so strong that the "some" stand to lose all they have gained.

It follows that repression will similarly not be a neutral phenomenon but will have a class basis. We can predict, with good accuracy, that when the state intervenes to repress an organization or an ideology, it will be a dissenting group, representing relatively powerless people, that will be repressed and the interests upheld will be those of the powerful. But to say that is not to say enough. Who are these powerful interests? Who are the powerless? Without some discussion of the specific groups that fill these categories, repression will be an abstract phenomenon unrelated to this world at this time. It is essential, in short, to address the question of who benefits from repression and who is hurt by it.

Locating Power

Many have realized the importance of making statements about who holds power in democratic societies, so a lack of literature on the subject is not the problem. The opposite of that is more likely to raise difficulties, for no clear consensus arises out of reading what exists on this subject. There are instead a series of mini-consensuses. One of these holds that power in America is no problem. The country is ruled by a series of minorities, each of these balancing out the potential power of others, thus making it impossible for any one group to dominate.[1] This pluralistic vision has been subjected to fairly severe criticism, so much so that there is no need to accept it here.[2] More insightful are two other approaches. One holds that there is a power elite which runs things. It is composed of the occupants of some key positions in American society, organized into rings of influence.[3] A similar view argues that it is not a power elite that is in command, but a ruling class centered not in the important political positions, but in key economic areas.[4] Viewing these claims, one is left with the impression that little clarity and much confusion exist on a theoretical problem of first importance.

In attempting to sort through the confusion, two positive steps might help. One is to accept neither side in the debate between those who advocate a ruling class model and those who prefer a power elite. Rather, following the example of sociologist Wldozimierz Wesolowski,[5] it is best to recognize the existence of both concepts. Power in a society such as the United States exists at both the economic and political levels. The point is not to subsume arbitrarily one under the other but to recognize the different kinds of power associated with each and to examine the conditions under which one is more important than the other; we will try to do so in this chapter.

Another step is to recognize that a bipolar model of power, in which one group is seen to have it all and the other is seen to have none, distorts reality to such a great extent that it becomes useless. Power is at all times a relational phenomenon. One only has a certain amount of power in relation to something else. It is quite possible for A to exercise power over B, but it is also possible that B in turn will be more powerful when compared to C. Does that make B powerful or powerless? The answer is neither. It means that B has power in some situations and not in others.

B would be at a middle level of power, a level that cannot be ignored in any meaningful discussion of who holds power in America.

These caveats leave us in the following situation. On a vertical dimension, power exists on a variety of levels, ranging from the most powerful institutions and people to the least. For the sake of convenience, we can begin to make sense out of these levels by calling them upper, middle, and lower, recognizing that each subdivision has gradations within itself. Horizontally, on the other hand, we have claimed that power has both an economic and a political dimension and that both are important. There are differences, however, in what they do. Because America is a capitalist society whose structure has continually evolved to accommodate changes in the nature of capitalism, those who are economically powerful, by their actions, shape the nature of the society in its most basic form. Within that form, the political leaders and political institutions decide on and implement policy matters. It makes a good deal of difference whether one policy or another is adopted, but in nearly all cases, *the range of available policy options are all perceived to be within the basic structure of a capitalist society.* In this sense, *the economic positions have a primary importance to which the political positions are secondary.* This is a controversial point, to which we will return shortly.

If we now combine all these levels together and attempt to represent them schematically, the result would look something like the following:

Table 1
Schematic Representation of Power in America

LEVELS	ECONOMIC ELITE (RULING CLASS)	POLITICAL ELITE (POWER ELITE)
Upper levels of power	corporation executives foundation heads, etc. (*function: shape the polity*)	president and state functionaries in executive branch, military, diplomats, etc. (*function: decide and implement policies*)
	Transmission belts	
Middle levels of power	corporate managers, high-level administrators, ex-military officers,	congressmen, judges, governors, lower-level executive branch

Table 1 (*cont.*)

LEVELS	ECONOMIC ELITE (RULING CLASS)	POLITICAL ELITE (POWER ELITE)
	national interest groups, local aristocrats	
	middle management, middle administrators, local interest groups, larger small businessmen, labor leaders	mayors, state legislators, other judicial, city, and state officials
	average small businessmen, professionals, highly paid workers	town and village officials
Lower levels of power	office workers, blue-collar workers unskilled workers youth, "deviant" groups, housewives unemployed, stigmatized, lumpen proletariat	

All diagrams simplify reality, and this one is no exception. It helps to use it only if it eventually leads to a clarification of complexity, not to its obfuscation. Whether this one accomplishes that goal or not should become clearer as we proceed through each category. The attempt here will be to differentiate the kinds of power that exist in America, and to isolate the kinds of institutions that possess different levels of power.

The Upper Levels of Power

The distinction between shaping the polity and deciding on policy within that shape is best seen at the highest levels of power. This is a point that pluralists often miss. Since their focus is on the relative influence of a group over specific policy outcomes, they may well be right in noting that various groups, ranging from corporations to labor unions, all have some say. But the question they never ask, the most important question to be asked, concerns the system in which the decision is being made. Pluralists accept liberal capitalism as inevitable, a given framework, and this leads to their unconcern with what brought it into being. But American capitalism did not mysteriously appear. It was brought into being by some very powerful people. It is continually reproduced by others who spend most of their time trying to ensure its reproduction. *In order, then, to speak of the ruling class, we would be mistaken to look at political decision making but must focus instead on those whose activities define the parameters of the system and reproduce those parameters on a day-to-day basis.*

America is defined by its consensus, by those political values that are alleged to be the only truly legitimate ones. Liberalism is the ideology of the consensus, and at the moment its most important aspects are three. One is that democracy of a representative sort, such as that enunciated in the Constitution, is the best form of government imaginable, which should be tampered with as little as possible. (Americans pride themselves that they have changed their Constitution so little, which from another point of view simply indicates the inflexibility of the system.) A second significant aspect to the consensus is a commitment to the paradoxical notion that private enterprise capitalism is the only legitimate economic structure, but that it does create problems which require substantial roles for the state to play: watching the "public" interest; intervening to ensure stability; and providing benefits to those displaced by the free market system. Finally, America is also united around the idea of America itself, i.e., the notion that the previous two things have been best accomplished in America and thus a preservation of this country against its foreign enemies is essential. Anticommunism, in other words, is part of the consensus as well.[6]

The important point to realize about the nature of consensus, and one that many theorists of democracy seem to forget, is that it is not received but made.[7] It does not arise through magic, but is the work of real people in real situations. It is not inevitable, but could take quite a different form under different circumstances. *The consensus that does exist does so because it fulfills the needs of those who rule the democratic state.* For example, the commitment to modern corporate liberalism came into being in the years 1900–20, when a group of men associated with the National Civic Federation rejected both Social Darwinism on the Right and socialism on the Left, combining elements of both into a new ideology that has essentially governed the United States since that time. As James Weinstein has shown, the change in American liberalism from one of free market capitalism to one of state intervention was the work of a group of strong-minded and intelligent men who, through their diligence, brought it into being.[8] It didn't just happen.

Those who created the modern American state in those years could be considered the ruling class of their time. (Interestingly enough, as chapter 8 will show, those same men were also instrumental in creating the modern system of repression.) *Today we would define the ruling class as those who play the greatest role in reproducing the dominant ideology and the structure that services it.* Who they are may become clearer if we first show who they are not.

The members of the ruling class are not necessarily "America's sixty families,"[9] that is, the richest people in the United States, for many a Howard Hughes is concerned more with making money than with shaping the nature of a system. Nor are they necessarily the entire social aristocracy, the people who go only to certain schools, join certain clubs, work in certain firms, die of certain diseases, and are buried in certain sacred resting places.[10] These people constitute an upper class in the social sense, but not in the economic (for not all of them are wealthy and many with wealth are not among them) or political (for not all of them have political power) spheres. Chances are good that a member of the ruling class will be a member of the social aristocracy, but an aristocrat need not necessarily be a ruler. In addition, the ruling class is not composed of all heads of corporations which do X number of dollars worth of business or more. Some corporations are much more concerned with rulership than others, the difference between First National City Bank and Texas Instruments. Finally, all members of the ruling class do not possess last names of distinguished family lines.[11] Many of them do (Harriman, Rockefeller, Bundy), but this is neither a necessary nor a sufficient condition for membership.

Instead, *the ruling class contains what could be called the politicized members of the upper class,* those who, from training, innate desire, upbringing, decide that they will rule and accomplish their objective. Therefore, position and social class are important, vitally important. A member of the ruling class will most likely spring from an aristocratic and rich family. He could easily head a corporation, be on numerous boards, and possess a distinguished last name. Similarly, he would undoubtedly occupy some crucial positions. It would not be surprising if he ran the Ford Foundation, chaired the Chase Manhattan Bank, edited *Foreign Affairs*, partnered in Dillon Read or Sullivan and Cromwell, or directed NBC.

John McCloy, former high commissioner to Germany, is a trustee of the Ford Foundation, a director of the Council on Foreign Relations, a former chairman of the board of the Chase Manhattan Bank, a member of the National Advertising Council, an entry in the Social Register (New York), and a partner in a powerful law firm. McGeorge Bundy was a Harvard dean, key presidential adviser on defense, and is now president of the Ford Foundation. He is the son of a Lowell. His brother William, also a high-level policy maker, married Dean Acheson's daughter, while his sister married an Auchincloss closely related to Jacqueline Onassis's stepfather.[12] If the objection is raised that those men are atypical because of their public visibility, consider the case of W. T. Moore of

Centre Island, N.Y.[13] His name may be unfamiliar, but aside from running Moore-McCormick Shipping and serving on the Council of Foreign Relations, he serves both his business and his country through the influential role he plays in the following three international organizations: the Pan American Association, the Argentine American Chamber of Commerce, the American Brazilian Society.

The impact of this definition is that the ruling class is small in number, composed of no more than a few thousand individuals, nearly all of them living in the Boston-New York-Philadelphia-Washington axis. They are all rich. Nearly all are white Anglo-Saxon Protestants or German Jews. They are all either businessmen or descendants of businessmen. They are born to power and grow up in an atmosphere that cultivates power. They recognize each other, and each of them is fully conscious that he belongs to the ruling class. They are chairmen, directors, trustees, vice-presidents, consultants, partners, secretaries, advisers, presidents, members and relatives. They, in other words, are the "they" that people (with acute perception) blame for their troubles. And the blame is deserved, for they have taken the responsibility of shaping the society in their interest. They are conscious of that responsibility, and they want to be thanked when popular and shunned when unpopular. For amusement, they read books (often written with support from their foundations) which "prove" that no ruling class exists in the United States.

The ruling class rules through transmission belts, institutions that do not make formal policy as much as they shape alternatives. We have already made reference to an early ruling-class transmission belt, the National Civic Federation, which preached state capitalism and industrial harmony. Its ideological descendant at this time is the Committee for Economic Development. The CED was founded and run by internationally minded businessmen who realized that after World War II there would be no such thing as an American economy, that industry would become worldwide under American control. Originally a group that concentrated on internal education, convincing businessmen with parochial mentalities of the importance of its mission, it now has mostly external functions, delivering its message to the public in direct and indirect ways.[14] Other transmission belts whose focus is on the shape of the economy include the National Planning Association, the Business Advisory Council, the Brookings Institution, the Ford and Rockefeller Foundations, and others of similar inclinations.[15] In 1976 a new transmission-belt organization, the Trilateral Commission, received extensive publicity because of its close ties to the Carter administration.

It is with foreign policy that the ruling class is most directly concerned. Since many of its members are businessmen, there is an immediate interest in preserving the structure of world business. Of the twenty largest corporations in the world, only two are not principally American (Shell and Unilever).[16] In 1967 U.S. banks had branches in fifty-five different countries.[17] The percentage of total foreign investments by all capital exporting states controlled by the United States increased between 1914 and 1960 from 6.3 percent to 59.1 percent.[18] No wonder the American ruling class looks outward. The Senate Armed Services Committee calculated in 1966 that a total of fifty-three different treaties or official declarations were in effect dealing with American defense.[19] Presumably to enforce those treaties, American troops were represented in sixty-four countries throughout the world.[20]

The primary ruling-class transmission belts for dealing with foreign policy are the Council on Foreign Relations and the Foreign Policy Association. The membership, financing, and activities of the CFR have been dealt with well by William Domhoff and need not be repeated here.[21] It is enough to say that writers as diverse as Joseph Kraft, Douglass Cater, Lester Milbrath, and the *New York Times* have all noted its power, that its membership is explicitly and proudly ruling class, that its ties to the government are so close that it is the government in many respects, that *Foreign Affairs* (its publication) is a forum for the conduct of American foreign policy, and that its involvement extends (though local committees) to "grass roots" opinion. The last function is not stressed heavily because the Foreign Policy Association primarily deals with local areas. Beyond these belts, the ruling class feels strongly enough about foreign policy to serve directly in government. The diplomatic corps has always been dominated by members of the ruling class. Key positions in the State and Defense Departments traditionally have gone to members of the ruling class. A study of foreign policy decision makers by Gabriel Kolko found that key law firms such as Sullivan and Cromwell; Carter, Ledyard, and Milburn; and Coudert Brothers; and such key investment firms as Dillon, Read and Brown Brothers, Harriman dominated the key departments.[22] Another study of the five most recent administrations found business domination of those that were vital to international affairs (Navy, Defense, etc.) compared to less domination where no foreign activity was at stake (HEW, Agriculture).[23]

One of the more revealing examples of how ruling-class organizations dominate policy-making positions is the representation of the Trilateral Commission in the Carter cabinet. The secretaries of State, Defense, and Treasury are all members of this "private" organization, as are many of the officials in less publicized positions. Four top jobs in the State Department are held by Trilateral members. The vice-president of the United States is a member, and the president's national security chief was a founder of the organization. In all of American history it would be difficult to find a transmission-belt organization that was so thoroughly dominant in one administration.

What all this means has been described with respect to one foreign policy area and decision (the Dominican Republic) in such a way that the reason for ruling-class domination cannot be ignored:

> . . . prominent New Dealer Abe Fortas was a director of the Sucrest Corporation for 20 years, third largest East Coast cane sugar refiner; Adolf A. Berle, Jr., known Latin American expert and advisor to several presidents, was Chairman of the Board of Sucrest for 18 years and is still a director and a large stockholder; Ellsworth Bunker was Chairman, President, and 38-year Director of the second largest East Coast cane sugar refiner, National Sugar Refining Corporation (partially founded by his father), and one-time stockholder in a Dominican sugar mill; Roving Ambassador W. Averell Harriman is a "limited partner" in the banking house of Brown Brothers, Harriman, which owns 5 percent of National Sugar's stock (his brother, E. Roland Harriman, sits on the board of National Sugar); J. M. Kaplan, molasses magnate, is a large contributor and influential advisor to many Democratic Party candidates and the ADA; Joseph S. Farland, State Department consultant and ex-U.S. Ambassador to the Dominican Republic, is a Director of South Puerto Rico Sugar Company; Roswell Gilpatrick, Deputy Secretary of Defense, is the managing executive partner on the Wall Street firm of Cravath, Swaine, and Moore, legal counsel to National Sugar; and Max Rabb, partner in the Wall Street firm of Strook, Strook and Lavan, legal counsel for Sucrest, is an influential Johnson supporter. The above sugar refiners, plus the largest U.S. refiner, American Sugar, depend directly on the Dominican sugar and molasses supply for their operations.[24]

The point to be emphasized from all this is that a distorted picture of the ruling class emerges if we speak of its economic, political, and foreign policy activities as separate. It acts as a cohesive unit and does not see distinctions between these activities. Without liberalism, there is no capitalism. Without capitalism, there would be no need for a specific kind of foreign policy. Therefore, it is not surprising that ruling-class individuals dominate all the positions and transmission belts that shape the nature of the polity in any way. Besides the cases of McCloy, Bundy, and Moore mentioned above, the following interconnections can be detected. Forty-seven trustees of the Committee for Economic Development were also members of the CFR. In the year 1960, 8 of the 19 members of the NAC's Public Policy Committee were in the CFR; 41 of 190 trustees of the Business Advisory Council were members of CFR; 48 of 190 trustees of the CED were also CFR; 10 of the 43 directors of the National Planning Association were on the CFR, while 8 of them were on the CED.[25] The mass media, obviously influential in shaping attitudes, fit in nicely. Time, Inc., the Knight papers, the Times-Mirror Corp., the Cowles firm, are all directed by people who share in the interests of the groups listed so far. National television companies, directed more by the Jewish members of the ruling class, are also interlocked. Given the enormous numbers of people who live in the United States, the fact that important consciousness-shaping institutions are directed by such a phenomenally small group, leading to such overlaps of membership, is evidence of the importance with which the ruling class treats its positions of power.

The members of the ruling class often seem to be above politics, and in a sense they are. Their enormous power comes not from political positions (though they have held them), or from direct corporate links. It comes from their role, often euphemistically described, as "public servants." America needs a group of leaders who at all times consider the interests of the whole society over the interests of any given segment of that society. But since the whole society is a capitalist one, the resulting "public interest" will in most cases be the interest of the capitalist class, rather than the interest of any one particular capitalist. It is because these men (and they are all men, or so it seems) shape a system based upon the power of a few that they can be considered to be at the highest levels of power in that society. When affairs are running smoothly, one hardly notices them.

The political governing class, which also exists at the upper levels of power on our diagram but which has less power than the ruling class, is more likely to be composed of individuals sensitive to the interests of the ruling class than it is of individuals who are members of the ruling class. There is no need for the ruling class to dominate all the political positions. If it did, the class nature of the democratic state would be all the more apparent, and claims about its openness would be harder to make. Furthermore, a distinct political governing class means that positions can be opened up for talented men from other classes. This has two advantages: (1) preventing stagnation, which was perceived by E. Digby Baltzell when he suggested that the only way to preserve aristocratic authority (to him a vital need) was for the aristocrats to be receptive to ambitious men from outside their ranks;[26] and (2) providing the illusion of social mobility (anybody can grow up to be president). Given these advantages, so long as the ruling class finds little opposition to its interests in a distinct political elite (it may even be willing to lose a little, if necessary), it has a reason to maintain the political elite's autonomy. There is little danger that such a strategy will backfire, and if it does (nomination of a populist, for example), control over the transmission belts can be used to win over the "public" to personalities and policies more in keeping with the purview of the ruling class. As moderate as he was, George McGovern's defeat in 1972 is an example of the treatment given to one who challenges, even a little bit, the fundamental aspects of the consensus. By 1976 the lesson had been learned; Jimmy Carter was able to portray himself as a populist without offending the sensibilities of any powerful group.

It may seem somewhat odd to suggest that the power of the American president, as a member of the political elite, is less than the power of others within the society. This is especially true when it is often asserted that "no mental effort is required to understand that the President of the United States is the most powerful single human being in the world today."[27] With the president's authority as commander-in-chief combined with the need for instantaneous decision making in an age of foreign policy crisis, the most frequent criticism of the American president is that he is too powerful. The series of events generally described as Watergate also convinced many people that the president's power had become too great. Since there would appear to be a consensus on the enormous power of the president, this would be a good place to state the position that the political class works within limits set by the ruling class.

One should not confuse the president as a person with the presidency as an institution. Personally, the president of the United States may well be the most powerful individual in the country, in the sense that his actions may do more to shape the society than the actions of any other single individual. But the power of the presidency is not much greater than the power of the president, while the power of the ruling class is much greater than the power of any single member. The collected membership of the ruling class is instrumental in nominating the president, financing his campaign, aiding in his accession to power, and advising him on policies. Its members not only shape the environment in which he makes his decisions, but they also give him all their help when those decisions have to be made. It is he who is more likely to recognize their power, rather than they who will recognize his. There has been no American president in this century who has crossed the ruling class for any length of time. (When influential segments of wealth and power made up their minds that Richard Nixon was no longer to be president because of his Watergate transgressions, his removal from office was only a matter of time.) This fact alone testifies to the severe limits placed on the presidency by an elite group which exists outside of it.

The same is true of Congress, including the Senate, which might also be listed as the highest level of strictly political power. The many studies of political institutions and political decision making in the United States that focus on this political elite unconsciously emphasize this, for example, the data collected on the background characteristics of political decision makers. In spite of the fact that the political elite is "elected" and not "anointed,"[28] there is a surprising homogeneity about it. The most comprehensive study of the U.S. Senate notes that "the 'typical' senator during the [World War II] years was a late-middle-aged or elderly, white, Protestant, native-born man with rural or small-town and upper-middle-class origins, a college-educated lawyer, and a 'joiner.' "[29] The percentage of non-Protestants in the House of Representatives is higher, but the same general trend continues there.[30] The same is true of Supreme Court judges, federal political executives, lobbyists, governors, military officers, and other sections of the political elite.[31] These findings reaffirm the relational aspects of the political elite. Its members are not generally from the most prestigious and the wealthiest families (although many senators, and an occasional governor or general are), but neither are they randomly distributed among the population. They remain a fairly closed group, because their function of deciding policies is important, but they are more open than the ruling class, since deciding policy is of a lower level of priority than shaping the system. Socially situated as they are, they can at once share the interests of the ruling class yet appear to be independent of the ruling class.

None of this is meant to suggest that the political governing class, as symbolized in the presidency and the Senate, is weak and ineffectual. It generally makes a substantial difference, especially to middle-range groups involved, whether one policy or another is followed, hence the lobbying efforts that surround Congress and the presidency. Without the cooperation of these political institutions, the ruling class could not rule, at least in the system as it presently exists. There have been times when either Congress, or the president, has refused to adopt the views of the ruling class (for example, the defeat of the League of Nations, the vengeance of McCarthyism, the attempt to defeat the nomination of Paul Warnke as head of the SALT negotiations). These situations do give the political institutions power, but that power is either a negative one (as in the examples cited) or it is relational. The political institutions have room for discretion, but the limits are set outside themselves. In the area of foreign policy particularly, the realization of these limits has led to tremendous frustrations on the part of many senators who want to have more say.

The Middle Levels of Power

The most important segment of the economic grouping within the middle levels of power is composed of the corporate managers. The claims that have been made for this group are extensive, such as their ability to constitute a new class, to run societies regardless of their economic systems, and to save capitalism from the ravages of the capitalists.[32] Ralph Miliband has uncovered the ideological basis of these claims and shown how the empirical reality of capitalist society is different from the premises of the managerial theorists.[33] The managers, he argues, while not owners in the classical sense, nevertheless are from the propertied classes and hold enough stock in the companies they manage to make the profit motive very real to them. But the most important question is not whether the rise of managerialism has changed the nature of capitalism, for Miliband has effectively shown that it has not. The question is whether the managers are part of the ruling class, and the answer is, *as long as they are only managers, they are not.*

Managers are to the ruling class in an economic sense what the power elite is in a political sense. Just as the power elite carries out *political* decision making within alternatives that the ruling class makes official, so the managers carry out and make *economic* policy within those same alternatives. Thus, their power is roughly equivalent to that of the political elite, leading some to see them as a new class. The view is incorrect, for neither the political elite nor the managers are a class in the sense that the ruling group is a class. Nor is it particularly helpful to idealize the corporate managers in the manner of A. A. Berle:

> . . . the really great corporation managements have reached a
> position for the first time in their history in which they must
> consciously take account of philosophical considerations. They must
> consider the kind of community in which they have faith, and which
> they will serve, and which they intend to construct and maintain.
> In a word, they must consider at least in its more elementary
> phases the ancient problem of the good life, and how their operations
> in the community can be adapted to affording or fostering it.[34]

The managers most certainly do consider their communities, but they do not and will not define the good life. That task has already been performed by the ruling class; it is up to the managers to make relatively narrow decisions concerning prices, distributions, products, and advertising. The combined impact of these decisions has an enormous influence over the community and what it considers good, but no one manager spends the great percentage of his time directly in value shaping, as a member of the ruling class would.

Another nongovernmental group whose power is often equal or even slightly more than that of the political elite is the directors of powerful national interest groups. Various writers have shown how organizations such as the American Farm Bureau Federation, the National Guard Association, trade associations, and others exercise quasi-governmental authority.[35] It is they, and not the governmental officials whose area of jurisdiction concerns them, who establish rates, police themselves, and decide policy. Such concentration of power in private associations goes far to destroy the pluralist myth of a neutral state, but it also shows the importance of differentiating between levels of power. For although such groups generally make policy in an uncontested fashion, they are not as powerful as ruling-class associations, for they do not shape the consensus. The American Farm Bureau Federation, which may well be the single most powerful private organization of this type, is still at the middle level of power. Its influence extends only to specific matters of policy, and its power exists primarily in local areas. This means that such a group, when it supersedes the government and makes policy for itself, is not replacing the state; it is only assuming power over a governmental apparatus that exists within a state over which it has little control.

In fact, it could be established as a rough general rule that any class or elite whose power is local in scope is not in the highest level of power, no matter how strong it may be locally. This differentiation between a local and a national elite is helpful in unraveling some of the problems involved in studies of "community power structures." Any individual or group that dominates a community will *not* be the major power in that community. The major power will always be a national ruling class, which may not have a single member living in that community. In narrowing one's focus to one specific area, one will nearly always miss the operations of the national elite, unless, like Vidich and Bensman,[36] one is studying that very interaction. From this perspective, the flaws in the books by the Lynds and Floyd Hunter[37] are not, as some have charged,[38] that they found local elites (for surely these exist), but that they did not examine how the power of community influentials is tempered by the existence of a national ruling class and power elite. The two families of Middletown are undoubtedly influential in the affairs of that community, but they would be humbled before the eastern ruling influentials.

Below these kinds of groups are other economic elites that are in more of a transitional situation, exercising power themselves and having power exercised over them. Middle-level businessmen, for example, often conduct their operations with very little flexibility because of the oligopolistic structure of American industry. Such is the case with independent oil producers, for rates and regulations are set by firms that dwarf them. But within either specified localities or a specialized section of the industry, smaller firms may be able to dominate other businesses even smaller, some local officials, and employees.[39]

This "betwixt and between" situation is partially responsible for confusions in the ideology of small business. Traditionally, American small businessmen have believed in the virtues of localism, agrarianism, and individualism. But these beliefs are being shattered by what one observer calls the "growing powerlessness of the small businessman today to direct and control his life chances."[40] Reacting against this loss of power, the small businessman becomes even more attached to the perceived virtues of preindustrial society. But in recent years the bitterness of business, as represented in a group such as the National Association of Manufacturers, seems to have become less visible. Such businessmen probably have realized that industrial concentration is the order of the day and that, recognizing this, there is still power to be exercised. It is a difficult pill to swallow, but that is the nature of being in the middle of the middle levels of power. One can take comfort when he realizes how many are below him each time he is depressed by the number of people above him.

As a group, labor leaders have been included at the middle level, although it is obvious that some may occasionally be more powerful and others will always be less powerful. This is because the most powerful labor leaders not only operate within an ideology established and maintained by a business-oriented ruling class, but also because labor—as a private association—does not have the power of a group such as the American Farm Bureau Federation. Labor is not the type of private association that can make governmental policy by itself and for itself. Whatever power it holds nationally is always achieved through bargaining with other groups with similar or more power. Alternatively, labor is said to exercise power in certain local areas through its control of the Democratic party. Once again, this points to the middle-level character of labor's influence. For not only is its power localized, but even where it is strongest, as in Detroit, it would be difficult to conclude that the influence of labor was all-pervasive. In Detroit, where according to Greenstone, the UAW "achieved as much . . . as any metropolitan labor movement could expect to accomplish" from 1937 until 1961, "the UAW never supported a successful mayoral candidate who faced significant opposition in a closely contested election."[41] Furthermore, the UAW-controlled Democratic party found itself consistently outflanked at the state level by a Ford-American Motors-Republican party grouping symbolized by George Romney. Even the most politically powerful union in the country, therefore, had no choice but to bargain for its position with more powerful groups.

Businessmen and labor leaders are joined at the middle level by interest group leaders whose scope is less than the most powerful national interest groups and by middle-level administrators and managers. The former would include organizations with a local character (Pennsylvania Economy League), with a constituency not as influential as business (National Association for the Advancement of Colored People, National Education Association), with a national constituency but less powerful leadership (National Farmers Union, Grange, National Association of Manufacturers), with primarily ideological interests (Americans for Democratic Action), or with an interest in a highly specialized area (Amateur Athletic Union). All such interest groups would have power over limited areas, but none could dominate a larger area or participate in any way in conducting the affairs of either state or government. Middle-management people speak for themselves; their position on an organization chart hierarchy is roughly their position in the hierarchy discussed here.

Finally, there is a category for those nongovernmental individuals and institutions whose power is less than all those discussed so far, but still more than those at the lowest levels of power. Professionals are a good example of this group. The traditional professions of law, medicine, and theology are all composed of individuals whose very work gives them some amount of power over most of the people with whom they come in contact: their clients, patients, and parishioners. But with the exception of the few who become active in the American Bar Association, the American Medical Association, or the leadership of their national church organization, such professionals are acted upon more than they act upon others. This generalization is even more accurate for those professionals who have reached that status recently. College professors, schoolteachers, nurses, insurance agents, and policemen are still achieving legislative status as professionals. All exercise power over others in the very nature of their work. Yet all are essentially middle-class people (except for the police) whose political influence at both local and national levels tends to dwindle to nothing. Such an ambiguous relationship to power often makes such professionals authoritarian in their work, for lacking real power over their lives, they overemphasize it in their classes, wards, precincts, or districts. A study of policemen found, for example, that they were cynical about power in the nation but authoritarian about their own power on the job.[42] Similarly, research into the political life of schoolteachers shows a pronounced need for respect but an enormous apathy about one's ability to change society.[43] The relational character of their power was clear, in other words, to both groups. The same kind of situation is faced by others at the lower points of the middle levels of power, such as store owners, very small businessmen, and highly paid blue-collar workers.

The political side of the middle level exhibits a similar gradation. Diagramatically, the middle level of the political elite can be defined as those governmental positions that are less powerful than both the governmental positions at the highest level and the nongovernmental positions at the corresponding middle level. The first part of that definition means that the scope and the depth of the political decisions dealt with will be more restricted than those of the power elite. In other words, these are the governmental figures responsible for policies that are either nonnational (governors), highly specialized (lower-level executive branch), or essentially negative (judges). The other gradations of power at the middle level are defined by those whose power is similar but who utilize that power at smaller and smaller levels of government, from states to cities to villages. This means that within certain areas, a member of the political elite at the middle level could have influence that is meaningful, but such influence will always be exercised within highly restrictive limits. For example, when a state legislature is called on to make a decision on the amount of tonnage that trucks within a state will be allowed to carry, the trucking industry and the railroads will mobilize their forces for a legislative battle that will be vitally important for them. Every citizen of the state will be affected by the decision, because questions of revenue will be raised. The governor, members of the legislature, and commissioners of transportation will be beseiged by pleas (and more) from both sides, and for the duration of the struggle, they will be influential in the controversy. But they will not have the authority to nationalize transportation, to build totally new means of transport, or to alter substantially the question that has been presented to them for their decision. Only at the highest levels of power could those things be done, and even there certain limits would also be present.

At the same time, decisions made at the middle levels of power are shaped by nongovernmental forces at the same level. Evidence for this has been uncovered by political scientists concerned with explanations of why certain states produce policies different from other states. In an early study of this type, the investigators tried to discover the factors that led to variations in state public policy, such as why some states spent more on welfare, education, and similar items than others. They found that characteristics of the political process in the state, such as degree of interparty competition, could not explain these variations. Nor could the nature of the state as a political system, since all were the same. The authors were therefore led to conclude that ". . . the evidence points to the relatively greater influence of certain external conditions over one aspect of the political process in the formulation of selected public policies."[44]

Since that study, a large body of literature has accumulated, distressed by the basic findings and trying to explain it away or further modify it.[45] But most of these attempts, as a recent critique points out,[46] can only do this by ignoring the context in which state political decisions are made. The reality of the situation is simply that political units at the middle level have relatively little autonomy. One of the reasons for this has to do with the relatively greater amount of power of the nongovernmental groups.

The amount of power that state-level economic associations can exercise over state legislatures is probably greater than the amount national groups can exercise over Congress. The reasons are many. State legislators are paid less and are therefore more receptive to outside help. They have little or no staff. Turnover is rapid, so representatives of corporations and farm bureaus are in the capitol much longer than the legislators. Little publicity surrounds the work of the legislature. Younger legislators are ambitious and do not wish to alienate powerful individuals. All these factors combined mean that political bodies at lower levels of government will be less authoritative than the national bodies are. The situation of a private group making policy for itself, which does occur in the Congress, is much more prevalent than at the state level.[47] Therefore, many of the economic positions at the middle levels of power will, as on the national, rank higher in overall influence than their corresponding figures in the political category.

The effect of all these pressures is to produce in officeholders at the middle level a sense of frustration. They have been told that to occupy a public office is to assume a public trust. Yet reality and their political sense make it clear that the actual amount of power they have is relatively little. Hence, even as high up as in Congress, there are feelings of resentment and anomie, against civil servants, members of the high executive branch, and members of the ruling class.[48] In fact, legislators will often strike out verbally against a ruling class that limits their ability to make decisions. Often this takes reactionary political forms, but the sense of frustration is real enough. In one case, resentment at the state level led to a national issue when in 1970 members of the Illinois constitutional convention refused to allow former Secretary of HEW and former President of the Carnegie Foundation John Gardner to address them. At another time, such resentment takes the form of a movement like McCarthyism, which was hardly a lower-class revolt. McCarthyism can be more realistically seen as the outpourings of a middle-level group of officeholders protesting the existence of an even higher level of nongovernmental power.[49] In the 1970s state and local governments are expressing their resentment against modernity by restricting the rights of homosexuals, limiting the availability of abortions, denying women equal rights through nonpassage of a constitutional amendment, and experimenting with the death penalty.

In short, a career at the middle levels of power is neither particularly glamorous nor particularly desirable. Sixteen percent of the members of the California legislature interviewed by one group of researchers said they entered upon their political career when no one else was willing to run. In four states, generally between 30 percent and 40 percent of the legislators, by their own admission, were aspiring for higher office. In Ohio and Tennessee, 60 percent of the legislators had one or more relatives in politics, indicating that a primary motivation for holding office was family tradition.[50] Although no one has studied the reasons perceived by local politicians for their general lack of interest, political impotence is surely one. Those who wish to exercise power will still be more likely to fulfill their ambition outside politics to a greater degree than inside. Such corporate executives as George Romney and Charles Percy, who leave business for politics, most likely do so not to gain power but to win prestige. There is still some of that left at the higher political positions.

Those at the middle levels of power play an important role in the repressive apparatus of the modern democratic state. Since repression is carried out as policy it follows the same procedure as any other policy. The consensus that repression is sometimes (reluctantly) necessary is shaped by the ruling class. But the means of carrying out that repression often fall to political institutions at the middle level, particularly Congress and the state legislatures. Similarly, in the long run the corporate elite benefits from a repression that reproduces liberal capitalism, but in the short run, middle level and local elites benefit most from repression, for it removes groups that threaten their power. Since being in a relational situation of power at the middle level is frustrating, groups here often vigorously support repression as a way of affirming their status. So zealous are they in supporting repressive policies that the ruling class often appears to be more "liberal" and hence less repressive than the middle power holders. But this difference is not one of degree but of kind; both groups are repressive, differing only as to means. The ruling class prefers subtle repressive apparatus, while those at the middle level use more blatant methods.

But, and this is the key to understanding relational power, in a sense people at the middle level are repressed themselves, even by themselves. There is nothing fulfilling and glamorous in being a county judge or an assistant district attorney in a midwestern American city. To the extent that our hypothetical official supports repression against those he sees as threatening, he is repressing himself, for he supports a system that will not allow him to realize anything better than a life of frustration. The point is to keep separate those who carry out repression from those who ultimately benefit from it. The agents of a policy may be as directly hurt from carrying it out as those against whom it is directed—an important irony of repression in the liberal state.

Life at the Bottom

There is a relational aspect to power at the lowest level, as there is at every other. The blue-collar worker who is constantly told what to do on the job may well come home and play boss with his wife. She, in turn, out of frustration with being a slave to her husband, may decide to command her children, who will respond by kicking the family cat, which has just chased a bird away from the window. Nonetheless, all the people at this level have in common a lack of power that is most explicit, and a resulting oppression that is most pronounced.

As with the ruling class, it is important to understand this category. Its members are not necessarily the poorest people in the society, for many a middle-class housewife is powerless. Nor are they necessarily those whose oppression is directly measurable through tangible indicators, such as authoritarianism or alienation scales. Much oppression can be so internalized that it is as hidden to the psychologist as it is to the bearer. Instead, *the lowest level of power is composed of those who routinely (sometimes willingly, sometimes not) allow the character of their existence to be shaped by those higher up in the hierarchy of power in the democratic state.* They are the people who cannot act to impose their will on others in an institutional way. The lowest level of power contains *those for whom being acted upon becomes a general way of life.*

There are some who argue that blue-collar workers experience feelings of belonging and influence through a series of associational contacts, such as unions or social club memberships.[51] This may lead to an identification with power, but it hardly leads to the real thing. One reason is that even the collective association can be relatively powerless in national terms, as we have seen in the case of unions. In addition, mere membership does not give a blue-collar worker influence within his local, for unions in the United States are not renowned for their excessive participation and democratization. No matter how many benefits a union brings, and no matter how "privileged" a union member becomes, then, it is possible to say in general that most blue-collar workers will be among the least powerful of groups.

Workers themselves know this, if social scientists do not, for the latter often write from a point of view unsympathetic to those who tend to be powerless. S. M. Lipset, for example, discovers in workers a deep authoritarianism, which, he implies, is not shared by elites in democratic societies.[52] Yet his own evidence, when properly anlayzed, indicates how insubstantial his proposition is. For example, Lipset takes as a measure of authoritarianism the lack of voting support for democratic parties. The assumption is that such parties are nonauthoritarian, and that any "democratically" inclined individual would inherently be likely to vote for one. This reasoning is tautological. If we start from the premise that "democratic" parties are the ones that most make the working class powerless because of their bourgeois orientation, then it follows that a refusal by a worker to vote for such a party is the most rational, least authoritarian act he could commit. Like a member of the ruling class, he is simply acting out of self-interest. Lipset is simply imposing values on the working class that they do not, and should not, have. This is true of all his evidence. Workers do not support civil liberties because civil liberties have never supported them. Workers feel, in Lipset's typology, isolated, insecure, and powerless because the democratic state renders them isolated, insecure, and powerless. What Lipset's research has discovered is not authoritarianism, but a sophisticated self-perception on the part of workers about their power and interests in the democratic state.

This example illustrates the major problem in trying to make statements on the powerless groups that exist in the democratic state. Studies of the powerless are often made because such groups are docile. The motive in such work is often to extend the mystique of the democratic state. Since democracy in its present form has been defined beforehand as a condition that is good, a certain missionary zeal characterizes the research. The powerless, like residents of Third World countries, are seen as underdeveloped and in need of political modernization. When such people ape middle-class notions about democracy, they are celebrated as mature and healthy. When, on the other hand, they give free rein to their perceptions about the operations of the system, they are a problem to be dealt with in the way that only liberal social science research can deal with it. Exceptions to this rule are often made for blacks, for no one wants to be called a racist. Yet a very real class chauvinism often exists in social science research; the only difference between it and racism is that a different group is harmed.

Support for the notion that workers have intelligent and perceptive notions about their own power comes from the few studies of this problem that take any pains to be relatively objective. Lewis Lipsitz, for one, lets the workers he studies speak for themselves. He found that perceptions of political powerlessness on the part of workers varies with their powerlessness on the job:

> Those workers who are conscious of having the least control over
> their own lives at work show the most pronounced tendency to view
> the social and political worlds as unalterable.[53]

That seems reasonable enough. Beyond that, Lipsitz found that workers were aware of reasons for their sense of fatalism and cynicism about political life in a democracy:

> First, they see a society directed toward profit-making. Second,
> they are aware of wide disparities of power. Out of these elements,
> these men have constructed a suspicion of human nature.[54]

There is some false consciousness here. The workers blame their problem on human nature, and not on the specific system under which they live. But at least a reasonably accurate picture of the perceptions of working-class males comes out of this study. Lipsitz's conclusions buttress those of an earlier work by Chinoy, who painstakingly analyzed how workers dealt with the contradiction between what they had been told of American democracy and what they perceived to be its true meaning.[55]

Others besides workers are at the lowest levels of power; in fact, manual workers tend to be at the higher reaches of the lower levels. Unskilled workers and the unemployed, many of whom happen also to possess what has come to be defined as a racial stigma, share powerlessness with workers. A clear sign of this is the way these two groups often seem to fight with one another, indicating the extent to which they have been both divided and conquered. Blacks in the United States have long been studied as an economically and psychologically exploited group. Combined with these characteristics is an element of powerlessness. One of the few studies of this specifically political problem found that 5 percent of the 1,088 policy-making positions in the public sector of Cook County, Illinois, were held by nonwhites.[56] Since these positions were at the middle of the middle level of the political side of the diagram, one could hypothesize that the percentage of blacks higher up the diagram and in the economic positions is even less. The evidence bears this out. The same study showed that only 2 percent of the policy positions within nongovernmental institutions in Cook County—banks, insurance companies, universities, labor unions, law firms—were held by nonwhites.[57] Most of these institutions existed at the same level, but on the economic side. As for the higher levels, racial data are not reported in nearly all the studies of the composition of the power elite or the ruling class, but it can safely be hypothesized that the percentage is even lower than 2 percent. It is probably closer to zero.

These statistics indicate that the feelings of powerlessness on the part of blacks that are perceived in both psychological terms and political terms[58] are based on reality, as in the case of workers. It may be true, as Wilson Record suggests,[59] that blacks in America have never tied their powerlessness to a radical critique of American democracy, but this is more a statement of the effects that paralyzing powerlessness and violent repression can have upon a group than it is a commitment to something called the American way of life. At any rate, the powerlessness of blacks is one area where the existence of powerlessness needs little documentation.

In discussing the phenomenon of powerlessness, mention must be made of those groups whose lack of power does not stem from a lack of money. Unlike workers and blacks, there are in the democratic state a variety of individuals who may be economically secure, but because of various stigmata can be considered powerless. While this enumeration does not exhaust the list, women, youth, and so-called deviant groups can be cited as illustrations of the general tendency.

In terms of formal positions, women may be even more discriminated against than blacks. The most thorough study of high political positions under five presidents shows that women held 12 of the 1,041 jobs, for a total of 1.1 percent.[60] Among those who could be defined as the ruling class, it would not be surprising if the percentage of males was 100 percent. It was not until the middle of 1970 that the first female generals in the history of the United States were appointed, and it will be longer still until one of them becomes a policy maker rather than just a high officer. The number of women in the leadership of the largest corporations in American society is so small that it is not even noticed as discrimination. On the other hand, women occupy in disproportionate numbers the less enviable economic positions. According to the U.S. census of 1960, the median annual wage of white females was lower than that of nonwhite males, with nonwhite females the lowest paid category.[61] The average salary of women in all occupational categories—professional, managerial, clerical, etc.—was lower than that of men.[62] There is severe disproportion, with women getting the worst end of the economic stick.

Many women, therefore, are economically exploited and underrepresented in the political positions of the democratic state. The latter problem is not of direct concern; it merely means that few women act as repressors in the United States. Those women's groups that push for equality in political positions simply want to give women an equal chance to be the oppressors, rather than to abolish repression. But the realization that women are an economic category (whether they are a class is much debated[63]) that is oppressed because of economic powerlessness contains the seeds of a real radicalization of the society. That kind of analysis holds that, stemming from economic oppression, an ideology of cultural and psychological oppression exists that can outweigh in its tenacity the economic. In this way the oppression of women, their powerlessness, is rooted into the structure of the democratic state. Women, it has been pointed out, are given the function of making up for the inequities of the system.[64] They are then ones who bring in income when it is needed, hold the family together when it starts to fall apart, and transmit this generation's values to the next. In short, through production, reproduction, socialization, and sexuality, women are called upon to maintain a state that renders them powerless.[65] These points have been well demonstrated; it remains here only to assert the point that the democratic state requires the oppression, not only of the poorest elements, but of many others as well.

Women are not the only group that is powerless for other than economic reasons. The American version of the democratic state has long had a xenophobic strain that turned against various kinds of people seen as unwelcome. At one point in time it was directed against immigrants,[66] who survived to become intolerant in turn. It has always existed against those labeled as deviant, radicals, and homosexuals particularly. The former group has never been well received, and repression against it is usually the very definition of repression. The other group, particularly in the 1970s, is beginning to fight its own repression, a sure sign of stirring among the traditionally powerless. The Gay Liberation movement is on the scene, and others will be sure to follow. In other words, many of those traditionally defined as powerless are recognizing their condition and attempting to do something about it. Whether they, like immigrants, become established only to be repressive in turn will have to be seen, but the chances for that seem dim.

It is from the ranks of the powerless that the objects of repression most often come. The most intense repression in the history of the United States came against workers who were trying to organize. In the 1960s, when the National Guard was called out to repress a group, that group was most likely to be blacks. Both groups were repressed when they tried to get together among themselves for purposes of advancing their class interest, something the ruling class does every day without being repressed. Recognition of this is basic to understanding repression in America. A powerful double standard exists, and it is biased against those who do not hold power. People are repressed not because they have done anything illegal (the determination of what is and is not legal is very much a class-biased phenomenon) but because they have understood their powerlessness and have tried to do something about it.

This chapter has tried to show that there is a realistic and meaningful hierarchy of power in the democratic state that remains relatively constant over time. Social mobility has been a much-debated concept in economic terms, but political mobility within the democratic state seems to be of diminishing importance. Entry into the ruling class is all but closed to nearly all Americans; its membership now comes exclusively from a few families that combine social connections, a business background, and a tradition of leadership. The political positions, traditionally those to which young men of lower status aspired, are still open, but heavily dominated by an upper-middle-class element. More and more, the politically powerless group is becoming homogeneous around three or four clusters: white working-class people of ethnic background, rural Protestant poor, urban blacks and Spanish-speaking individuals, and those powerless but not poor collections of women, youth, and stigmatized groups.

One implication is clear: *one class of people consistently benefits from repression, another carries out the policies of repression and feels benefits therefrom but is repressed in a sense as well, and a third is the object of repression.* In addition, each group is composed of fairly well-defined institutions, which enables the observer to rank any person reasonably accurately on a scale of repression, given certain socioeconomic information. In short, just as the state has a very definite bias in the way it operates, repression, as a policy of the state, is biased as well. The "who" that benefits from repression is not randomly decided, some days one group, other days, another. The objects of repression do not continually vary throughout the social structure. Instead, *repression is an aspect of class society,* a method in the class struggle. Repression is a way by which those at the top keep themselves there. From this chapter, it should now be clear what those at the top are like, as well as those at other levels. Every reader of this book should be able to place herself or himself on the scale and determine his or her relationship to the problem of political repression.

part ★ two

the dynamics of repression

chapter
four ☆
violent
repression

Violence is a tricky phenomenon, to which people often apply double standards. If a group of people attack the government by burning down a bank, many see that as anarchy, something that a democratic society cannot tolerate. On the other hand, were the government to respond by raiding the offices of those held responsible and smashing their furniture, those same people would see that as "law and order"—perfectly legitimate behavior, however zealous in application. Reflecting this bias, the sociological literature on violence generally refers only to the violence of groups, not to state violence. The scholarly papers of the President's Commission on Violence, for example, never address the violence of the state, and by doing that, they ignore a substantial part of the violence that has characterized American history.[1]

State violence is "normal" behavior, in liberal democratic societies as in others. It is a way in which a society reproduces itself. Those who rule democratic societies have a number of means at their disposal for maintaining their rule. Among these are traditions, the propagation of ideologies of obedience, the provision of rewards (consumer goods, for example), and socialization patterns. In most cases, particularly when things appear to be "stable," these methods will suffice to preserve the existing order of things, and state violence will not be necessary. But two factors interfere with that stability. One is that there are certain periods when the existing ideologies are not sufficient to instill obedience. In those periods of rapid change and delegitimization—in America, the years 1877–90, 1916–20, and 1964–68 are good examples—challenges to the existing rulers occur, and violence is needed to subdue those challenges.

In addition, at any time certain groups are likely to dissent from the status quo and want to see it changed. From the beginnings of American history, there have been movements, some small, some not so small, that have refused to abide by rules that put them at a permanent disadvantage. The response of the state has been violent repression, since the dissenting consciousness is immune to appeals of tradition or ideology.

Despite its claim to fairness, then, the liberal state, given its biases, will be disposed toward the violent elimination or control of groups whose existence is seen as a threat, whether they are in reality one or not. It is astounding, given the amount of violent repression that has existed in the United States, that few serious treatments of the subject can be found. This paucity necessitates at least three steps to be rectified. First, the process of violent repression must be examined—through what means does the state engage in violence? Then, it is important to show that these means are a permanent feature of American liberal democracy, not ugly aberrations that mistakenly appear from time to time. Finally, given the centrality of repression to liberal democracy, an explanation of the correlation is in order. With those goals addressed, we will have moved a bit farther along in trying to understand a phenomenon such as repression.

Legal Repression

The experiences of the Black Panther party, summarized in chapter 2, sensitize one to the key role played by laws in a system of violent repression. The use of the legal system to control or destroy political organizations is a form of violence, even if no physical harm actually takes place.[2] The arresting act involves physical detention and is therefore an aspect of force. In addition, the law has behind it sanctions that are quite harmful, and the threat of imposing those sanctions constitutes a form of violence even if eventually they are not imposed. Finally, the use of laws against a group is often designed to intimidate, encouraging the group to initiate a violent response, at which point more directly violent forms of repression will be used. These factors suggest that the term *legal repression* should not imply legality—the idea that legal means of repression are fairer or more pure than other forms. It simply means that laws are the means of repression. Legal repression is neither better nor worse than illegal or extralegal repression; in many ways, its use by the state is preferred, since it gives the state's actions a covering of legitimacy.

The kinds of repressive laws used by the governments of the United States are so extensive that a classification system is needed to discuss them. Most examples of legal violence can be subsumed under the following categories: harassment laws, obligatory laws, inclusion laws, process laws, public order laws, preventive laws, and directly political laws.

When a simple law that was originally passed with no political purpose is used to repress, it is an example of a *harassment* law. Many laws can be used to harass, and many groups have been harassed. The laws that may be the most frequently used to harass are narcotics laws, and the groups most frequently repressed are Marxist groups, so the combination of the two provides an illustration of the use of such laws. On March 1, 1966, Attorney General Katzenbach announced that the Justice Department was asking the Subversive Activities Control Board to classify the W. E. B. DuBois club as a "Communist-front" organization, thus forcing it to register as such with the government.[3] The purpose of the move was only partly to make the group register; it was also a signal to others that the group could be repressed in whatever ways were convenient. On the night of November 5, 1966, the DuBois club, needing money to contest the Justice Department's actions, held a fund-raising party in Manhattan. Their attorney describes what happened next:

> The apartment door was apparently unlatched, and seven
> plainclothesmen walked into the party. Witnesses testified that they
> pushed away at least one boy who asked them for identification,
> searched a sport jacket hanging on a chair, and cornered the
> hostess for questioning before the guests, mostly teen-agers, combined
> to push them out. Uniformed men arrived shortly afterward and
> arrested the entire party—some eighty-seven persons—for loitering
> for the purpose of using narcotics.[4]

All the young people were held for fifteen hours by the police, then charged and cleared for arraignment. As there were no narcotics present (the DuBois club, the group's infiltrator must have informed the police, was opposed to the use of drugs), the charges were eventually dismissed.

No convictions were seriously entertained. The purpose of the raid was just one of nuisance. Its effects were tempered somewhat when the police commissioner expunged from police records notations of the arrests, but the example is illustrative nonetheless. One should not get the idea, however, that all harassment serves only a nuisance value. Sometimes nonpolitical laws that are very serious are applied. Members of the Black Panther party have been harassed with murder charges; and a sit-in by black students at Ohio State University resulted in kidnaping indictments. It is up to those doing the repressing to make the punishment fit the noncrime.

Besides harassment laws, there are others—*obligatory* laws—that create for everyone in the society certain political obligations. These become political when it is known by the state that a group cannot comply with the obligations created but is forced to anyway. In such cases, when repression is not the desired end, exceptions can be created. When repression is desired, the exceptions will be drawn tightly, thereby excluding from the scope the group which is to be repressed. Selective Service legislation is the obvious example. There was little interest in repressing the Society of Friends, since its pacifism had so easily become passivism. Exceptions to the law provided means whereby that group would not be repressed. But political opponents of the war had to be repressed, so the exception to the obligation did not apply to them. Here there is no use arguing that one's avoidance of the obligation is more "sincere" or "well-founded" than the other's. We are dealing with a political phenomenon, and one group's politics were more of a threat than the other's. The interesting thing about obligatory laws is that in many cases the obligation does not really exist until someone challenges it. Then the challenger finds that his obligation is greater than anyone else's. That is when an obligatory law becomes an example of political repression. The group must either obey the law and thus deny its purpose or disobey it and be repressed.

Obligatory laws provide positive actions that everyone in the society is expected to perform. They can thus be distinguished from *inclusion* laws, which define who everyone in the society is supposed to be. One of the easiest ways to repress is not to allow someone associated with a political group access into the country in the first place. This was done in the case of an internationally famous woman author, and then repeated for a former Yale professor.[5] When they would not swear to pick up arms to defend the country, they were excluded from entering it. In more recent years a number of prominent European Marxists, including Ernest Mandel and leaders of the Italian Community party, have been notified that they are unwelcome in this country. Alternatively, once in the country, those considered repressible, if they are not yet citizens, are easily deportable. Deportation of immigrants was one of the most popular repressive laws against radicals, especially after World War I.[6] Vietnam war draft resisters who flew to Canada were deported in fact, even if they have the "right" to return home and face charges. Laws that define membership in the political system will always be used, when appropriate, for political repression.[7]

Process laws have proved effective for repressive purposes. A process law is one that punishes, not the specific actions discussed above, but the process of carrying out those actions. The most famous process law—indeed, the most remarkable of all the repressive laws in the arsenal of the democratic state—is the one that alleges the existence of a conspiracy to commit an offense, whether it was committed or not. Conspiracy laws generally carry the greatest penalty for the least offense; for example, in California a conspiracy to commit certain misdemeanors is a felony. In addition, standards of proof for conspiracy laws are lax; the conspirators need never have met. Finally, the action around which the conspiracy allegedly took place need never have occurred: a conspiracy to rob a bank is still a crime even if no robbery was ever attempted. With all these advantages to the state, and with a corresponding lack of defenses available to the political group, conspiracy laws are most popular for purposes of repression. Eugene Debs, who was too old to avoid an obligatory law (the draft), was sent to jail on a process law (conspiring to obstruct the operations of the draft). The federal trials to repress the IWW, referred to in chapter 2, were organized around the same conspiracy law. The same tactic has proved effective in disrupting the operations of labor unions, civil rights organizations, and antiwar organizations.

One other flexibility provided by conspiracy laws is that they cannot only be substituted for direct violations of other types of laws, but they can also be tacked onto indictments based on other types of laws to compound the punishment. This is what happened with the Chicago Eight in 1969. They were alleged to have conspired to break the law, and they were also charged with breaking the law itself, giving the state a legal method of imposing double jeopardy. In that case, the specific law was a form of *public order* law, also popular for purposes of repression. Public order laws say that in the interests of public order, certain penalties will have to be paid by those who are alleged to have created disorder. Inciting a riot is a public order law, as are local ordinances dealing with crowds, curfews, and sound equipment.

There are two interesting aspects to public order laws. One is that they express the liberal dilemma well, for in the name of order they impose repression. Thus, public order laws are often supported because they contribute to the maintenance of "liberty." It is not surprising that the law under which the Chicago Eight were tried was passed as part of a law designed to expand civil rights; this is the very essence of the dilemma. The other aspect of public order laws is that they assume that the group, not the state, caused the disorder, reflecting the bias toward violence previously mentioned. It must be the group that created the disorder, for the state by definition can only further order. Thus, it is difficult to use public order laws to punish agents of the state if they were responsible for the disorder, for such a notion is beyond the ken of these laws. This built-in political bias can be illustrated with two examples. When a number of Arizona residents were deported to New Mexico in an illegal action in 1917, clear evidence was uncovered that the local sheriff and officials of the Phelps Dodge Corporation instigated and executed this "vigilante" action. Federal criminal proceedings were brought against them, but they were never convicted.[8] In the other example, eight policemen were indicted along with the Chicago Eight. All were found not guilty even though evidence of a "police riot" was strong.[9] In both cases, juries could not conceive that public authorities could possibly contribute to disorder, for they shared the misconception that it is always the political groups and never the state that "cause" disorder to take place. In 1977 charges were brought against the FBI for taking illegal actions against the Weathermen; a violence-prone group. This is the first time that formal charges have been brought against the most famous of repressive agencies. It will be interesting to see whether any agents ever go to jail for crimes performed while on active duty.

This society also contains *preventive* laws and practices. The purpose of these laws is not to repress people who have become active dissidents, but to control those segments of the population that are viewed as potentially disruptive, before they have become overt political opponents of the regime. One example is the violence associated with repressive institutions, such as prisons and mental institutions, where regulations and practices are designed to isolate and make impotent those who are defined as "not fitting into the society." (Ironically, both institutions can have a countereffect, leading to politicization. Witness recent U.S. prison rebellions and the creation of a Mental Patients Liberation Front.) Also illustrative of these laws and practices are the conditions of everyday life in the urban ghettos. Police brutality, frequent arrests, police sweeps, and racism are often designed to prevent potential rebellion from a class that has a self-interest (whether recognized or not) in being critical of the existing political, economic, and social system.

Finally, there are explictly *political* laws. When the state is confident of its ability to repress, it needs few subterfuges or symbolic actions. It can simply declare that certain political groups will be repressed and rely on popular hostility to those groups to support their actions. The Smith Act and the residue of anti-Communist legislation of the 1950s were all explicitly political laws. When the Smith Act was upheld in the *Dennis* case, it served as an impetus for the state to be even more explicitly political in its legislation.[10] Later judicial undercutting of such efforts was irrelevant, for by the time the Court began to remember the matter of civil liberty, the laws had taken their effect and the groups were significantly weakened. The important point to remember about political laws is that they are rarely needed to repress; other types of laws will do just as well. Political laws, therefore, are passed as a test of strength. It is as if the state is proudly declaring repression and daring the group to do something about it. In most cases, political laws will be passed when the group is already on the way to impotence. Because of this, it would be in error to conclude that a paucity of explicitly political laws in a certain period, or even the repeal of political laws, is a sign that repression is on the wane. It is a sign that it is about to take a different form.

One other word should be added here for the sake of clarity. All the forms of legal repression discussed so far can take other than legislative forms. Specifically, in the United States repression can be investigative, judicial, and administrative. Investigatory repression needs little comment. Hearings of what was called the House Un-American Activities Committee are familiar enough. It is sufficient to say that when little evidence for conviction was present, HUAC hearings provided repression in two ways: social and economic, by relying on public pressure to discredit the individual; and punitive, by seeking to result in a *process* indictment, contempt of Congress.[11]

The judiciary plays a contradictory role in the repressive apparatus of the democratic state. It receives much publicity when the Supreme Court upsets the conviction of a political group. To many this is a vindication of the democratic state, a sign of its fairness. But periods of leniency toward dissidents are short-lived; while the Warren Court did try to apply the Bill of Rights, the Nixon-appointed Burger Court has shown only minimal concern with protecting the rights of dissidents against repressive agencies. In addition, the judicial system below the high appellate courts is often in the forefront of repression. Judicial restraining orders are used against political groups, rarely against the state. In addition, the courtroom is frequently used for purposes of a public political trial. Here the state does not simply want a conviction. It wants to hold the dissenting group up to public ridicule by proving to the world how impotent the group is in the face of the state's repressive procedures. (In the Chicago case, this seems to have worked for older Americans, but failed completely for younger ones. The state discovered one of the contradictions of the political trial as repressive procedure—that it can win sympathy for the group being repressed.) Finally, by its interpretation of legislation, the judiciary can strengthen repressive laws, even adding repressive dimensions when they were not intended to be there. Thus, it was the courts, not Congress, that discovered that the Sherman Antitrust Act could be used to imprison Eugene Debs.

Administrative edicts, executive orders, and general bureaucratic procedures can also be used for purposes of repression. Like judicial interpretation, presidential executive orders clarify and sharpen repressive laws. Furthermore, it is through the administrative branch that the prosecution's case is made, an important step in any legal repression. Administrative actions can also be concerned directly with political attitudes. A loyalty-security program was created by the executive branch before Congress passed any comprehensive legislation, before the start of what is now called the McCarthy period. Japanese-Americans were repressed during World War II by executive action. President Nixon's staff debated a plan for centralizing repression in the executive branch (the Huston plan), which was stopped only because FBI director Hoover saw it as a threat to his power. Also under the executive branch are those forms of repression related to members of the armed forces, an area in which repression is usually more explicit and harsh than in the civilian realm. Finally, the growth of the welfare state has led to a policy of repression through implementation. Welfare recipients are denied certain political rights through bureaucratic procedure, not through legislation, as are residents of public housing projects, students, and other recipients of state aid.[12] In short, repression through administrative action has to be added to the list to make it reasonably complete.

That there is a class basis to law is an often asserted truism. Oliver Goldsmith once wrote that "laws grind the poor and rich men rule the law," while Anatole France is sometimes remembered for his remark praising the "majesty" of laws that prohibit rich and poor from sleeping under the same bridge.[13] Stemming from this class bias, there is a political bias toward law as well. Groups perceived as a threat by state officials will find laws enforced, often harshly, while those who are held to be respectable, if arrested, will find leniency the order of the day. Laws exist in a political context, and the political reality of America is such that laws are too convenient to the rulers of the democratic state to be ignored. In America, the existence of a government of laws and not of men is sometimes praised, but when the laws are used by the men to preserve their own power, the law itself becomes the problem.

Repression Through Political Intelligence

A second form of violent repression in liberal society is political intelligence and espionage. Here it is of no concern whether the state's activities are formally defined as "legal," that is, whether they are supported by legislative statute. Much of domestic political espionage is legal in that sense; much of it is also illegal or extralegal. It makes little difference. This form of repression is characterized by the use of covert means by the state to control political dissidents. Since, by definition, this form is covert, information on it is less available when compared to other forms of repression. Nonetheless, every now and then the state is willing to reveal how extensive its infiltrative mechanisms are, for if it did not, who would be intimidated by them? From these acts of revelation, enough information can be assembled to place the use of political intelligence by the democratic state into a meaningful perspective.

Obtaining political information covertly is an old human custom. In the Bible, Delilah would appear to be the first agent, working for the Philistines against Israel.[14] The use of spies and informers for domestic political purposes has been traced back at least as far as medieval England.[15] Since Americans think of themselves as both religious and shaped by English law, it is not surprising that Delilah's techniques were quickly adopted. What is interesting is that political intelligence was first used by private groups and only later by the government.

The Pinkerton Detective Agency—which flourished at the end of the nineteenth century—was instrumental in developing tactics of repression through political intelligence. Of the many colorful individuals who rose to prominence in this profession, the career of the most well known is illustrative of a whole pattern. James McParland—subject of a Hollywood movie in 1970—caught the eye of Allen Pinkerton when he successfully infiltrated the semisecret labor organization known as the "Molly Maguires" in the Pennsylvania coalfields.[16] Eventually becoming a key leader of the organization, he often acted as a *provocateur*, pushing the group into an illegal action and then informing the authorities so that the group could be suppressed. McParland was highly successful, and his testimony against the group in court ensured its demise. This led to a promotion for the young intelligence officer, and he went farther west to continue roughly the same sort of work.

In 1906, McParland and the Pinkertons reemerged to work actively in repressing the IWW. Arrested and charged with the murder of former governor Frank Steunenberg of Idaho were three key leaders of the IWW—William Haywood, George A. Pettibone, and Charles H. Moyer. The arrests were illegal; the men were kidnaped across state lines so that Idaho could ignore extradition proceedings. Since little evidence was presented linking the men to the crime, McParland, instinctively understanding the tortured mind of a self-confessed murderer, obtained a confession that implicated the three officials, and a political trial was begun. In this case, Clarence Darrow broke through the confession, and the men were found not guilty. Nonetheless, the expense and harassment associated with the trial hurt the IWW and was a sign of its future treatment.

What is the role of the state in this tale? At one level the state (of Idaho) cooperated with McParland and the Pinkertons in their work. But more important is something revealed by McParland himself in a letter to his boss, written during these events:

> This is one of the most important operations ever undertaken in the Portland District, and if through our offices we are successful, it will mean a great deal to the Spokane office so far as the mine operators are concerned, in fact all mine operators in the whole district.[17]

It did mean a good deal to the mine owners. In situations of this sort, the Pinkerton Agency was explicitly working for those who constituted the ruling class at that time. One could infer that repression by the state was contracted out to a private organization with all the advantages (fewer scruples) that such a move entails. Intelligence of this sort, though conducted privately, is clearly an affair of state and should be considered as such.

Private intelligence intensified after this period. The use of industrial spies led to strikes and resulted in violence in Kentucky in 1933 and 1934.[18] In fact, the amount of industrial espionage leaped in the 1920s and 1930s. Fortunately one aspect of the American government investigated the actions of another, resulting in the hearings before the Subcommittee of the Senate Education and Labor Committee, often called the La Follette Civil Liberties Committee.[19] These 1936 hearings, the most comprehensive collection of information about industrial espionage ever gathered, reveal a vast system of private intelligence, working for the powerful, designed to repress labor organizations of all varieties, including the least revolutionary. The hearings uncovered the existence of at least 225 private detective agencies engaged in the business of spying on labor unions.[20] Spy reports, filed by agents, covered in meticulous detail every event at meeting after meeting of a labor union. Employers knew union affairs more thoroughly than union leaders themselves. Also informative from these hearings were lists of contributions made by various corporations to "employer's associations," money that went immediately into espionage.[21] The La Follette hearings show an extensive network of intelligence operatives working for corporations—with the expressed sympathy of the state—whose sole function is the violent repression of those groups whose interests run counter to the interests of the rulers of the democratic state.

One should not get the impression that because private groups were engaged in repression for the state that the state itself was idle. In 1917, the Bureau of Investigation of the Department of Justice gave its blessing to a group called the American Protective League, a private organization that would ferret out "subversives" and others endangering the war effort.[22] So zealous were these patriots that vigilantism mushroomed throughout the country. The violence became so intense that the bureau realized it must itself take on the job of political repression, in a more covert and "professional" manner. Repression, it discovered, is a tricky business best left to the experts. Shortly thereafter, in June 1917, an assistant to the attorney general was hired to coordinate "war work," and he in turn hired an assistant named J. Edgar Hoover. In September, the first raids by the bureau against the IWW were taken. In those few months, the foundations of the modern FBI were laid, and national government increasingly became involved in repression through political intelligence.

The proudest moment in this period occurred in 1922. In 1920, while the Soviet Union was being undermined by the presence of American troops aiding the White Army, Francis Morrow was hired by the Department of Justice to spy on radical organizations, eventually including the American Communist party, which was formed in 1921. Morrow became a party official in Camden, New Jersey, and he periodically sent reports to Washington. It was Morrow who relayed enough information to make possible a raid on the party's Bridgman (Michigan) Convention, an affair held after the most elaborate precautions were taken to ensure that the government would be unable to find the then "underground" organizations. Many leaders were arrested, documents were seized, and the importance of a professional intelligence system for purposes of political repression was demonstrated to all who remained skeptical.[23] What soon became the Federal Bureau of Investigation had a major part of its mission defined.

What is the current status of repression through political intelligence? The general use of intelligence techniques in law enforcement seems certain to have risen. At least twelve federal agencies keep extensive intelligence records: FBI, Federal Bureau of Narcotics, Bureau of Customs, Alcohol Tax Unit, Immigration and Naturalization Service, Internal Revenue Service (Intelligence Division), Civil Aeronautics Administration, U.S. Maritime Commission, Post Office Department, Interstate Commerce Commission, Department of Agriculture, and Department of Labor.[24] States and municipalities also keep such information; California, for example, has five state agencies that perform key intelligence operations.[25] The importance of effective intelligence for police work in general has been summarized in a police textbook on the problem:

Police operational intelligence has probably made more advances in the last twenty years than it did in the previous century. Though an embryo service, *the future appears exceptionally bright, full of vast unexplored areas for research and development not yet unveiled. Police agencies throughout the country are experimenting in one degree or another with the application of intelligence techniques.* The product of this experiment coupled with *current research in the fields of psychology, criminology, sociology,* and data processing techniques should bring forth a highly effective tool for future police administrators.[26]

One would expect, given the increasing reliance on intelligence for general law enforcement, that the use of such techniques for political repression is bound to increase as well. This is especially true when we consider that to those who enforce the law, political dissidents themselves are just a special sort of criminal. The standard police textbook on intelligence discusses communism in the same chapter with crime, right after Al Capone and Salvatore Luciana. The authors' reason for making this linkage is to emphasize the "true nature" of the Communist *conspiracy:* "Any idiot or pseudo-intellectual that thinks Communism has any relationship to the Latin root is grossly ill informed." They must realize instead that "Communism is a pseudoscientific, atheistic philosophy perpetuated by a criminal conspiracy of power hungry dictators."[27] (This is in a textbook designed for professional use.) If political dissidents are indeed so dangerous, they are criminals and all law enforcement tactics can be used, including intelligence.

In a 1955 speech to the International Association of Chiefs of Police, J. Edgar Hoover told those responsible for law enforcement this:

> It is through the efforts of confidential informants that we have been able to expose the Communist conspiracy in the past and *through which we must stake much of the future security of the United States.* That is why such a vicious attack has been made against former Communists who have firsthand knowledge of the secret diabolical purpose of the Communist Party.[28]

If Hoover is considered a biased spokesman, the speech at the same meeting by Assistant U.S. Attorney General William Tomkins is even more interesting, because it illustrates the legitimacy that liberal intellectuals like Learned Hand have, in their desire to ensure balance, given to the more nefarious aspects of political repression:

> With reference to the propriety of using informants, very little need be said. Judge Learned Hand, in affirming the conviction in the celebrated Dennis case, tried before Judge Medina in New York City, announced this contention simply and succinctly by stating that

"courts have countenanced the use of informers from time immemorial." *What our critics fail to, or will not recognize, is that those who are engaged in a criminal enterprise have no right to be free from such surveillance. . . .*[29]

The function of repression through intelligence is more than merely to render a group ineffective. One reason for keeping tabs on political dissidents is to strengthen other forms of political repression, especially of the legal variety. The information gathered through the intelligence network is dramatically "revealed" to the public in a highly visible political trial. A close examination of the evidence at *all* recent political trials indicates that the only "evidence" presented by the state is the word of informers. In the Dennis trial, the government's case consisted of four converts (those who joined the party sincerely and were "sickened") and seven informers (those who joined the FBI and then joined the party).[30] In the Chicago conspiracy trial of 1969, one of the defendants noted that "as for concrete evidence of lawbreaking activity, the government puzzled us further by introducing almost nothing."[31] All the government did was to parade its undercover agents on the stand, and their number alone seems to have convinced the jury that the defendants were indeed dangerous and, therefore, guilty.

In addition, repression through intelligence provides to the repressors of the democratic state continued reason for their own existence. There are now many liberals within the United States who would like to deemphasize this form of repression, but those who control it have entrenched themselves within the bureaucracy and with the public and are unmovable. Since the death of J. Edgar Hoover, various directors have spoken of reforming the bureau in order to inspire public confidence. But the bureaucratic infighting is fierce, and little has so far been done. It remains to be seen how successful Carter will be in imposing his plans on the agency. Intelligence, after all, is more than one man. It is an apparatus, and what keeps an apparatus operating is its work. Parkinson's law is accurate for intelligence work: the information uncovered will expand to match the number of people doing the uncovering.

At the present time, this problem has become most serious. Sophisticated technological improvements have been combined with traditional espionage techniques to create a repressive apparatus that is truly startling. Electronic surveillance is widely used,[32] which creates a dilemma. In reviewing the conviction of a labor leader convicted on the basis of a wiretap of his phone, the Supreme Court recently noted that ". . . the use of secret informers is not *per se* unconstitutional."[33] There is the rub. Since liberal theory does not want to render the state powerless, it admits in principle the legitimacy of the new devices. But once admitted, these devices have a way of multiplying to their technological limits. (It is, after all, a capitalist economy that makes and sells the new equipment.) Thus, one has reason to believe that the new techniques are seen as highly relevant to the control of political dissidents. Nobody knows how much wiretapping takes place; the very secrecy of it leads to wild rumors. The feeling that one's phone is tapped is effective in shaping political conduct, whether the phone actually is or not.

In spite of the secrecy surrounding surveillance, new facts have come to light that begin to reveal how extensive practices of this sort are. We know that the FBI devotes twice as much money to watching political groups as it does to fighting organized crime. We know that Lyndon Johnson sent thirty agents to "cover" the Democratic convention of 1964 and that a significant number of delegates to the 1972 convention were being watched. We know that the CIA, in violation of its charter, operates at home, conducting extensive mail-opening operations. We know that military intelligence agencies regularly patrol demonstrations, even though their authority to do so is tenuous. We know that the Internal Revenue Service will release "confidential" information to curious presidents. We know, in short, that interventions into private life in America are far more extensive than we had dreamed.[34]

This discussion would suggest that repression through intelligence cannot be explained in totally rational terms. Further evidence of this comes from the heavy emphasis on converts in this sort of work. In the speech quoted earlier, J. Edgar Hoover indicated the importance of apostates to political work. Indeed, the Bridgman raid, the first successful federal repression of the Communist party, was directed by a Russian who sympathized with the Russian Revolution.[35] The presence of so many converts adds a psychological dimension to the problem. It is possible that the democratic state finds itself controlling so many groups because the state needs to manufacture its own opposition? The possibility must at least be admitted. If order is an end of the democratic state, what would be more ordered than controlling one's own antithesis? *There is evidence, in short, that the function of repression through intelligence is not to destroy such groups but to keep them functioning.* Their existence is needed, sometimes desperately. In 1964, when the Communist party of the United States was weak, divided, and a threat to nobody or nothing, by any objective standard, the director of the FBI said:

> The Communist Party, USA, stepped up its programs on all
> domestic fronts during the 1964 fiscal year. . . . The Party worked
> unremittingly to increase its influence in the racial struggle; gain
> new members through an intensive youth recruitment campaign; and
> promote the false impression that it is a legitimate political
> party.[36]

Many people manufacture their own devils. What made this man's devils so interesting was not that he was just another person, but that he was in charge of repression through intelligence in the democratic state. He could have reached such a position only with the support of the whole system.

One should not, however, conclude that such repression is totally irrational. Kirchheimer has noted that "Informing will be a somewhat smaller threat to larger movements, which neither need nor want to consider violence a necessary or exclusive means of undermining the foundations of an existing regime, but are intent and able to concentrate their efforts on a broader front. Due to the wider nature of their appeal, they are more immune to turncoats and traitors."[37] It follows that this form of repression is most used against small groups. If they are not engaged in violence, and hence no threat to public order, infiltration is little justified, though heavily used. If they are a threat by their emphasis on violence, it must be remembered that the group might not have decided on a violent course were it not for the agent in their midst urging violence upon them. In short, the function of repression through intelligence is not to allow the group to have a choice. The democratic state can no longer draw the line between groups that threaten order and those that do not. Control is the basis of the democratic state, and repression through intelligence is still an effective and highly rational form of control.

Such repression bothers some people. Writing in 1863, the British historian Sir Thomas Erskine May expressed the problem eloquently:

> Men may be without restraints upon their liberty; they may pass to and fro at pleasure; but if their steps are tracked by spies and informers, their words noted down for crimination, their associates watched as conspirators—who shall say they are free?
> [Espionage] haunts men like an evil genius, chills their gaiety, restrains their wit, casts a shadow over their friendships, and blights their domestic health. The freedom of a country may be measured by its immunity from this baleful agency.[38]

If that immunity is to be the measure, it is unfortunate for the government of the United States. For it is not only clear that the government will fail the test, but every indication is that it will continue to fail it, perhaps with even lower scores.

The Role of the Military and the Police

The last general form of violent repression to be discussed is the use of direct violence for political ends. So far the means discussed have only implied actual violence; that is, what makes repression through laws and intelligence effective is the threat of violence that exists behind them. But it is clear that sometimes the direct application of force is needed. When that occurs, the state takes what can be considered military action against dissidents. The importance of this ultimate form of state violence should not be underestimated, for its use has been quite consistent.

Military-type repression often takes place in conjunction with the other forms discussed. This is true of one of the most popular forms, the raid. Material uncovered through raids on the homes of dissidents and the headquarters of political groups is usually effective evidence in a public political trial. But if the IWW is an example, this is not the only purpose of the raid. Before the mass trial of the IWW, as was mentioned in chapter 2, the organization had offered to open its books for the government, confident that no "evidence" of a criminal charge would be found in them. The government chose to raid instead. This suggests that its purpose was something more than data collection. Periodic raids may be considered a form of repression by harassment. The purpose is simply to keep the group defensive, never knowing when a raid is coming. It is hoped that this will have an anticipatory effect on the group. Constantly anticipating raids, the group will change its conduct, becoming more defensive. Thus, its original purpose—say, to transform society—becomes transformed itself, into the task of simply maintaining the group's existence. This reasoning may explain the popularity of and frequent use of raids. We have already seen the number of raids made against the Black Panther party and the use of similar tactics against the Communist party. In the first case, the raiding was done by local police (although evidence of federal encouragement exists); in the second, it was done by the FBI. Other institutions also practice raiding. For example, the files of an organization called the Southern Conference Educational Fund were raided by agents of a legislative committee.[39]

Related to raids are those occasions when actual pitched battles are fought between political groups and agents of the state. Here the purpose is to commit serious injury or death to key individuals who are held to be a threat to existing social relationships. If a trial might be too embarrassing, repressing through intelligence not devastating enough, an individual can be enticed into a fight and shot. In past times, such activity was often undertaken by private guards under the employ of corporations. Extensive killing—twenty strikers, for example, in one steel strike[40]—has the effect not only of removing some individuals from the scene, but also of modifying the conduct of others. Few people wish to give up their lives for political goals. Serious evidence that their lives are in danger should in most cases temper their spirit and make more conservative their politics, whether they are conscious of the problem or not.

One of the most thinly disguised attempts of this form of repression occurred in December 1969. Here the perpetrators were not private guards but city police. Fred Hampton and Mark Clark of the Chicago Black Panthers were murdered in their beds; all the evidence points to that. How could the state have been so bold in its moves? Consider what happened afterward. Although every investigation has uncovered that the police killed the men before they even picked up their guns, only one serious effort to discipline any of the policemen has taken place and that was the result of a feud in Chicago politics. It also culminated in a "not guilty" verdict against the official who was charged. The extraordinary nature of the incident has been lost in bureaucratic detail, possibly intentionally. This incident has shown that the democratic state can use the most violent forms of terror associated with "totalitarianism" against a political group within its borders and risk little loss of legitimacy; the Chicago incident is still written off by many as an accident. Presumably, the lesson will not be lost on future generations of repressors.

The most common form of military repression is the use of the military itself in domestic politics. The rationale for the existence of a domestic army is the government's obligation to keep order. If all the troops did was to keep order, assuming a neutral role without aid to any group in a given conflict, then a case could be made that repression was not being practiced. But in an actual conflict situation, such a judgment is often difficult to make. For example, consider a case in which, according to one scholar, "Martial law has never been used on so broad a scale, in so drastic a manner, nor upon such sweeping principles."[41] The case was a strike in the Paint Creek section of West Virginia during 1912–13. Violence associated with the strike had assumed the status of a civil war, with battles constantly being fought throughout the countryside. The major precipitants of the violence, according to West Virginia Governor Glasscock's Senate testimony, were guards employed by the miners. Martial law was declared to stop the violence being perpetrated by employees of management. Here is a case where the state would appear to be intervening in a neutral way, or even on the side of the miners. Yet given the nature of the democratic state, such a situation did not come about in practice.

The proclamation declaring martial order noted that danger to property was apparent. It sought to "execute the laws, and to protect the public peace, lives, and property of quiet and orderly citizens."[42] Thus, there was a conservative bias to the proclamation from the beginning. One could argue that the purpose of martial law was not to protect the miners but to acheive a stability in which industrial production could continue. But one need not go that far, for the enforcement of martial law penalized the strikers, even though it was admitted that the cause of the violence was the company. Under martial law, for example, a socialist newspaper that published outside the martial law zone, with few readers inside the area, was suppressed by the governor in an action upheld by the state supreme court. In addition, the existence of martial law meant that all cases arising out of the strike were tried in military courts, even though civil courts were "open." Testifying before a committee, the governor pointed out that the purpose of the sentences handed down by the military courts was intimidation, not punishment.[43] These military measures combined finally to end the strike and restore peace. The settlement reached was more beneficial to the employers than it was to the union.

Consideration of the use of troops to restore order must begin with a recognition of who benefits most from it. Commenting on a study of labor violence, Graham and Gurr noted:

> . . . most labor violence in American history was not a deliberate tactic of working class organization but a result of forceful employer resistance to worker organization and demands. Companies repeatedly resorted to coercive and sometimes terroristic activities against union organizers and to violent strike-breaking tactics. The violence of employers often provided both model and impetus to counterviolence by workers, leading in many situations to an escalating spiral of violent conflict to the point of military intervention.[44]

What happened when military intervention took place? Again, in spite of the employer contribution to violence, in nearly all cases the use of troops served the interests of the dominant groups.

Restoring order came to mean restoring the status quo. The only weapon the labor unions had was the threat of a strike. Yet to engage workers in a strike was a feat of organizing, for most workers were more concerned with their own problems of security and family. Enormous momentum was needed to keep a strike going. When troops disrupted that momentum, it was the workers who were hurt. The employers had a class consciousness. They knew what their goals were and were united in their desire to obtain them. This was not true of the unions, and it is why "keeping order" meant to many of them an important defeat.

There are other reasons to question the "neutrality" of the use of troops. The National Guard, which was relied on for these purposes, was composed of human beings who held a place in the social structure. After World War I, the Guard became close to groups like the Rotary and Lions. When the American Legion was formed in 1920, according to one authority, "the two organizations overlapped." Furthermore,

> The Guard had strong ties also to local business leaders. Again, the two groups tended to overlap. Many high-ranking Guard officers were among their community's leading businessmen. In this period, as in

the late nineteenth century, the Guard served the interests of
business in conflicts with labor.[45]

The CIO, a group that should know, frequently found cause to denounce
the National Guard throughout the late 1930s. No wonder. An official of
the Cleveland Chamber of Commerce was a newly retired commander of
a National Guard division. "This case," writes Derthick, "was probably
not unusual."[46]

Thus, in labor disputes throughout the 1930s, the National Guard
was engaged in the business of repression when it intervened in strikes.
Some commentators admit this, but see an end to the pattern in recent
times. Writing in 1956, two political scientists claimed that the function of
the Guard had changed. "From an embodiment of force it has become
largely an instrument of rescue and relief."[47] The very next year the
Guard was used to restore order in Little Rock, Arkansas. Here was a
case where the use of troops did not necessarily mean repression. The
troops aided the blacks, helped integrate Little Rock schools, and set
back the plans of segregationists. But the pattern established by this
exception did not continue. The Guard increasingly was used for purposes of force, and increasingly the force was against the less privileged
groups. Beginning in 1964, the Guard saw extensive use—more than at
any other time in its history—in "restoring order" to racially troubled
areas. Here its function was again analogous to the labor situation. Restoring order meant an end to a protest by people who were challenging
the conditions of their lives. To them the use of National Guard troops
meant a return to passivity and poverty. In addition, the social characteristics of the Guard were again relevant. The Guard was nearly all
white and highly racially prejudiced. Strenuous efforts to integrate the
Guard, to improve its legitimacy as an instrument of repression, were
undertaken, but these have all failed. The Guard continues to represent
conservative interests and its use in racial situations continues to be a
repressive one.

In the 1960s, repression through military means was oriented to the
preservation of racial peace. Yet there are other aspects. The year 1970
saw the National Guard use its weapons against middle-class white students, an "accident" that seems to have changed many people's minds
about repression. While the use of violent repression has decreased since
the turbulent sixties, the reemergence of a student movement in 1977
(against apartheid and in favor of equal opportunity) may lead to a
situation resembling the previous decade in its intensity.

Occasionally troops are used against more privileged groups, this
being a form of exception that says something about the rule. For example, in 1948 President Truman ordered the secretary of the army to

seize America's railroads. What happened next was interesting: "In August 1950, however, the seized railroads were placed under the direction of the Assistant Secretary of the Army, while the entire country was divided into several regions headed by army colonels recalled to active military duty. Curiously enough, all these colonels happened to be railroad presidents in civilian life."[48] *In other words, from the least violent form of repression to the most, the class bias of the state is the most important factor in determining the severity of the means.*

The Ubiquity of Violence

Violent repression has been a fairly constant feature of the American political landscape in the twentieth century. As previously indicated, repression in the nineteenth century was concentrated in private hands. Corporations repressed challenges to their power by hiring private agencies to break strikes, infiltrating attempts at unionization, and engaging in armed warfare with workers. It was during the administration of Woodrow Wilson that this pattern began to change. The same urge of leading figures of that time to engage the state as an active partner with corporations in the economy also led to an active role of the state in the task of repression. The need for a centralized and professional agency of repression culminated in the attempts by the Department of Justice to eliminate so-called subversive elements from the country, through new laws (like the Espionage Acts), deportations, and raids.[49]

The trend toward systematic repression by the state culminated in the year 1919, a crucial year, as Arthur Waskow has noted:

> When John Dos Passos sought a date upon which to center *U.S.A.*,
> his trilogy about intense social conflict and a crisis in American values,
> he chose 1919. In the development of American attitudes toward
> the public and private use of violence in dealing with intense social
> conflict, 1919 was a crucial year.[50]

It was crucial because, unlike any other time in this century, both labor unions and blacks were struggling, at the same time and often violently, to obtain their ends. There was a (peaceful) general strike in Seattle (unique in American history), vigilante attacks on the IWW, coal strikes, a racial pogrom in Chicago of major proportions, another racial disturbance in Arkansas, and a final one in Omaha, during which, according to one writer, the military "took over the complete administration and control of an American municipality."[51] With all this at stake, Waskow's conclusion is apt:

> In 1919 the new American "state" that had emerged from the First
> World War was forced to decide whether to enforce its monopoly

of violence or instead to allow private violence full sway. Although federal officials were not conscious of making a momentous choice of the future role of "state" power in America and did not theorize about their choice, their actions did in fact embody a decision.[52]

The decisions made around 1919 were never changed and in fact have been consistently reiterated. The 1920s continued the pattern. National Guard use was frequent. In addition, between 1919 and 1921, twenty-three separate states and territories enacted legislation that outlawed "criminal syndicalism." Idaho's law was typical:

> Criminal syndicalism is the doctrine which advocates crime, sabotage, violence or unlawful methods of terrorism as a means of accomplishing industrial or political reform. The advocacy of such a doctrine, whether by word of mouth or writing, is a felony. . . .

California's was similar, but included "means of accomplishing a change in industrial ownership or control, or effecting any political change."[53] Though passed at this time, these laws did not just die out. One black militant was arrested under New York's criminal syndicalism law as late as the 1960s.

The only period between the end of World War I and the present in which no substantial acts of state repression occurred was during the 1930s. This does not mean that no repression existed; National Guard use was frequent for breaking up major strikes in nearly every year of the decade. But the New Deal was a period in which the obvious economic disaster required that attention be directed toward saving the system. Since many radicals supported the New Deal (it is interesting that the Communist party did, but the less radical Socialist party did not),[54] their cooperation was asked for and obtained. Events moved too fast—and the stakes were too high—to permit overt repression to take place. It was more effective to pass legislation that broadened the social base of the country, thereby having the effect of stabilizing a fairly unstable situation.

Whatever was lacking in the 1930s was compensated for in the next decade. These ten years began with the one incident in American history generally considered to be the most disgraceful action ever taken by the United States: the internment of Japanese-American citizens during World War II. So much has been written on these events that these need not be recapitulated here. It is enough to say that national security had very little to do with these acts. Rather, it was a classic case of repression in which some groups stood to benefit economically from the action. In spite of fantastic discrimination and unfair legislation, the West Coast Japanese had done well economically. They owned or managed 226,000 acres of farmland valued at $66 million. In addition, Japanese youth were going to college in higher numbers than any single ethnic group in the United States. Not only were they going, but their success was to be envied. Although less than 1 percent of the student population at the University of Washington, Japanese-American students comprised 10 percent of the Phi Beta Kappas.[55] These figures indicate what many West Coast whites felt, that repression against this group would remove a threat to their economic security. The Federal Reserve Bank of San Francisco estimated that the land confiscated during the internment period amounted to about $400 million.[56] Since the land was claimed by prosperous whites, the group that benefited from these acts of repression became clear.

Not only did the 1940s begin with repression, they ended with it as well. The emergence of a national security consciousness preoccupied the Truman Administration, and the basis of repression through anti-Communist legislation was started then. In the words of one historian:

> More often after 1948 the liberals, not the McCarthyites, sought to
> restrict the political dialogue, to define certain subjects as beyond the
> pale of responsible criticism. Asserting that they were protecting
> the national security, Truman administration supporters dismissed
> criticism as dangerous and subversive.[57]

Thus, when McCarthyism characterized the repression of the 1950s, it did not come as a surprise but as the continuation of policies started after the war. In any case, phobias about national security defined repression throughout the decade of the 1950s, and their effects have tapered off only slightly at the present time. Legislation against "communism" is still prevalent, and it is still used, not to repress Communists, but to quell dangerous thinking which might lead to the wrong questions about the democratic state.

Given this basis, it is no wonder that repression did not go away in the 1960s. If anything it increased, for the political quiet of the earlier decade was replaced by an intense concern that eventually led to activism. Signs of the new repression were many. The National Guard was used as a repressive force more heavily than ever. Infiltration seems to have skyrocketed as a repressive tactic. The federal government's treatment of the Black Panther party shows that the fate of the IWW is not simply a historical curiosity, but can be repeated whenever a group seems to have found an effective way to organize its constituencies. The trial of the Chicago Eight was symbolic of an entire atmosphere of repression that characterized the last part of the decade. Judge Julius Hoffman was in some respects perfect for this trial; he symbolized in a Dickensesque way every aspect of the democratic state that stood for repression through violence. He was not subtle; he did not try to give his actions the appearance of neutrality. In that sense, he represented well what violent repression means as another decade came to a close.

The 1970s began with a horrendous act of repression, a murderous attack upon prisoners at the Attica State Facility in upstate New York. But the major lesson of the 1970s was this: not only dissidents need fear the repressive aspects of the state. Under the Nixon presidency, traditional acts of repression were undertaken against pillars of the establishment: the Democratic party, journalists, even prominent members of Congress. Nixon carried repression further than any other president, but the wrath against him was caused by the fact that his targets were more "respectable." Nonetheless, we owe Nixon our gratitude. By his actions, repression became an everyday word; and the seamier aspects of state power were revealed for all to see. Since his resignation, events have returned to normal. Congress is now considering a major revision of the federal criminal code, which will have a major impact on the practice of repression. Prominent liberals like Senator Kennedy may spend more time reforming repression than working to eliminate it.

Just as there has been a major act of violent repression associated with each decade of the twentieth century, an examination of one specific means of repression also indicates the constancy of the phenomenon. It is not possible, generally, to measure statistically something like repression, but there are some helpful indicators. In the discussion of military repression, the point was made that the use of the National Guard in political disputes should not be seen as a "neutral" device to keep order but as a way of protecting the interest of dominant groups in a conflict. Therefore, statistics on the number of times the National Guard has been called out for political actions would reflect the extensiveness of one aspect of military repression. Ignoring those times when the Guard is used for charity, disaster relief, and other nonpolitical purposes, the political side of National Guard work in this century can be divided into three categories: labor disturbances, when the Guard interceded in a strike for the purpose of ending it; racial disturbances, when the Guard was sent into an area to stop a civil disturbance or keep racial peace (included here are a few occaisons when governors threatened to use the Guard but did not; this serves a similar political purpose); and other political uses, such as keeping order at elections or intervening in student or youth rebellions. Table 2 summarizes the use of the Guard in such situations, and compares it with other gross acts of repression already discussed.

The most striking fact that emerges from this table is that the National Guard was *not* called out in only four years out of fifty-one. The use of the National Guard, in short, is clearly not sporadic. As measured by the frequency of its use, it seems that such forms of state violence have to be considered a rather permanent feature of American politics.

Table 2
Forms of Violent Repression, 1919–69

NATIONAL GUARD USE

YEAR	LABOR	RACE	OTHER	OTHER REPRESSION
1919	2	2		"Palmer raids"; naturalization hearings
1920	5			Criminal syndicalist laws
1921	9	2		Criminal syndicalist laws
1922	24			Criminal syndicalist laws
1923	8			Criminal syndicalist laws
1924	5	1	1	
1925	4	1		
1926	3	0		
1927	6	3		
1928	1	0		
1929	3	1	1	
1930	1	3	1	
1931	1			
1932	2			
1933	9			Labor repression
1934	13			Labor repression
1935	9			Labor repression
1936	11[a]			Labor repression
1937	3			
1938	2			
1939	2			
1940	0[b]			
1941		1		Japanese-American exclusion
1942	1	3		
1943	0			Conscientious objectors
1944	1	2		Conscientious objectors
1945	1	8		Conscientious objectors
1946		1	1	
1947		2		
1948	0			National security legislation
1949	1			National security legislation
1950	1		1	McCarthyism
1951	1			McCarthyism
1952	0			McCarthyism
1953	1			McCarthyism
1954		1		McCarthyism
1955	1			
1956		2		
1957		1		
1958				

Table 2 (*cont.*)

NATIONAL GUARD USE

YEAR	LABOR	RACE	OTHER	OTHER REPRESSION
1959	1	3		
1960		2	1	
1961		2		
1962		1		Infiltration of civil rights organizations
1963		6		
1964		2	3c	
1965		7	0	
1966		11	1c	Repression of antiwar groups
1967		25	3c	Repression of Black Panthers
1968		101	7c	Repression of Black Panthers
1969		50	7c	Chicago Eight trial

ᵃ Refers to fiscal year, 7/1/35–6/30/36.

ᵇ In 1940, it was found that a semifascist organization, the Christian Front, was intimately connected to National Guard units (*New York Times*, 15 January 1940, p. 1).

ᶜ Primarily campus disturbances.

Sources: All incidents on the National Guard were taken from one or more of the following: Philip Taft and Philip Ross, "American Labor Violence: Its Causes, Character, and Outcome," in *Violence in America*, ed. Hugh Davis Graham and Ted Robert Gurr (New York: Signet Books, 1969), pp. 27–376; *Annual Report of the Chief of the Militia Bureau* (Washington, D.C.: Government Printing Office, 1920–32); *Annual Report of the Chief of the National Guard Bureau* (Washington, D.C.: Government Printing Office, 1933–69); *The New York Times* (various issues, 1919–69).

To be sure, there were periods when Guard activities were more intense. After World War I, the Guard was used extensively to repress workers, and in the 1960s, its use skyrocketed for purposes of repressing black rebellions. But these peaks must be interpreted, not so much as abnormal, but as supernormal. They are an intensification of what already exists and not a new development.

By now, Americans must be used to repression. The number of years in this century in which violent repression has not taken place is so small that one conclusion is inevitable: *violent repression, not violence in general, is as American as cherry pie*. It is no longer possible to conclude that each individual act of repression is an aberration, a mistake, something that could have been avoided if only different people were in power. How many mistakes can there be? Instead of trying to explain away each act, when so many acts exist, a more valid sociological procedure would be to attempt to account for the ubiquity of the phenomenon. It has occurred often enough to have a cause.

One Reason Why

Liberalism and violent repression have an ambiguous attitude toward one another. It is not enough to say that the idea of liberty, as it is expressed in the liberal tradition that has shaped American society, is incompatible with repression. The political thinkers who most shaped the liberal tradition in England like Hobbes, Locke, and Mill (discussed in chapter 1), all upheld the necessity for repression. Men should be free to engage in pursuits, especially economic ones, according to Locke and Mill, but—and this is how the ambiguity enters—such freedom can take place only in an ordered society. Therefore, liberal society requires both liberty and order. The later is maintained, among other ways, through repression. The constitutional justification of state violence (see chapter 1) was used to suppress an insurrection in the first term of the first president (the so-called Whiskey Rebellion),[58] and it has been solidified and revised in the basic statutes of the United States.[59] The right of the government to suppress "insurrections" is not challenged. Nor has it been unused. Between 1794 and 1901, there were seventy-seven incidents of the use of troops for purposes of enforcing domestic laws. Included in that number is the use of troops in labor strikes, racial disturbances, Indian uprisings, Reconstruction politics, and what the government has called "Chinese outrages."[60] When repression was needed, repression was used.

The Constitution has been interpreted by the Supreme Court to meet changing conditions, but the need for repression is a condition that has never changed. Liberals who have served on the Supreme Court have gone through agonizing attempts to develop a theory that would permit both liberty and repression to take place. The most extreme statement of this attempt are the "balance" theories of the late Mr. Justice Frankfurter. In any given situation, one must balance the interests of the state in protecting itself against the interests of the individual in exercising his freedom. If the former is more important, then it must be given preference. Since the state is a collective entity and the individual only an individual, most balances would be struck in favor of the state, which is exactly what happened when the balance theory became the ruling doctrine of the Supreme Court. Very little state action seemed to upset Frankfurter, for example. He found the Smith Act, which essentially outlawed the Communist party, to be valid along with a host of other repressive actions taken by local, state, and federal governments.[61] The only action he seems to have found truly repellent was a nonpolitical one, the use of a stomach pump to force out of a man's body some evidence that he swallowed.[62]

With the exception of a few judges, and for a brief period during the Warren Court, the Supreme Court has accepted balance theories of one sort or another. The Burger Court has shown a positive predilection for weighing individual rights against the state in a manner favorable to the latter. The result has been to give repression the sanction of the Constitution; only when the repression is too oppressive is an attempt made to stop it.

Liberalism, then, is a series of agreements, not to stop repression, but to allow it to happen. Assume for the moment that liberalism's goals could actually be reached. The result would be something like the following: (1) access to the means of repression, open only to a few, would be egalitarian; anyone would have as likely a chance as anyone else to obtain those positions; (2) the practice of repression would always be done according to certain well-defined rules; it would never be arbitrary; and (3) any group would be as likely to be repressed as any other group, the distribution being without regard to class. That would be the case for an ideal liberal society, but none so far has existed. Instead, access to the means of repression is closed to most of the population, due process is rarely followed when it is against the interests of the state, and a ruling class exists that benefits from repression at the expense of those who challenge their rule. But phrased in this way, it is clear that much liberal criticism of repression covers only the failure to reach the ideal. What must be understood is that the ideal itself is a rationalization for repression, a more perfect system.

Why must liberalism be a theory of repression? Could it not be possible to emphasize the libertarian components of the doctrine to the exclusion of the repressive elements? The answer is no, as long as liberalism is the political ideology of capitalism. Liberalism and capitalism have continually been allied with one another.[63] Much of the origins of liberal theory can be traced to the need to justify the emergence of a new capitalist class. Since that time, liberalism has operated to solidify the power of the class. When capitalism changed from a system of laissez faire to one of state aid and monopoly, so liberalism changed from its Social Darwinist phase to its positive-state phase. The political goal of liberty has been continually sacrificed for the economic goal of order. (This subject will be expanded in chapter 9.)

Capitalism requires an ordered society that is predictable and explainable. It requires a stable political universe in which the foundations of the society are held to be justified by all. These needs presuppose a substantial amount of repression, particularly of the ideological variety. But beyond that, capitalism continually produces dissatisfaction. It sets goals (e.g., prosperity for all, freedom, and democracy) and then it fails to reach them (e.g., through depressions and poverty, concentrations of private power, ineffectual reforms, bureaucratic vested interests, racism, sexism). Any society that creates expectations it cannot meet is a society geared for heavy repression, and American capitalism is a perfect example.

Repression exists because needs are unmet and people have gotten together to find a way to meet them. Such an action threatens those who hold power and who are responsible for unmet needs. They try to accommodate the demand by meeting the needs. But when they cannot be met, when the system refuses to bend to satisfy those who do not benefit from it, the challenges become persistent, and repression is needed. This cycle has occurred time and time again in American history, and it explains why repression has occupied such a permanent place in the dynamics of American politics.

Need all repression be violent? The answer, theoretically, is no. If ideological repression (to be discussed in the next two chapters) works, then people will accept the given order and not challenge it. But ideological repression, in practice, has not worked. The existence of unmet needs has been continually realized by segments of the population. When a group no longer accepts being told that it should comply, force will be used to encourage compliance. *The existence of violent repression in America, then, is not something to be bemoaned. It is an indication that people are thinking for themselves, that they are trying to create a better society than the one which now exists.* The response of the state might be to smash the attempt, but the more important fact is that the attempt is being made.

chapter five ☆ private ideological repression

In the United States, when a group of people develop an organization that threatens existing power relationships, violent repression will likely result. But few people like violence, including those in power who are responsible for it. They view excessive violence as a sign of instability, an indication that all is not well. Those engaged in repression realize that ideology precedes organization; without a dissenting consciousness, no groups will be doing any organizing. From their point of view, it is clearly a major task of governance to prevent the formation of alternative ideologies among the population. Given the importance of this task in the perpetuation of the system, we would expect that a goodly proportion of time and energy would go into ideological manipulation, and our survey of repression in the democratic state would be incomplete without paying attention to this phenomenon.

Direct ideological repression involves both a direct attack on potential competing ideologies—such as a return to the free market from the Right or socialism from the Left—as well as a continued defense of the existing ideology of corporate liberalism. The problem that arises in trying to discuss how this works is not that the work is obscure, but that it is omnipresent. In his discussion of the capitalist state, for example, Ralph Miliband realized the need to talk about this phenomenon—he called it the process of legitimization—and his discussion covered political parties, religion, patriotism, the business ethic, the media, education, and the development of false consciousness.[1] Though the list is long, it is still incomplete, since Miliband left out one of the most important legitimizing institutions: the family. The point is that ideological repression takes place everywhere in liberal society.[2] It is difficult to think of a single activity (athletics, popular music) that does not in some way attempt to support existing ways of thinking and doing. Everyday life in capitalist society is suffused with ideology.[3]

Our problem here is one of limiting the phenomenon in order to make it discussable. This can be done by dealing only with those institutions and people whose conscious and direct purpose is ideological repression, ignoring, except to note their importance, other institutions that support the existing ideology as a by-product of their activity. Thus, important as it is, we leave a major discussion of the family (a minor one is included in the next chapter) to others, particularly since some good work has already been done in that area.[4] We will be concerned in this chapter with those private institutions that are most clearly ideological and most clearly repressive, and in the next chapter with both public institutions and intermediate associations.

Ideological Repression as Conscious Activity

Do those who are engaged in ideological repression know what they are doing? In the twentieth century, those who hold power in liberal democracies have come to realize the importance of ideology. Acceptance of received ways of thinking, it has been found, is not accidental but has to be worked at. This need has given rise to a group of experts at ideological indoctrination, and a review of the career of one of the most important of these people will tell us some things we need to know about ideological repression.

After World War I, many servicemen returning from Europe found themselves unable to obtain work. Indications were that if conditions remained the same, in the words of one of the participants in these events, "they might vent their frustrations on the government."[5] Here is an example of an area where an unregulated capitalism worked itself into one of its periodic contradictions, leading to a crisis. The obvious solution was economic: change the structure of employment. But being at that time relatively unregulated, the economy could not simply change itself. Time was needed, and unemployed ex-servicemen were not very charitable with their spare time, of which they had too much. Something was needed to gain time, and few knew exactly what to suggest. Into this picture stepped Colonel Arthur Woods, assistant secretary of war.

Woods was a crucial person in the ruling class at the time. Holder of an important position in the military, Woods—a Harvard and Groton graduate—had been police commissioner in New York and would become director of the Rockefeller Foundation. In addition, Woods' wife was a close relative of J. P. Morgan, which further established his political power. From this perspective, Woods realized that along with any actions he took, "public opinion" would have to be mobilized, both the opinion of the employers, who would have to be convinced to hire these people, and the ex-servicemen, who would have to maintain their loyalty. Woods hired Edward L. Bernays, a publicist, who attacked the problem with zeal, using all his contacts with newspapers and other forms of communication. The "public" was informed of the problem in various ways. The news media of the country were sent massive doses of material, including information on

> leaders who had re-employed servicemen, pledges made by groups to do so, an appeal to patriotic motivation, and the economic advantages in re-employing ex-servicemen.[6]

Announcements of major reemployment pledges were manipulated to give what Bernays called the "bandwagon effect," appearing as if spontaneous. Slogans were invented (naive compared to more modern ones: "A job inside is worth a hundred 'welcome home' signs in the window"). Optimistic interviews were conducted and given substantial publicity. The huge staff given Woods to deal with the problem thus worked in an atmosphere in which the public assumed that progress was being made, when none actually was. Not yet cynical about manufactured news, the public assumed that things happened the way the media told them, not knowing the planning that was going on. Encouraged by an apparent success, the public tempered its criticism of the situation, which gave Woods enough time. Soon, postwar prosperity provided enough jobs, and the crisis passed. But a new weapon had been given to the ruling class to win crucial, albeit temporary, support at times when it was needed.

Woods certainly recognized this. After the crisis passed, he wrote to Bernays:

> I want to let you know how highly I think of the work you have been doing for us. The results you got were quick, and grew in steadily increasing measure. *You have shown that you know how to reach all classes of the public and to get the facts before them.* . . . The success of the work we have been trying to do here depended more than on any single thing on *having the people of the country realize the situation and cheerfully take up themselves* the duty of looking after the welfare of men discharged from the service.[7]

It would not be long before Woods would again be calling on Bernays for his help.

When, in the last year of the Hoover Administration, unemployment reached new high peaks, the president called on Woods to head a committee that would work to relieve public anxiety about the problem. The situation was roughly the same: a crisis in the economy, which was leading people to question whether capitalism should retain their loyalty, was being met by a systematic attempt at consciousness manipulation. When consulted, Bernays' first recommendation was to change the name of the committee from the National Committee on Unemployment to the President's Emergency Committee for Employment (PECE). Here is linguistic manipulation in a nutshell: dropping the "un" to give the group a more positive direction; using the office of the president to put an authoritative ring to it, allowing people to transfer their allegiance to the office directly to the committee; indicating that there was an emergency to show importance; and, finally, providing initials to make the group more easily identifiable. Bernays later described the work of the committee:

> It was really a public relations committee. Its mission: to co-operate with the Federal Department and national organizations to further employment, to point out the value of expediting necessary public and semipublic construction work with industry and to indicate specific methods that might be used to share the work.[8]

PECE had a large budget, and it worked extensively to convince the public that solutions to unemployment were not only possible but just around the corner. Some of its ideas now seem ludicrous. At one point it advanced a share-the-work idea, "which put the onus of sacrifice on the shoulders of the wage earner instead of the employer."[9] Later, it advanced a campaign based on the idea that "prosperity is largely a state of mind." From one point of view PECE failed. The Great Depression came, and no amount of tinkering with ideas could prevent it. The committee bought time, but the economy now needed more than that. But, in another sense, PECE succeeded admirably. In a crisis in which the future of capitalism looked in doubt, many retained their allegiance to the system. Surely part of this was due to the efforts of the rulers of the system to convince people that the crisis was not systematic and could be solved by mutual aid.

These examples suggest that the role played by such men as Bernays is an important one in preserving the democratic state. If these men can prevent people from seeing the defects of the system, there will be no need for violent repression. The Bernays of this world have come to occupy a cruicial position in modern liberal societies. Bernays has written extensively about what he does, apparently because he believes in promoting himself as much as he promotes others. Also, so proud is he of his work—he insists that he is really the first to make a profession, a noble calling, out of publicity, and he constantly searches for a term that would describe to others what he does to his own satisfaction—that he writes in a pleasingly direct manner. He has justified his work to himself, obviously defensive about his new profession; that self-justification is quite revealing.

The essence of what is called "public relations" is that it serves the rulers of the democratic state—those who benefit from repression most—and nobody else. Bernays occasionally denies this by taking a pluralist point of view:

> Today the privilege of attempting to sway public opinion is
> everyone's. It is one of the manifestations of democracy that anyone
> may try to convince others and to assume leadership on behalf
> of his own thesis.[10]

Here is a statement of democratic theory, completely divorced from the realities of who actually holds power in the society. It is Adam Smith liberalism, in twentieth-century form. There is even the notion of an invisible hand:

> Propaganda will never die out. Intelligent men must realize that
> propaganda is the modern instrument by which they can fight for
> productive ends and help bring order out of chaos.[11]

Yet, Bernays cannot really believe in pluralism. Surely he must realize: (1) that although he has done work for the NAACP, he never did any work for people from the lower classes, and (2) that none of his techniques were ever directed *against* those who hold power. Thus, when he aspires to political theory, a more honest self-evaluation evolves. Who, after all, are these "intelligent men" who will use propaganda?

When realistic, Bernays contradicts the ideas that all have equal access to the new instrument: "But clearly it is the intelligent minorities which need to make use of propaganda continuously and systematically. In the active proselytizing minorities *in whom selfish interest and public interest* coincide lie the progress and development of America. Only through active energy of the intelligent few can the public become aware of and act upon its new ideas."[12] The "intelligent few" are obviously businessmen. Bernays knows who has power in the democratic state and he is appealing to them directly: "And it is my conviction that as big business becomes bigger the need for expert manipulation of its innumerable contracts with the public will become greater."[13] No wonder that Bernays found himself "excited"[14] when the American Tobacco Company asked for his services, even though he himself was the victim of an elaborate espionage plot designed to keep him away from American Tobacco's competitors. The section of his autobiography dealing with his move from Broadway and the arts to work with big corporations is called "fulfillment."[15]

Not only was Bernays aware that business was the place to go, he also realized that the days of entrepreneurial and personalized business were over. His mission was to make acceptable to the public a new conception of business and businessmen; and, for doing that, he has to be considered one of the more important individuals of the twentieth century. Times were changing; the public had old prejudices toward business. "Occasionally the manipulation of the public mind entails the removal of a prejudice. Prejudices are often the application of old taboos to new conditions. They are illogical, emotional, and hampering to progress."[16] Progress being an important product, it was Bernay's job to manipulate public opinion to support the new type of industrial capitalism that emerged after the Great Depression. There might be public resistance to such things as industrial concentration, mass production, similar goods, similar prices, modern advertising, private enterprise itself. These resistances (prejudices) could, however, be overcome

> by trying to control every approach to the public mind in such a
> manner that the public receives the desired impression,
> often without being conscious of it.[17]

To those who charged that work such as Bernays' was incompatible with democracy, he had a ready reply. Bernays, who was influenced by antidemocratic writers such as LeBon and others who stressed irrationality (e.g., his mother's brother, Sigmund Freud), answered that he was saving democracy, not destroying it, by keeping it pure from the hands of common people:

> . . . a public that learns more and more how to express itself will
> learn more and more how to overthrow tyranny of every sort. So that
> every man who teaches the public how to ask for what it wants

at the same time teaches the public how to safeguard itself against its own possible tyrannous aggressiveness.[18]

If allowed to get out of hand, the public might respond antidemocratically, destroying the democratic state (and thereby capitalism). This is why consent has to be *engineered*.[19] Some must channel the public mind so that it can be controlled: "No matter how sophisticated, how cynical the public may become about publicity methods, it must respond to the basic appeals, because it will always need food, crave amusement, long for beauty, respond to leadership."[20]

From Bernays a number of things about ideological repression become clear. One is that it is a short step from the assumptions of elitist democracy to direct manipulation. The science or art of public relations is inherently elitist, and it shares the anticommon-man bias of most academic literature on democracy.[21] In addition, practitioners of this form of repression cannot hide the beneficiaries of their work, no matter what their formal commitment to pluralism. It seems that they must convince themselves of their neutrality while being directly partisan (in the class struggle, not the party struggle). There is a cycle here: the public appears "ignorant" because its teachers teach them ignorance; then these teachers marvel about how ignorant their students are, leading to the conclusion that only more ignorance should be their lot. Finally, as the democratic state undergoes repeated crises, we can expect that a greater percentage of its attention will be directed to Bernays-type functions. What was once a luxury to those companies that could afford a unique service has now become an integral aspect of the work of all those who wish to retain privileged positions. Ideological repression (sometimes called "propaganda") has become institutionalized.

One result of this process of institutionalization is that it is difficult to isolate individuals who do the work at the moment. It is more a group phenomenon now. Yet occasionally one person will rise to the top of the field and, through his many activities, establish himself as a leader. If one had to pick the individual who most clearly followed the paths established by Bernays, for example, it would probably be William Benton.[22] Benton founded the advertising agency of Benton and Bowles (with Chester Bowles, later ambassador to India), a firm that pioneered in the development of new techniques for selling goods. Not content with private work, Benton expanded his ideological role to include government service. He was an assistant secretary of state (responsible for information), a key position for exporting repression (see chapter 7). In addition, he was a U.S. senator from Connecticut, where he fought bitterly the blatantly repressive techniques of Joseph McCarthy, leading to his own defeat. Returning to private life, Benton, still dissatisfied with advertising, engaged in other forms of ideological repression. He presided over Muzak Corporation, a business that provides subliminal background music to soothe the feelings of people who are in anxious surroundings, and, as president of Encyclopaedia Britannica, he was responsible for passing along the wisdom of one generation to another. In 1972 he emerged again, this time to push for a somewhat conservative platform at the Democratic Convention of that year. Less blunt than Bernays, and much more liberal, Benton represents the sophistication of ideological repression as it matures and becomes more institutionalized.

There is one other difference between the Bernays period and our own. Whereas Bernays worked on isolated problems, e.g., unemployment, contemporary repressive techniques focus more on indirect approaches, maintaining certain values, rather than indoctrinating certain attitudes. *The goal of ideological repression now is to win support for the capitalist system, not for any one of its policies.*

What has been the effect of men such as Bernays and Benton? There is no easy way to answer that question, since attitudes and values have a way of changing rapidly. But it is also true that, among the working class, ideological repression has had a significant effect. *Those who do not benefit from repression, who are in fact harmed by it, but who nonetheless believe that their own repression is in their own best interest and who therefore give full support to those who are repressing them, express the importance of ideological repression.* The ultimate goal of ideological repression is to help people support their own repressors.

The success of this work can be seen in the experience of one person living in America. Joe Kelly, a young construction worker from Staten Island, New York, was recently written about in a national newspaper.[23] His income is fairly high for a construction worker, but he is by no means rich. His working-class background prevented him from developing an interest in school, and though he went to college for a short time on an athletic scholarship, he never graduated and took his present job because it was the best he could aspire to. He owns a home and has a family and a variety of consumer goods. He thinks of himself as well off. Yet he is not, whether he knows it or not. His income, though at first impressive, is hardly enough for a family of five to live on in New York City. Furthermore, Joe Kelly is ignorant. He is not stupid, he is simply unaware of a whole world that exists outside his narrowly defined one. In short, there is no reason, theoretically, why he should be a passionate defender of the existing order. In a more rational world, he could live without the tyranny of credit systems, private medical services that would wipe out his income with one sickness, unsure working conditions, the risk of accidental death, an unhappy wife who lives for little except to be oppressed by him, and a political system in which he is continually forced to compete with his fellow workers. He could also broaden his horizons and learn something about the rest of the world.

Yet Kelly loves his capitalist system. The president's authority to him is unchallenged, just like the pope's. "He's in charge." Because he is, his policies must be supported, regardless of what they do to other countries and to the homeland. The symbols of loyalty attract his attention: "I think of all the people that died for that flag. And somebody's gonna spit on it, it's like spitting on their graves. So they better not spit on it in front of me." Metaphorically speaking, someone did. Joe Kelly carried a flag in a patriotic march of construction workers. He also threw some punches at peace demonstrators. It is clear where his sympathies lie. "No one's more Establishment than I am." In short, Joe Kelly is devoted to those who keep him, his wife, and his family oppressed, and he is not even aware of it.

Ideological repression can do things like that. Joe Kelly didn't develop his political ideas in a vacuum. He has the ideas he has because he learned them. And he learned them in and from a series of institutions that exist for the purpose of teaching them to him. He learned his lessons well; others have had a harder time and in fact have tried to throw out the teachers. But the work goes on, and the everyday attitudes and values of Joe Kelly indicate how crucial ideological repression is in the democratic state.

The Values of Liberal Society

From the discussion to this point, it is possible to see two kinds of ideological repression that are important. One has already been mentioned: the attack on alternative ideologies and the defense of existing ones. Since this is directly political, we call it *direct* ideological manipulation. But it is also true that various ideologies have associated with them certain values; if people uphold these values, belief in the ideology will almost automatically follow. Those who wish to maintain the hegemony of liberal society, therefore, can do so not only by continually informing the population that liberalism is good, but also by trying to inculcate certain attitudes whose effect will be the perpetuation of liberal society. This kind of *indirect* repression is as crucial as the other form, but since it is often not recognized as repression, a few words are needed.

What are the values that maintain liberal society? There are many, but the most important would seem to be these: individualism, competitiveness, fatalism, distrust, parochialism, dislike of theory, and a respect for constituted authority, sometimes called authoritarianism.

It may seem peculiar to begin with *individualism*. Did not an entire generation of sociologists ten to twenty years ago point out the importance of conformity to the average American? This was seen, say, in the work of David Riesman, as a change in the national character, from one that was inner-directed to one directed by others.[24] In what another group of sociologists called "mass society," the problem is not individualism, but the lack of it.[25] In some books, individualism is alleged to have declined to such a degree that we are all in danger of falling victim to totalitarianism. Yet, in spite of all these books testifying to the importance of social conformity, the rhetoric of American life continued to be individualistic. We are still urged "to do our own thing"—the latest popular expression of this value. In spite of the apparent contradiction, an explanation can be advanced.

The most plausible explanation is that those who were observing conformity were wrong. The indicators of conformity actually indicate something else. When the sociologist shows that people own similar homes, drive similar cars, and work in similar places, he is not showing conformity but the effects of monopoly capitalism. People drive similar cars because there are no other cars to drive. The more important characteristic—often overlooked in those studies of suburbia—is that, even though the houses are built alike, each family chooses to live by itself. Individualized living patterns are reflective of a basic anticommunal attitude shared by citizens of the democratic state. People are expected to do things by themselves, even if, because of the nature of the economy, what they do is exactly what everyone else is doing. Thus, what those who found conformity did wrong was to look only at the results of public behavior. More important is the process, and the process indicates a fractured and highly atomistic picture of the world. There is a sacredness attached to the unit, be it the family or the individual. When the coffee klatch, so important to William Whyte's study of the organization man,[26] was over, what Whyte forgot to mention was that each housewife retreated to a house where her feelings of loneliness and alienation from a nonexistent community were so great that she often contemplated suicide. "Going it alone" is still what Americans do, both in rhetoric and in practice.

The importance of individualism is that it works to prevent collective action for social change. People who cannot work toward the same end are ineffective. Their impotence reinforces the status quo. Thus, individualism is not only important as a value in itself that prevents a true consciousness from emerging, but it is also of vital tactical importance. To promote individualism is to fracture and divide those who, while trying to change the society, are part of it nonetheless.

Closely related to individualism is *competitiveness*. This does not mean the "competitive spirit," which has been seen as vital to the formation of capitalism. Modern competitiveness is a by-product of individualism. It is a less exalted, more destructive form than the older type. People compete, are taught to compete, over everything: their children, their possessions, their jobs. More than economic competition, this value is best expressed simply as the opposite of cooperation. So long as people are competing in this way, they will be unable to transcend their individualism in order to work constructively. At one time, the competitive spirit may have been revolutionary in that it led to a constantly evolving new economic order. Present competitiveness is counterrevolutionary, designed to keep the existing order in place by reinforcing attitudes and behavior that will accomplish that end.

Fatalism is another important political value that is integral to the received consciousness of most citizens of the democratic state. Once again, it is important to specify the things that people are expected to be fatalistic over. For example, Americans are often held to be optimistic, continually assuring one another that things will work out in the long run.[27] This may well be true, but it does not contradict the point about fatalism; one can be optimistically fatalistic. Fatalism instead refers to the belief that things in any significant way cannot really change. "That's human nature" or "That's the way the cookie crumbles" or "You can't fight city hall"—these are expressions of fatalism. What they imply is that no revolution will ever really change things. The Chinese gentry before the revolution had a cryptic expression that summarizes the basic notion of fatalism. When confronted by demands that the feudal system of agriculture be changed, they philosophically replied, "Can the sun rise in the West?"[28]

It is often said of Americans that they believe anything is possible. If it would make huge profits for the sun to rise in the West, then someone would figure out how to do it. It is important to realize that such a nonfatalistic attitude was necessary to the development of capitalism, and it was only to be held by those capitalists who were controlling the system. In a mature capitalist economy, it is more important that those values that kept the industrial proletariat working—particularly fatalism—be made a part of nearly everyone's consciousness. Only then will the order be safe.

By *distrust* is meant a certain cynicism toward everyone outside one's immediate world. Americans distrust everybody; anybody one comes into contact with is out for himself. Strangers are not to be talked to, because if friends are not trusted, how could strangers be? Even the leaders of the system are not to be trusted. In many cases, reformers who uncover the existence of graft contribute to feelings of satisfaction on the part of the electorate. "I told you so—all politicians are crooks" is a favorite expression of those to whom the existence of graft has just been revealed. Believing that all politicians are out for themselves thus confirms one's fatalism; it is living proof that a more perfect human will never be created. One antirevolutionary attitude reinforces another.

The leaders of the democratic state can continue to lead without trust. In fact, when they are distrusted, their power is enhanced because it removes them somewhat from everyday affairs. Those who are hurt by pervasive distrust are the potential leaders of a new society. They are told that reformers are only out for themselves; revolutionaries are working only to fulfill internal needs; people engaged in collective action have ulterior motives. In short, without trust, significant change is impossible. But without trust, a continuation of the existing system is quite possible. This is why distrust is such an important value for people to hold.

It is also important that people believe that their world is the only one that is really good. Commenting on high taxes, Joe Kelly said: "If this is what it takes to run this country, I don't mind paying them. You couldn't live anyplace else like you do here."[29] Since he has never lived anyplace else, this is a rather remarkable statement. It indicates that *parochialism* is something more than patriotism. Patriotism is simply a love of one's country; contact with other countries can even improve and sharpen one's patriotism. But parochialism is purposive ignorance, and it is the ignorance that the democratic state needs. For contact with other countries is bound to deflate parochialism and thereby make people more aware of the nature of their own world. Since the awareness engendered could lead to a questioning of all established institutions, the importance of parochialism to the rulers of the democratic state is enhanced. Often unconsciously—but many times consciously—they encourage expressions of parochialism, for they understand how it works to their advantage.

Another important characteristic of the citizens of the United States (though not of other capitalist societies such as France and Germany) is that they should not be able to relate isolated events one to the other in a way that makes sense out of them. This can be called *atheoreticalism*, a confusing term simply meant to imply a distrust of theory. Thus, the anti-intellectualism of Americans, a characteristic often remarked upon,[30] is only indicative of a wider attitude toward systematic and contextual explanation in general. The democratic state has a vested interest in preventing the emergence of patterns of thought in which two things can be related to a common third thing that caused them. One is not expected to see the connection between the high price of milk in the stores and the needs of a defense-oriented economy. The one is not caused by the other. Insofar as causation exists at all, the attributed cause is held to be something of simple origin. "Outside agitators" cause campus unrest, not alienation from the system. The importance of no causality, or a false and simple one, is obvious. It prevents people from making the kinds of connections that would lead them to an understanding of their world. Like parochialism, the distrust of theory is a form of ignorance that the democratic state values highly.

The final value to be discussed is *respect for authority*. This may be difficult to reconcile with pervasive distrust, but most people seem capable of doing it. Those in positions of authority may be there for their own purposes, but their position entitles them to respect nonetheless. For it is not the individual per se who is respected, but the position of authority he holds. Much has been written about the need for authority among individuals, including the famous "authoritarian personality" studies and their critics.[31] Whatever methodological disputes these studies have led to, they at least make it clear that respect for and appreciation of authority are important characteristics of the minds of many Americans. What they do not give is an explanation. From this discussion, authority is related to the phenomenon of ignorance. Without an explanation, a theory of why things are as they are—yet with a feeling that some explanation is necessary—a belief in authority becomes a surrogate for the lack of a theory Again, there is a reinforcement of basic attitudes. Respect for the office of the president is called for most at those times when the legitimacy of the presidency is most in doubt. It has to be that way, for if the call is not needed, the respect not given, then a valid explanation for the cause of the disrespect may soon be forthcoming. Few, in other words, are inherently authoritarian. Belief in authority is a learned response, and those who run the system are the teachers.

A population that possesses the values just discussed is a repressed population, one against which violence would never need to be used. If these ideas were held by all, the primacy of liberal society would never be in doubt. Yet they are not; though many in power would like to see these values held by all, the transmission of them to the population has not been totally successful. Examining some of the institutions responsible for transmitting the values of liberal society, then, is the obvious next step in this investigation. This can be done by looking at private ideological repression first, reserving a separate chapter for the role of the state.

Corporate Ideological Repression

The institutions engaged in ideological repression range from those that are close to the individual to those that are remote. Some of them practice repression as a major goal, others as a by-product. Some are primarily involved in indirect repression, others in the direct form. In short, many things could be talked about here. Dealing in general terms with the most important, it is possible to approach the subject in a manner similar to the way power was discussed in chapter 3. There will be both economic and governmental institutions working in this area, and these institutions will exist in a power hierarchy themselves. The results of such a conceptualization are represented in figure 1.

Enormous amounts of paper have been devoted to each of these institutions, and in what follows no attempt is made to summarize that literature. Only the following themes are emphasized: Does the institution repress directly or indirectly? Is it public or private? Who controls the repression; who are the decision makers? How effective is it? It is necessary to restrict the scope of the discussion, for much that has been written about these institutions, while notable, is of little interest here. The various cultural critiques of the media, for example, which show how much poor taste is to be observed, are only relevant if the poor taste can be shown to play a role in repression.

The first group of ideological repressors are those who repress privately (outside the government), similar to the role played by Edward Bernays. Included in this category would be foundations, advertising agencies, public relations firms, the media, and "opinion makers." Since the role of foundations will be discussed in chapter 7, we can begin on Madison Avenue.

Advertising involves the selling of goods. In the words of Rosser Reeves, board chairman of Ted Bates and Co. and the man most often responsible for television's more offensive commercials: "Advertising is the art of getting a unique selling proposition into the heads of the most people at the lowest possible cost."[32] Selling goods is important and it does lead to excess. Based on the writings of Reeves, Jules Henry has written a trenchant commentary on modern advertising, stressing the "pecuniary motivation" and the ideology that has grown up around it.[33] Yet both Reeves and to some extent Henry fail to examine the other aspects of advertising besides consumerism. Without meaning to play off one ad man against another, Pierre Martineau is more willing than Reeves to examine the social functions of advertising:

> . . . its primary function is that it integrates the individual into our
> kind of society. Its secondary function is to sell goods. But *its*
> *primary function is to relate people to our American system,* helping
> them to feel that they are participating in the best the society has
> to offer, causing them to aspire and to work with willingness and high
> productivity. Just as the training of its formative years socializes
> the child, so advertising continuously socializes the adult.[34]

In other words, a critique of advertising must go beyond showing what type of people advertising men are trying to mold in order to show why

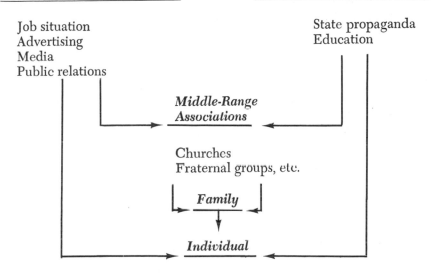

Private Ideological Repression   *Public Ideological Repression*

Figure 1

Institutions of Ideological Repression

they are doing it. Martineau provides a good reason: advertising produces in people those values necessary to sustain the capitalist system and the resulting modern democratic state.

One way modern advertising does this is by reinforcing traditional role conceptions, making people think that the role society has defined for them is the only one they can possibly have. Nowhere is this seen more than in sex roles. Most advertising is directed toward women. David Ogilvy's *Confessions,* for example, used the word "he" when he talks about how to start a business and the word "she" when describing the watchers of television ads.[35] The inference is obvious: under modern advertising, the female sex role is translated into consumer. In Ogilvy's characteristically flip way: "The consumer isn't a moron; she is your wife."[36] This constant equation of women with consumer is indicative of a range of role reinforcements stressed by advertisers. Woman-as-consumer plays a role supportive of the existing system. A change in role would harm the system; therefore, advertising must constantly reinforce the role. Someone from outside the planet whose picture of women was formed only by seeing advertisements would no doubt conclude that there were two kinds of humans: people and women, the latter existing to serve the former.

In the content of its messages, advertising upholds all the values discussed before, those that tend to maintain the present state of affairs. Consider, for example, distrust. One could argue that one of the consequences of the many comparative demonstrations between a product and Brand X that repeatedly occur on television is to instill distrust of *all* evaluative attempts. Thus, the advertising men know that the tests are dishonest (many cases exist where the product identified by the advertiser is actually a chemical created for purposes of passing the "test"),[37] and the public knows it too.[38] Consumers respond to who has made the test the most outrageous, admiring the gimmickry, thinking, "Wow, they sure are trying to put something over on people." There is a mutual self-serving interchange going on, and the only people not part of it are those who believe that real differences exist between things, including political and economic systems. Such advertising reinforces the present arrangement by suggesting that all human arrangements are gimmicks, so why change what we have now? In a similar way, advertising encourages the other repressive values as summarized in the following outline:

Table 3
Examples of Value Reinforcement
in Television Advertising

VALUE	SITUATIONS	SLOGAN
Individualism	Marlboro man alone on horse	"Camel Filters—they're not for everyone" "There's nobody else exactly like you" (Equitable) "I'd rather fight than switch" (Tarryton)
Competitiveness	Mother-daughter comparisons (over hands, hair, weight)	"Look, ma, no cavities" (Crest) "Be the first on your block . . ." (various)
Fatalism	Cumulative effect of all commercials Dishonesty of "tests"	"No money down—years to pay" (various) "What will happen to your wife if you are suddenly taken out of the picture?" (life insurance)

Table 3 (cont.)

VALUE	SITUATIONS	SLOGAN
Distrust	Any commercial about smells (body, hair, underarms) or dandruff	"Coke—it's the real thing" (as opposed to others) "Even your best friend won't tell you" (mouthwash) "If he kissed you once, will he kiss you again?" (Certs)
Parochialism	Settings of all ads (small town or suburb; no real diversity, even with black and oriental actors) Romanticization of other countries and cultures (West Indies, especially)	"See America first"
Atheoreticalism	Purposive mystification (peas do not grow; they are from the land of the Jolly Green Giant)	"Take a puff—it's spring-time (false causality) "What do you want—good grammar or good taste?" (false causality)
Authoritarianism	All product endorsements Commercials with doctors or other experts	"You don't just rent a car—you rent a company" (Hertz) "Three out of four doctors recommend" (various)

Advertising is done through media, so we would expect the means of mass communication to be heavily involved in ideological repression. This is especially true because the media, like the advertising agencies, are allowed to exist in private hands. Communications is an industry, and it bears the characteristics that affect all American industry, including the fact that it operates to benefit the few rather than everyone. The major television networks are monopolistic. ABC owns almost four hundred movie theaters in thirty-four states, as well as numerous television and radio stations.[39] Many cities resemble Philadelphia, where newspapers and television stations and magazines are owned by the same company.[40] Companies as large as General Tire, AVCO, Westinghouse, and Kerr

McGee own television stations.[41] Television regulation, like other forms, was created in the interest of television network owners and has served their interest ever since.[42]

Because the media are part of the capitalist system, and because a change in that system would significantly alter the power of a small group of men, it is not surprising that the media engage much of their time in preserving the existing state of affairs. They do this by being conscious propagandists for the system, by reinforcing indirect consciousness manipulation, and by *not* serving as an informative vehicle. This last aspect of the problem was observed in 1948 by two social scientists who soon thereafter lost their critical perspective on the problem:

> To the extent that the media of mass communications have had an influence upon their audience, it has stemmed not only from what is said, but more significantly from what is not said. For these media not only continue to affirm the *status quo* but, in the same measure, they fail to raise essential questions about the structure of the society. Hence, by leading toward conformism and by providing little basis for a critical appraisal of society, the commercially sponsored mass media indirectly but effectively restrain the cogent development of a genuine critical outlook.[43]

In their more positive aspects, the media contribute to false consciousness mostly by reinforcing values, rather than by direct activity in supporting existing institutions. This is especially the case with specific groups in the society, women and children. The most comprehensive study of broadcasting content—an analysis of themes of radio "soap operas" done in 1942—reveals the importance of all the values discussed above. It is worthwhile to interpret these conclusions in terms of those values:

> The egotistic and individualistic concept of a world in which the community appears mainly as a threat from outside is supported. . . .
>
> Only private problems exist.
>
> Dissatisfaction with her own achievements and with the state of affairs around her, which could serve as a spur towards striving for improvement, is drained off by substitute gratification.
> There is little effort to make the listener aware of her prejudices and resentments; rather, she is carefully flattered. Men are shown to be inferior to women, the working class is ignored, learning is deprecated.[44]

The rise of mass television does not seem to have changed this. If anything, visual effects have probably reinforced all these characteristics that previously had been communicated with less closure. There is no reason why those who control the media had to pick these things; in another society, different values may be stressed. But the content of media programming in this society is purposive; there is repression in the soap opera.

As with women, so with children. The young, in fact, are more important. They are the ones who, if not properly manipulated, may (as many in past years have done) take away their loyalty. So a tremendous amount of energy goes into the task of repressing the consciousness of youth. It has been estimated that the average child in America will watch 4,000 hours of television before he or she begins elementary school.[45] That is a fantastic potential given to the manipulators, and they have been quick to use every minute of it. The most thorough studies of the relationship between television and children have been done in England, but their results are clearly generalizable to the United States. By intensive questioning of children, and by content analysis of television programming, Himmelweit and her associates found that:

> Television influences the way children think about jobs, job values, success and social surroundings. It stresses the prestige of upper-middle-class occupations: the professions and big business. It makes essentially middle-class value judgments about jobs and success in life.[46]

In addition, television makes children materialistic and keeps them in adolescence longer. The only effect they discovered contrary to repressive values was that television slightly enhanced respect for other cultures. When this study notes that "Television may be used too easily as a pacifier for young children,"[47] it unwittingly points out the role that television plays in guaranteeing that today's children will not have to be repressed through violence tomorrow.

The media also play a role in direct ideological repression, a role that becomes more apparent when we turn to the ways in which the media present reports of daily events, often called news. Again, the process by which news is disseminated to the public is left to corporations expected to make a profit. This suggests that the business aspect of news gathering and news presentation will affect the result. When a television viewer complained to CBS News about its not covering important events as they happen, instead showing "I Love Lucy," the president of CBS pointed out "the necessity to maintain a sound and viable economy within the company. The cost of maintaining television and news organizations is enormous, and the major part of it must be borne by income from entertainment programming."[48] In a business-dominated economy, business considerations must come first.

But the fact that news media leave things out is not as important as the ways they shape what is put in. The existence of a corporate order surrounding news has many more implications that bear direct ideological repression. Two of these implications are not of direct concern. One is the fear that the press will be partisan, that during the years of the Republican ascendancy it supported Republicans, and now supports Democrats. Given minimal differences between the parties, this is not a major issue. The other idea is that the media find it hard to be "objective" in their covering of news. It is of no concern here whether the news is presented subjectively or objectively. Even assuming the presentations to be objective, what has to be kept in mind is that *the very definition of objectivity is what gives the media their bias.* For when the media try to be the most "objective," they most often serve those in power in this society. The managing editor of the *New York Times* once said: ". . . a reporter knows pretty well when he is being objective, and so does his editor. The *important thing is that they should appreciate the need for objectivity,* and its relationship to the role they play in our democracy."[49] In other words, objectivity serves certain functions. Objectivity is the best way to ensure ideological repression. Replying to those who argued that too much attention had been given to the Soviet Union in American newspapers, the UPI's Moscow correspondent replied:

> It seems to me that Western journalism has not taken full advantage of all the available opportunities to serve the reader a complete, balanced and accurate report of the Soviet Union, *so essential to the moulding of public opinion in a democratic society.*[50]

The media are objective only about events that take place within a certain ideological framework. They need not choose between two different ways to reach a goal; all that matters is their consensus on the goal. Thus, the media uphold the consensus: capitalism, democracy, and an anti-Communist foreign policy. It can be no other way. In order for the press to be allowed to exist without itself being repressed, and in order for it to make a profit in the economy, any organ of the established news media must conform to the basic ideas, regardless of more minor differences regarding how those ideas could be realized. Newsmen differed on whether to send reporters to China when they were invited in 1956. Bowing to the wishes of the Eisenhower Administration, no reporters went. Clifton Daniel of the *New York Times* now regrets that decision. Why? Not because news on China, its social system upholding values outside the existing one, might educate Americans to a new consciousness, but because ". . . any effort by journalism to . . . see that the American people are informed about China would be a contribution to our national security."[51]

The "news" then, is interpreted within an ideological framework.

This is revealed in a manual prepared by CBS News for those who would like to enter the business. "Television often must wait for the news to happen before it can film it."[52] *Often?* This is a remarkable sentence because it indicates that some news is filmed before it happens. Yet, this is probably accurate, since before an event occurs, the ideological framework specifies how it will be treated when it does occur. One example should be sufficient. Suppose that our visitor from another planet saw some foreign dignitaries being given enthusiastic receptions by many people. He might conclude that the men were popular. Here is where the anti-Communist bias enters. CBS's description about how it treated an actual situation involving a foreign reception is highly revealing:

> The East German Communist party has made a statement which
> creates a furor of anti-communist reaction in West Germany. These
> facts are duly reported by the newscaster. He then observes
> that on this day of furor, the leaders of Russia's Communist Party are
> creating a different kind of furor far from home, in India. Then
> the film of Bulganin and Khrushchev in India shows the two through a
> succession of parades and festivities, Indians in vast bodies of
> humanity crowding around the two Russians, showering them with
> flowers. The film testifies that in India these two are creating
> considerable furor. No one says it, but the thought is conveyed
> instantly to the viewer's mind that the ruthless energy of world
> communism seeks its outlets in many ways; with voluminous
> propaganda from East Germany, with elaborate politeness in the Far
> East.[53]

It is interesting that as we move outside the consensus, the media admit exactly how they manipulate consciousness, sure that everyone who reads what they say will be inside the consensus and will, therefore, agree with their treatment of the news. In any case, this passage reveals—not an idiosyncratic policy that can be corrected from within—but an inherent bias that will always exist so long as news gathering takes place within the liberal, democratic state. The opportunities to manipulate, while giving the appearance of objectively presenting the news, are too great to be passed up.

The institutions discussed so far—media, news, advertising—are all industries that occupy a goodly portion of their time in the business of ideological repression. They spend much of their time winning support for a certain order directly and indirectly, much of it directed to women and children. But, it is also important to mention that all private industry performs a similar function, whatever it does. In their actual work experience, people in the democratic state are taught the values that will keep them loyal. Men, working women (a very large group), people who do not watch television, and the uninformed not concerned with news—

these people are also reached, directly on their jobs. The nature of work in capitalist society has an important repressive aspect.

At one time corporations were heavily engaged in the business of direct ideological repression. Those who ran the company dispensed heavy doses of propaganda in the general direction of those who worked for it, ranging from "requests" (that had to be supported) to support tariffs, personalities, parties, and programs. For example, Thomas Watson, the man who founded and directed the International Business Machines Corporation, constantly made known his thoughts to his employees, through his heavily financed company organ, *Business Machines*, and through his periodic walking tours through headquarters.[54] Employees were told (both by word and by deed) what Watson thought of God, cleanliness, thrift, and other verities. Men (IBM did not hire women, not even as secretaries) who did not conform lost their jobs. When Franklin Roosevelt passed the National Recovery Administration—which as we saw in chapter 2 was a boon to the corporations even though it recognized labor unions—Watson came to the rescue when NRA was under attack. "We have no right to think or talk of the NRA failing," he cried. "It is not going to fail." Watson then mobilized the propaganda apparatus of his company. In the words of his biographer:

> He ordered company employees to take part in NRA parades, and
> the IBM press became a thunderous propaganda organ in support of
> business cooperation with the agency FDR and the Congress
> had set up to cure the great depression. Issues of *Business Machines*
> were devoted to it.[55]

The company engaged in a wide range of activities to win support for the measure. Here is another case when, in a period of crisis, the institutions that manipulate consciousness came to the support of the capitalist system in crucial ways.

But at the same time, the nature of work in capitalist society was producing supportive values (indirect repression) in people, whatever the direct activities of the corporations. The consequences of work have been studied and thought about for years. In his early writings, Marx pointed to a number of values that the worker was taught on the job.[56] Since these values were antihumanistic and irrational, Marx claimed that the worker was *alienated*. To Marx, alienation was both psychological and economic, a synonym for exploitation. Are those same alienating values still taught on the job, or has capitalism become more humane? To some like Hannah Arendt, technological society, not capitalism specifically, produces worker "discontents," in many ways even worse than in the nineteenth century.[57] These writers agree with Marx that something is amiss. In more recent years, however, an attempt has been made to show that the consequences of work have changed. Robert Blauner has questioned whether "alienation" can be equally applied to all work; instead he sees it as varying between different kinds of jobs.[58] Melvin Seeman disputes both Marx and the neoconservative critique of industrial society by also questioning the uniformity of alienation.[59] Developing an interview schedule based on powerlessness, intergroup hostility, lack of political awareness, status-mindedness, normlessness, and orientation to expertise (characteristics that match almost word for word the values of the democratic state discussed above), Seeman questions whether the "alienated worker" exists, and if he does, whether his existence has any severe consequences. The critics, however, misinterpret the critique. Both Marx and Arendt were dealing with a concept of alienation that does not go away because the person does not recognize it. By basing their research on questionnaires, Blauner and Seeman change the concept and thereby take away its meaning. Their conclusions do not signify much about whether the nature of work has changed.

It would be impossible to summarize the current literature on work and its consequences. It is enough to hypothesize strongly that the values discussed above are still taught on the job, whether the job is in a factory or an office. In their study of "Yankee City," Warner and his associates examined the factory system. They found that increasing technological sophistication has increased the alienating character of work, in this case, making shoes.[60] What was before a craft had become routinized. One consequence was increased authoritarianism; the foreman and management could control the worker's behavior more easily. In addition, the fact that less skill on the worker's part was required made him less sure of himself, therefore, often made him more competitive and individualistic. The work situation had become so bleak that only through collective action—union membership—could the worker obtain any human satisfaction at all. In short, factory work reinforced conservative values. When the worker left the job, his day's experience qualified him for political quiescence. Studies of the home life of workers show how the values learned on the job have the consequences of making people individualistic and highly parochial in their daily lives.[61]

Working conditions in the modern office are probably more pleasant than they are in the factory. The pay may or may not be higher. But the values taught remain similar, whatever the differences in the work. Mills has discussed a change very similar to that noted by Warner.[62] The craft-oriented middle class is disappearing to be replaced by one associated with an organization. In spite of books like The Organization Man, which stress the conformity of bureaucratic life, there are grounds for believing—as noted above—that harmful individualism dominates the society. In the bureaucracy, one must be individualistic in the way one conforms.

What is required is that the individual go along, but that he or she do it alone. Conformism does not mean communalism, but its opposite. Robert Presthus's study of the difficulties faced by those who are forced to adjust to the modern organization is best understood as a discussion of the problems faced by those who find it difficult to walk this balance or resolve this paradox.[63] Similarly, the modern bureaucracy encourages competitiveness (even if people compete in order to conform); fatalism (by encouraging the Weberian notion that there is no other way to do something in the modern world except bureaucratically); distrust (by numerous checks and double checks of every action and operation); parochialism (by its insistence on conformity to certain rules)[64]; atheoreticalism (by encouraging specialization and frowning on general approaches to problems); and authoritarianism (by structuring a fairly rigid hierarchy of command). As a remarkable book by Harry Braverman documents, the lack of power and general proletarianization of work that characterize the factory now apply to the office as well.[65]

chapter six ☆
public
ideological
repression

An interesting parallel with violent repression emerges at this point. Chapter 4 showed how violence was first undertaken for the state by private groups, while the state stepped in as a repressive institution only when there was a need for "professionalization" and "centralization of command" in the development of the institutions of violent repression. In a similar manner, the previous chapter's discussion of ideological repression involved only private institutions. Nonetheless, all the institutions discussed in the previous chapter were in or close to the ruling class. All had the same interest in keeping themselves in power as the state did. Therefore, all were doing the state's work. It is now time to examine the role played by the state itself in this business. Generally, public ideological repression occurs through the use of what is formally called propaganda and through the educational system. Each of these deserves a few words.

State Propaganda

The state began to develop a major interest in violent repression around the time of World War I, and it is also possible to trace the emergence of a state propaganda machine from that period. The war was a modern one that required the support of the domestic population. Thus, in 1917 (at the same time it was learning how to raid), the government, through the Committee on Public Information—the first agency in American history to be devoted solely to ideological repression—released the *National Service Handbook*. Noting that "agencies of publicity by stimulating interest and publishing facts which will help the citizen to know what is going on and the work which needs to be done will themselves be performing a distinct war service,"[1] the Handbook became a guide to propaganda. Its second section, "Domestic Warfare," is devoted to the way in which a series of domestic institutions—including industry, social welfare, education, social work, philanthropy, and the YMCA—could further the war effort by altering perceptions of the war. The *Handbook* noted that the armies fighting the war were, of course, of vital importance, but one should not forget "an army of 10,000,000" at home that was also important.

If the Committee on Public Information had merely organized around the goal of supporting the war, one could say that it used propaganda, but not for purposes of repression. However, the CPI did more than urge support. Much of its activity was directed toward winning loyalty from two groups—labor and immigrants—which had fewer reasons than others to be loyal. And the loyalty sought was not simply to "America," but was directed to the whole complex of economic and social arrangements for which it stands. In that sense, the CPI was expressing the bias of the democratic state, and its functions must therefore be seen as repressive.

In order to win the support of labor, George Creel, CPI's moving spirit, realized that labor leaders themselves would be the best agents to transmit the message. He and his staff (including Edward Bernays, who learned many of his techniques working for Creel)[2] convinced (it did not take much) labor leaders such as Samuel Gompers and J. C. Phelps Stokes to work for the committee. This was done through what the historians of CPI called a "front group"[3] for the committee, the American Alliance for Labor and Democracy. It has been described as follows:

> In most respects the Alliance may be considered a field organization of the CPI charged with the special responsibility of keeping

labor industrious, patriotic, and quiet. The Alliance had support from high places.[4]

Three divisions carried out the work of the Alliance: organization, literature, and public speaking. All together 150 branches in 40 states were created; 1,980,000 pamphlets were printed and distributed; 200 meetings were held; and 10,000 columns of newspaper publicity were written. A pay-envelope plan—using patriotic messages in the pay envelope each week—was carried out, along with various poster campaigns.[5] Although Creel formally tried not to allow the Alliance to become a tool of the industrialists, he failed—or he did not try very hard. In many cases, employers administered the Alliance's plan. The group had the full support of many industrialists, including many reactionary ones. In short,

> . . . the military requirements of the government and the self-interest
> of capital tended to reinforce each other in seeking to ensure the
> patriotism of labor and to preserve industrial peace.[6]

At the same time the Industrial Workers of the World was being forcibly repressed, the CPI was developing the technique of repression through propaganda. In most cases when the government seeks to bring two groups together around a "harmony of interests," the weaker group is forced to accept the terms of the stronger.[7]

Foreign-born Americans were also a problem for the committee. For one thing, many of the more radical labor organizations were dominated by immigrants. In addition, in 1916 there were 14½ million American residents who had been born in foreign countries, a high peak in immigration figures.[8] Many were from countries that were fighting the United States (countries that also had more radical political traditions). From the viewpoint of unity, immigrants were a threat to the existence of the democratic state, or at least were perceived as one. Unlike the experience of World War II, Creel specifically rejected any attempt to handle this "problem" with violence.[9] He felt that the CPI's ideological activities could easily take care of whatever had to be done. What was needed was an organized campaign. In Creel's words, written later:

> The loyalty of "our aliens," however splendid as it was, had in it
> nothing of the spontaneous or the accidental. Results were obtained
> only by hard, driving work. The bitterness bred by years of neglect and
> injustice were not to be dissipated by any mere war-call, but had to
> be burned away by a continuous educational campaign.[10]

Groups were formed, under CPI leadership, for Swedes, Danes, Norwegians, Finns, Italians, Czechs, Poles, Hungarians, Germans, Russians, twenty-four ethnic groups in all.[11] As with labor, the best way to convince these groups was with their own representatives. This meant that CPI worked covertly: "We worked from inside, not from the outside, aiding each group to develop its own loyalty league, and utilizing the natural and existing leaders, institutions, and machinery."[12] Various activities were undertaken. All 745 regularly publishing foreign-language newspapers received voluminous copy. Conventions were attended, pamphlets published, lectures given.[13] The basic idea was to leave nothing to chance.

CPI was disbanded in 1919 by an increasingly isolationist Congress. Conservative congressmen did not understand the new functions of public information, to the annoyance of men such as Creel who realized the power of what the state could now do.[14] But the spirit of CPI did not die. What it represents—direct state attention given to the problem of ideological repression—has been carried forward in the United States in increasing amounts in recent years.

The New Deal was an example of the increased importance of Creel-type activities on the domestic front. Publicity and propaganda by the state increased substantially, because ". . . the national government was becoming increasingly involved in social and economic functions that were controversial."[15] As part of that controversy, Republicans in the 80th Congress investigated domestic propaganda during the Roosevelt and Truman Administrations. Their findings, while highly partisan and not very well thought out, nonetheless contained some information on the problem.[16] The Department of Agriculture, it was found, employed 525 persons in public relations work alone. In the Office of Information of the Department, a budget of $2,307,000 existed for fiscal year 1949, a substantial increase over the previous year. In the nine-month period terminating April 1, 1947, the Office of Information of the Agriculture Department issued 1,998 press releases (about 11 every working day); dispensed 837 radio scripts and 17 motion pictures; displayed exhibits to 2,100 state and county fairs; and sent weekly clippings to agriculture journals, science publications, general magazines, woman's page editors, and Negro newspapers.[17] The investigators also found that the total amount spent by the federal government in 1948 for publicity was $74,829,467 (an increase from the $28,000,000 in fiscal year 1941), with 42,000 employees. It would take 800 columns (100 pages) of the *New York Times* to print the press releases of government agencies written in one week.[18]

Later investigations showed increases in the publicity function. The 1950 Hoover Commission Report estimated that publicity costs increased to $105 million, with 45,778 persons employed. Most of this was directed to Americans, not overseas. The Departments of State, Treasury, and

Agriculture all spent more for publicity than the War Department and the Office of War Information. Every agency of the government was found to have a public relations staff. All together, government agencies in one year spent about $50 million for printing and $40 million for mailing costs.[19] Thus, a steady upward trend in state publicity can be observed. There have been no investigations of this sort in recent years, but a look at the federal budget gives some indication of the size of the publicity function. In 1969, the Commerce Department alone spent nearly $3 million on duplicating expenses. The printing budget of the Army Department in the same year was $43 million. More than half a million dollars was spent on printing by the Federal Bureau of Investigation, merely one branch of the Department of Justice.[20]

All these statistics are important only insofar as they reflect the understanding that the democratic state now possesses of the importance of direct attention to ideological repression. A major segment of the "propaganda arm" if the American government is directed overseas and will be discussed in the next chapter, but some interpretation has to be made of the domestic propaganda function. The most serious student of the problem has concluded that American democracy is still safe, even though publicity does constitute a threat. Francis Rourke maintains that a pluralistic political structure prevents any one body of power from dominating the publicity function and that governmental information helps democracy as much as it hurts it.[21] Such a conclusion presents problems. The pluralistic structure means that many groups use publicity; it does not mean that the direction of their attention is different. Indeed, this chapter and the previous one have tried to show that the direction is the same. But there are grounds to believe that, in a sense, Rourke is right: direct propaganda by the state is not overwhelmingly important at this time. The amounts spent are small compared to the activity of the media and other private groups in this field. Even with what is spent, government publicity (or state propaganda, depending on the impression one wishes to give) is directed toward winning support for specific programs and policies. It is generally true that the inculcation of general attitudes is more important for maintaining a repressed population. This the state does not attempt to do through its governmental publicity apparatus. It relies, instead, on the educational system.

The Educational System

Starting before World War I, a series of books called *The Modern Teachers' Series* began publication. These were handbooks designed to inform schoolteachers on current happenings and to give them hints concerning their work. In 1941 one of the volumes—written by the dean of the School of Education at the University of Texas—began with these words.

> This essay advocates the deliberate indoctrination for American democracy of children and youth in American schools. It maintains that a proper business of education, both public and private, in this country is to imbue young Americans with intelligent devotion to their country's basic principles and ideals. Indoctrination for American democracy is represented as not only a proper, but also a major and necessary, business of American education. It is a plain duty of schools and teachers to give vigorous support to the ideological pattern that sustains them.[22]

The author, B. F. Pittenger, went on to emphasize the importance of schools in serving this purpose, for no other organization reached as many people in as direct a way. He was aware of the role that education could be expected to play in ideological repression in the democratic state.

Pittenger, however, underestimated the extent to which education had historically played a role supportive of existing institutions. Nineteenth-century school-reform advocates, though they used a language that stressed the democratic aspects of education, were contributing to a system that served only the needs of certain classes. The more privileged groups supported the modernization of the schools because it matched their own economic interests. Michael Katz's study of Massachusetts documents this well:

> . . . the fable that the high school served the entire community was naturally attractive to middle-class parents because it justified having the entire community support an institution most useful to the middle-class. Through the high school they could spread among the population at large the burden of educating their children. The ideology of communal benefit served wealthy groups well, too.[23]

Thus, in spite of a formal commitment to egalitarianism, American education historically has at the same time served the interest of the more privileged groups and tried to convince other, poorer groups that middle-class values were the only ones people should have. Perhaps this explains why leading educational reformers of the nineteenth century, men such as Henry Barnard and Horace Mann, were also prominently associated with the developing capitalist order.[24]

At the present time, it is useful to think of the public system of education as contributing to ideological repression in the direct and indirect fashion already delineated.

Direct ideological repression in the schools is best seen in the way in which systems that challenge the democratic state are handled. The problem arose because so many educators wished to use the schools for political purposes, especially the promotion of something called "democracy." For example, immediately after World War II, the National Educational Association outlined a program for the postwar educational system. "It is important," they noted, ". . . that loyalty to the democratic ideal and appreciation of its possibilities be supported by an acute awareness of the factors which threaten it."[25] What were those factors? The document goes on to list "social ills" (e.g., depression, unemployment, insecurity, and general dissatisfaction), "the weakening of religious convictions," an unresponsive state, the resort to violence by deprived groups, and "conditions created by modern propaganda." In short, the NEA recognized that the schools were part of a system and had the obligation to preserve that system's basic structure. Therefore, when the United States discovered a "Communist problem" in its midst after 1948, the schools could be expected to play a direct role in repression by showing how democracy and communism were opposites and how the latter must be scorned under any circumstances. This was no mere matter of national security, since the democracy being compared to communism often meant American society in its present form, that is, benefiting those it benefited at that time. Thus, when schools took upon themselves the preservation of "democracy," they became repressive in a political sense (they had always been repressive in other senses).

The result was that a number of states passed laws regulating the "teaching" of communism. These laws were never repealed: in fact, years after the anti-Communist hysteria of 1948–54, new laws were being passed. In 1961 the Florida legislature passed a law providing that a compulsory course on "Americanism Versus Communism" would be taught in all public high schools in the state. This piece of legislation noted that ". . . the successful exploitation and manipulation of youth and student groups throughout the world today are a major challenge which free forces must meet and defeat." Therefore,

> The best method of meeting this challenge is to have the youth of the state and nation thoroughly and completely informed as to the evils, dangers and fallacies of Communism by giving them a thorough understanding of the entire Communist Movement, including its history, doctrines, objectives, and techniques.[26]

This law was similar to, if more explicit than, legislation passed earlier in Alabama, California, Louisiana, Nebraska, New York, Ohio, and almost every other state.[27]

Organizations such as the American Bar Association, the National Education Association, the American Legion, the National Congress of Parents and Teachers, and the American Association of School Administrators passed resolutions encouraging the schools in such activities and explaining why it was perfectly legitimate for schools to fire any Communists on their staffs.[28] The American Federation of Teachers, not to be outdone, found that membership in the Communist party was imcompatible with membership in the union.[29] With all this activity, the schools became propaganda vehicles touting the virtues of the democratic state. Education became highly political, completely involved in direct ideological repression. The situation envisioned by Pittenger in 1941 had been realized, but it came about—not at first through positive indoctrination, but by comparison with systems other than that of the United States.

Schools also play a role in promoting indirect ideological repression, but the picture is more confusing. One peculiarity of American education is that schools have by and large been under local control. Since states and municipalities could legislate about education, it was only when a threat was perceived—e.g., the "Communist menace"—that they banded together and acted in a uniform manner. At other periods, it is impossible to generalize about American schools, since what happens in New York is so different from what happens in Alabama. The national ruling class does not control the American educational system, a deficiency that some perceptive members of that class are trying to remedy. The Sputnik events, it is generally recognized, led to increased attention to education in America. But they also led to increased ruling-class involvement. Members of the ruling class became educational critics, calling for the establishment of totally new approaches to schooling.[30] Their words had effect; a sign of the changing nature of education is the increasing attention being paid to it by the federal government. Between 1962 and 1967, an estimated thirty pieces of new legislation passed by Congress gave money to education. The size of the U.S. Office of Education tripled during the 1960s.[31] The importance of such federal activity is that the resulting centralization will signify the creation of a national educational system that could more easily serve the ruling class than the present decentralized and essentially inefficient one.

It would be an error to take heart that schools are not yet under the control of a national ruling class, for in their present state they serve interests much more parochial. Many educational critics have pointed out how dreadful the American public school really is and their findings have not surprised anyone. Education is one of the few areas (if not the only area) where the status quo has no prominent defenders; *everybody* knows that something is wrong with the schools. And not only the schools of the lower class, but those of the more privileged groups as well, have been found wanting. The indictment of American education is familiar enough and needs no summary here.[32] What needs emphasis is the reason for the failure.

One answer may be that it is no failure at all. In their discussion of the "tracking system" found in most high schools, Paul Lauter and Florence Howe question those critics of stratification who point out how such systems reinforce class lines.[33] Perhaps, they suggest, the tracking system is a sign of how the schools have succeeded. For if the school is seen as an agency *designed* to preserve the class structure (and they make a good case that this is so), then methods that serve those ends have to be considered a sign of success, not failure. A similar conclusion emerges concerning ideological repression. When it is shown that the schools teach cynicism, passivity, powerlessness, conformity, dullness, incompetence, and many other such concepts, these results can be seen not as an unconscious by-product of otherwise well intentioned activity, but as the purposive consequence of the educational system. It is designed to teach those things. The resemblance between the powers of student government and the powers of many political bodies in the real world (e.g., pollution control agencies, regulatory bodies, even legislatures) are too similar to be coincidental. Because this society needs people who believe that power lies with government when actually it lies elsewhere, student governments play an important role in conveying that belief. Schools, then, teach well what the real world of the democratic state is like: people are powerless; don't try to change the world; vote like a good citizen and try not to understand your malaise.

Thus, the schools play a contradictory role. On the one hand, they foster those attitudes that the democratic state requires of its citizens. But they have done such a good job that the whole nation is in danger of turning moronic. The society needs passivity, but it also needs a certain technological intelligence to run the system in its present grooves. So some changes—some improvements—will have to be made in the schools, and we can expect more ruling-class criticism and attempts to control. An alliance may even be formed between the proponents of "radical school reform" and the corporate elite. Already a movement close to education reform—sensitivity training in its various manifestations—has received corporate support, making a sort of new approach to industrial happiness. Yet, such an alliance will doom the chances for a meaningful change in the educational system. Schools are such an important part of the democratic state that they will always be expected to uphold that state's basis. A truly human educational system will be created only when a truly human political and economic one is created.

This review of the instruments of consciousness manipulation by agencies of the state indicates that this form of repression is left in private hands to a much greater degree than violent repression. Yet, some changes are becoming apparent. Both direct state propaganda and a centralized educational system are increasing in importance. Perhaps the reason is analogous to the situation of violence. There, private violent repression eventually became too irresponsible and uncoordinated, giving it a bad name. Similar signs of irresponsibility appear in the private sphere of ideological repression as well; some television commercials simply go too far.[34] At that point, the state intervenes to regulate, so that a few bad repressors won't destroy the atmosphere in which the good ones work, to preserve the integrity of indoctrination, so to speak. If this trend continues, we could expect more and more of the means of consciousness manipulation to come under state control. This would be ironic; while the means of production were left in private hands, the means of repression would be socialized. Repression may become so important for the corporate elite that it will no longer be left in their hands, and at that point the state will increasingly do it for them. But little of this has happened as yet and private groups are still expected to play the major role in manipulating people's consciousness.

Other Associations and Institutions

Economically powerful groups and the state, between them, establish what values are to be indoctrinated and how they are going to be operationalized. They also propagate quite a bit by themselves. But psychologists have told them that a message is more likely to be favorably received when the communicator is less remote.[35] Since both private and public institutions generally are remote, an important form by which the consciousness manipulation function is transmitted is through intermediaries, of which there are many. They receive the message and (without being allowed to change it in any substantial way) transmit it in a more personal and effective manner to the individual. This process can be illustrated through the experiences of two such intermediate groups: private associations and the family.

Private associations are often assigned an important role in the theory of the democratic state. Generally, that role is seen in this way:

> The right of association is central to any serious conception of constitutional democracy. In the big states of modern times the individual cannot function politically with any measure of effectiveness

unless he is free to associate with others without hindrance. In fact, most people find much of their identity, in either economic, social, political, professional or confessional terms, in some form of group activity.[36]

All democratic theorists concur in such sentiments, making freedom of association a "right" of fundamental importance. Yet, those who write on totalitarianism have pointed out how group membership is used by the state in order to control dissidents,[37] and we have seen (in chapter 1) how writers on totalitarianism give many insights into the nature of the democratic state, albeit unconsciously. If true, this raises a question of fundamental importance, whether the right of association is used by the state more often for purposes of repression than for purposes of enhancing freedom. Here again is a basic paradox of democratic theory: groups are needed so that the individual can be free, yet those same groups can be used periodically to ensure his or her unfreedom. When the democratic state promotes the advantages of membership in groups, perhaps it does so knowing how important that membership may someday turn out to be.

The crucial operating fact is the undemocratic nature of private associations in the United States. This is a phenomenon of social organization that can be traced back at least as far as the study by Roberto Michels of the German Social Democratic party.[38] When Michels proved the existence of an oligarchy in the very party of Marx and Engels, he felt that he sufficiently disproved forever the idea that what would later be called "participatory democracy" could ever come into existence. The problem, however, is that the SDP, even at the time Michels wrote, had lost its revolutionary ardor and become bourgeois. In that sense, its oligarchic structure was a reflection of all organization in a developing capitalist state. What his book tends to prove is not that democracy within private associations is impossible, but that present forms of society render it impossible. The undemocratic nature of private associations in the United States is crucial to the operation of the democratic state for two reasons. First, it enables the leaders to form alliances with the rulers of the democratic state or their agents. In a crisis situation, the leaders then work for the state against the interests of their constituents and engage in ideological repression in order to justify their activity. Second, undemocratic private groups reinforce cynical and fatalistic values, as well as authoritarianism. With the privilege of leadership restricted to a few, the many are encouraged to remain passive, good citizens of the democratic state.

The relationship between the rulers of the democratic state and the leaders of America's labor unions provides the best example of the first situation. Labor is the one group that has the numbers and potential political power to be a genuine threat to the existence of capitalism; hence, its repression is most vital. This repression has very often taken the form of ideological repression by the leaders of labor unions operating as intermediaries. We have seen how George Creel used the American Alliance for Labor and Democracy to obtain support for President Wilson's programs. This was not an isolated example. It is repeated frequently, but one additional example might be enough. The American alliance with the Soviet Union during World War II resulted in a certain legitimacy for domestic radicalism. Members of the Communist party, for example, reached places of influence within many labor unions. If an anti-Communist, pro-capitalist society was to be strengthened after the war, such radicalism would have to be purged, and using labor leaders to do it was an obvious solution. CIO President Philip Murray cooperated with Secretary of State George Marshall in obtaining labor support for the Marshall Plan, the key to a stable, non-Communist Europe. Marshall spoke to the membership, but this was ineffective. Much more telling was the outright purging of Communists from important CIO unions. Done with the obvious blessing of the Truman Administration, this action continued from 1947 to 1949, by which time the CIO was fully able to support the cold-war foreign policy of the democratic state without dissent from within.[39] All alternatives to the existing state of affairs having been expelled from the unions, it is no wonder that the rank and file developed anti-Communist attitudes. Their leaders, working for the state, had ensured that there would be no other attitudes around.

The ways in which the undemocratic structures of private groups reinforce conservative values is nowhere better illustrated than with religious institutions. It is one thing to recognize religion as an opiate, but what can be overlooked is the strength of the addiction; in the previous chapter Joe Kelly indicated that the most important influence shaping his political attitudes was the Catholic Church. Indeed, that is as it should be. Since of all the major religious denominations in the democratic state the Catholic Church has (along wtih some southern fundamentalist Protestant groups) the most undemocratic structure, its members—if they are to learn from its undemocratic nature—should have the most antirevolutionary attitudes. A survey found exactly that: Catholics had fewer doubts about the existence of God than any other religious groups except southern Protestant sects. The same is true of belief in miracles, literal Biblical interpretations, and belief in an afterlife, each of which can be associated with fatalism and parochialism. At the same time, however, Catholics had less specific religious knowledge than other groups.[40] There is a political correlate to these religious attitudes. One study found that regular church attenders would be more likely to be intolerant of radicals, that is, would be more ideologically repressed.[41] In addition, the well-known impression that Catholics would be more politically conservative than Jews—whose religious bodies have a structure that is slightly more democratic—is borne out in every instance.[42] The general notion that the more authoritarian the structure of a group, the more ideologically repressed will be its membership seems confirmed.

It would be foolish to underestimate the importance of private associations in maintaining freedom. Without some leeway in which to organize, political movements would be repressed from the start. The "right of association" is an important right that should be struggled for at all costs. But it is also true that established associations can be agencies of unfreedom, when manipulated by those in power. The contributions that private associations can make to freedom are flawed and undermined when they are used by the state for purposes of repression. This occurs not only when a group is forced out of existence, but also when the state contributes to and substantially defines its activities. The democratic state engages in repression just as much when it works positively with labor leaders to win support for its policies as when it harasses labor union members into prison.

The family is the other important transmission group working toward the goal of political repression. Within it, the communication flow is generally a one-way affair, as Hyman has noted:

> While influence might conceivably flow from child to parent what is
> much more likely is that parents are the agents who transmit
> politically relevant attitudes to their children. The almost complete
> absence of negative correlations provides considerable evidence against
> the theory that political attitudes are formed generally in terms
> of rebellion and opposition to parents.[43]

Thus, the parents adopt repressive attitudes and values from the public and private repressive agents and pass them directly on to their children. (The same pattern even holds in families where radicalism is the norm; most studies of student rebels show that they are the sons and daughters of rebellious parents.)[44] The political functions of the family are, therefore, worth comment, although the size of the subject precludes extensive analysis.

Many studies have dealt with the transmission of specific political values, that is, ideological repression. In a series of older studies, family influence was found to be highly responsible for attitudes toward the New Deal and government ownership, communism and the Soviet Union, political party preference, and other such specific political events.[45] More recent investigations have challenged the notion that the family is the most important agency of socialization, stressing instead the schools.[46] In this case, the critics are probably right; specific attitudes are changing fast, and many children think differently from their parents about specific events. Nonetheless, the family still plays an important role. One of the more recent studies, which upholds the importance of schools in political socialization, notes that ". . . the family's primary effect is to support consensually-held attitudes rather than to inculcate idiosyncratic attitudes." The result is that the family's major importance is in creating support for things that will ensure "the stability of basic institutions."[47] Thus, *the chief importance of the family is in indirect repression, teaching values that support the political consensus, rather than inculcating any specific politics.*

An illumination of how this is done comes from an examination of the internal dynamics of the working-class family undertaken by Komarovsky and her associates.[48] Included in that study is material supporting the notion that the family reinforces general attitudes that are supportive of the existing society. The effects of individualism can be seen in the sources that family members turned to when in need of emotional support. When asked, "What helps you when you feel bad, unhappy or worried about something, or generally low?" a surprisingly high number did not refer to their spouse but stressed such activities as crying, exercising, or drinking, all done alone. This testifies to the isolation of the family member, his or her inability to relate to others when in need. Such isolation is also found in the tendency of the families to have very few friendships; nearly all social relationships (visits and entertainment) took place between kin, where parochial attitudes also would not be broken. Power relationships within the families existed, reinforcing patterns of authoritarianism. In many cases, husbands were dominant, but there were also others that were matriarchal and a few were egalitarian. Often patterns of dominance were transferred outside the marriage to others, giving the impression that the man (or woman) is "boss" in the family and, therefore, worthy of respect. In short, blue-collar marriages appear to be political worlds in miniature. By possessing many characteristics of the larger society, they help shape the child who grows up in such an atmosphere to a world that will not be totally unfamiliar when he or she becomes a citizen.

It has been long recognized that the family plays a conservative role, supportive of existing political orders.[49] Yet, attempts are often made at suggesting that the nuclear family in its present form is inevitable; as, with interest groups, many held that undemocratic structures were inevitable. That notion can be questioned.[50] To be sure, the family will have to exist as it does now if the present social order continues to exist. The isolation, competitiveness, parochialism, and traditionalism of the family are important, and without it, it would be difficult to find another institution that would be quite as successful as a conservative force; this is one reason why conservatives place the family so high (near God) in their hierarchy of values. There is no reason why a new society could not have a new method of raising children, but this is a question that simply cannot be addressed intelligently here.

The Diffusion of Ideological Repression

This chapter and the previous one have covered a wide range of material very rapidly; the result might be to leave the impression that all these institutions are working together with unanimity and with prearranged foresight toward the conspiratorial goal of repressing everyone in sight. Such a conclusion is unwarranted, for ideological repression does not operate that way in the United States.

What makes indoctrination and manipulation in democratic societies so interesting is that they are very often voluntary, haphazard, and even unconscious. They are voluntary because most institutions choose to do so for benefits received. If they do not choose to do so, they would no longer exist as the same type of group, which does add an element of compulsion—but there is an alternative. Some people within some of these institutions have been realizing their repressive role and trying to do something about it, the creation of alternative media for example. Indoctrination is haphazard because many institutions that engage in ideological repression (advertising, much of the media, and to some extent education are exceptions here) do so not as their primary activity but as consequences of other activities. This means they are amateurs and do not always do the best job. Manipulation can be unconscious because many groups repress ideologically without even knowing they are doing it. The family is often unaware of the repressive role it plays, which does not stop it (and may even help it) from playing its repressive role well. Far from being monolithic, ideological repression is dispersed and uncoordinated, except at the highest levels.

The important point to note here is that those who are engaged in ideological repression are not all-powerful and all-knowing. In an important essay, Hans Magnus Enzensberger has suggested that the very complexity of contemporary means of communication prevent their being used in a systematic and unilateral way, giving support to the point of view presented here.[51]

Dispersion, however, has not led to pluralism. In spite of being voluntary, haphazard, and unconscious, the institutions of indoctrination wind up being extremely similar to one another. But this very similarity is another sign of weakness. Those involved in ideological repression face dilemmas, just as those engaged in violent repression do. The nature of the work presupposes enormous rigidity. If one institution is allowed to change, to stop direct and indirect repression, to become an agent of change and a new consciousness, the whole structure of society would be in danger because the society is built on false consciousness. So those in power wish to change these institutions as little as possible. But this, in turn, causes enormous dissatisfaction on the part of those who are aware of discrepancies between what they are told of democracy and what they actually observe. When they, in their idealism, find that the institutions are unresponsive, they are likely to beome further alienated from the system. When that happens, their consciousness is altered, and they can no longer be repressed so easily.

Periodically, then, we should find that institutional dissatisfaction will be high in the United States. It certainly is in 1977, after all the revelations involving Vietnam and Watergate. Large numbers of people have indicated their lack of faith in the major institutions of American society, including business corporations, labor unions, and the church. Support for political parties has fallen off sharply. Respect for the presidency has declined. Factors such as these have led writers from all sides of the political spectrum to ask whether a legitimacy crisis exists in American society.[52] If it does, even in a minor fashion, then ideological repression has failed to win positive support for the existing order.

The reason why ideological repression succeeds only partially, and often fails, is really very simple. The reality of most people's lives in this society is so much at odds with what they are being told that occasionally the reality breaks through, and no amount of ideological repression will work. At any given time, there are likely to be a substantial number of people whose consciousness can no longer be manipulated. Sometimes they are quiet, passive, and hardly noticed; at other times they are quite vociferous. But, in both cases, some element in their lives has told them that things are amiss. It may be an education, a personal experience that shatters their preconceptions, a peculiar upbringing, a dreadful living situation, or a combination of all these. What is important to realize here is that, whatever the "radicalizing" experience, it grows not out of a whim, but out of one of the basic paradoxes facing liberal society. If an act of violent repression leads someone to question his or her political values, that is one way that those who rule America undermine their own support. Institutional rigidity is another. Conditions of poverty or feelings of guilt from overwhelming affluence are still others. *The society that creates the need for ideological repression also creates the conditions needed for immunity to it.*

chapter
seven ☆
exporting
repression

Earlier in this book repression was defined as the use of violence and ideological manipulation to reproduce existing power relationships. Those who hold power in capitalist society reap great benefits from that power, even though they are a minority of the population. Through repression, they protect themselves against the potential power that a majority could exercise if that majority were united, i.e., not repressed. It is in the nature of repression to prevent large numbers of people from realizing their potential as rulers themselves, to stymie the political growth and independence of people and to keep them in a state of dependency.

But who are the ones who constitute the target group to be repressed? If the answer is anyone who constitutes a threat to those who hold power in the United States, then we are faced with a problem. For the boundaries of the United States have been continually expanding. At one time, perhaps, it made sense to talk of national boundaries as constituting some kind of meaningful end point to political influence. But with the United States this can no longer be done. Powerful people in America now have interests all over the world, and along with the extension of those interests, has gone the expansion of methods to protect them. As repression developed domestically to prevent potential threats from those who benefited least from industrialization, so *repression must now expand outside the borders of the United States to meet a potential challenge from those who benefit least from imperialism.*

For those who hold power in America, this is one of the "problems" of having an empire. In his study of Latin America, Andre Gunder Frank has challenged the traditional view of economic development by suggesting that many Latin American countries are not (and never really were) autonomous "feudal-type" societies, but are part of a worldwide capitalist order. It is futile, he suggests, to examine the economic affairs of any of the "Third World" countries without reference to the metropolitan power, because doing so will never result in a total understanding of the situation.[1] Interestingly enough, Frank's model has always been understood by corporate and political leaders in the United States. They think of such places as South America as part of their world, and their political control mechanisms are used there, as they are used at home. At one time, for example, John D. Rockefeller sponsored a major act of repression at his mines in Ludlow, Colorado.[2] Now, his grandsons are as vitally concerned with the residents of such places as Venezuela, Thailand, and Indonesia. Coca-Cola is no longer the major export of the United States. Repression is sent overseas as well. (In fact, there is probably a relationship there; the gun may well follow the bottle.)

International repression is amazingly similar to the domestic variety. The export of repression has involved both the means of violence and the means of ideological indoctrination. Often these go hand in hand, but in order to make some sense of the subject, it is possible to separate them for a while and to review each one. Then some attempt to place the export of repression into perspective can be undertaken.

Exporting Ideology

Since the export of repression has not been generally understood as a policy of the United States, we can begin with an illustrative example.

In October 1947 members of an American congressional committee visited Italy, and after touring the country, issued a report that said, in part:

> . . . there is today a growing doubt whether Italy can solve her
> problems within the framework of a representative democracy. The
> country is under great pressure from within and without to veer to the
> left and adopt a totalitarian collective national organization.
> The extent of this pressure can be judged by the fact that there exists
> in Italy one of the largest Communist parties outside of the U.S.S.R.,
> with a membership of 2½ million.[3]

There were good reasons for the strength of the Italian Communist party
(PCI). The Italian economy had been devastated by World War II. Sixty
percent of the families in Italy earned less than $825 a year; 54 percent
lived on less food than they had before the war, and 56.9 percent had
fewer clothes. In addition, the PCI had been the country's most consistent enemy of Mussolini, going to periodic martyrdom in its opposition to
his policies. During the war, the PCI was widely hailed for its support to
the partisans, those who fought hardest for the liberation of their country.
Strictly for internal reasons (the Soviet Union, of course, helped the PCI,
but that help was more in the nature of moral support than anything else,
considering how Russia was devastated in the war),[4] the Smith-Mundt
Committee was right in asserting the strength of the Italian Communist
movement.

Without the use of any troops, the United States helped turn what
seemed like a sure PCI victory in the April 1948 Italian elections into a
much publicized defeat. First, the state propaganda apparatus was
mobilized. The Voice of America, for example, increased its daily programming to Italy by one-third. News programs emphasized the generosity of the United States, by stressing the importance of each foreign
aid grant announced for Italy. Entertainment featured such American
celebrities as Frank Sinatra, warning against a PCI victory. Italian-Ameri-
can housewives made broadcasts, designed to show the close ties between the countries. Private radio companies in the United States, of
course, contributed whatever they could. Many mobilized Italian-Ameri-
cans in letter-writing campaigns to their relatives in Europe. Anti-Communist Americans of Italian descent, such as Luigi Antonini of the International Ladies Garment Workers Union went on the air to deliver
frightening messages about the PCI. And in an extraordinary series of
broadcasts, various American officials went berserk with demagoguery,
promising to cut off all American aid to war-devastated Italy, and threatening outright to stop all Italian emigration to the United States, should
the PCI capture a majority of the votes.

From a more positive direction, the provision of ecomonic aid from
the United States was tied to a PCI defeat. Timing of the first announcement of the Marshall Plan was placed so as to cut into PCI's strength just

before the election. (The Marshall Plan gave huge amounts of money to European countries for economic "recovery.") Around the same time, a heavily publicized "friendship" treaty between the two countries was signed. The president of Italy continually announced supplementary grants of foreign aid, all strategically timed. Relief money was provided for disaster victims. In all cases, the message that went along with the money was clear: vote "Right" and the cornucopia will flow; vote PCI and starve.

Finally, the United States undertook a series of actions designed to have a symbolic effect on the Italian population. One month before the election, the United States proposed to the Soviet Union that Trieste be returned to Italy. Two weeks before the election, America demanded Italian membership in the United Nations. Both actions were obviously timed to coincide with the elections. When other international events occurred spontaneously, Italian opinion makers were mobilized to relate them to the election. Thus, a Communist coup in Czechoslovakia in 1948 was pictured as the consequence of what happens when international communism is treated like any other political force, while the American breakup of the Soviet blockade of West Berlin was interpreted as the triumph of freedom. On those occasions when Americans chose the wrong strategy, there was a well-publicized reversal. The announcement of economic aid to a right-wing government in Spain, which confirmed what the PCI had been saying about reactionary America, was reversed, and the Italian population notified accordingly.

It is difficult to determine the precise effect of all these actions. They did obtain the immediate goal· the PCI was defeated in the elections. But exporting ideology was still a controversial and a new idea. The whole question of how much to use this tactic had to be reevaluated after World War II, just as it had been after World War I, when George Creel's Committee on Public Information was discontinued by a hostile Congress. "Isolationists" still saw no reason why the United States should spend so much money in other countries.

In spite of its use in Italy, there was a reaction to the export of ideology in the late 1940s similar to the one that had occurred in 1919. The Office of War Information, involved during the war in propaganda work, was phased out of existence by being transferred to the Department of State, most of whose bureaucrats were hostile to the idea. But this time, more people in high positions opposed an end to the export of ideology. William Benton (see chapter 5), for example, as assistant secretary of state for public affairs, fought hard to continue such a program, as did his business partner, Chester Bowles. Their lobbying efforts helped produce the Smith-Mundt Act of 1948 (which grew out of the events in Italy). This law created a state information service, noting that

> The Secretary of State is authorized, when he finds it appropriate, to provide for the preparation and dissemination abroad, of information about the United States, its people, and its policies, through press, publications, radio, motion pictures, and other information media.[5]

When the new institutions, particularly the Voice of America and the predecessor of the United States Information Service, the International Information Administration, came under attack from conservative quarters in the early 1950s, some rethinking of the export of ideology was again undertaken.[6] A presidential commission (composed of Defense Department and army officials, college presidents, and, naturally, the head of the country's most renowned advertising agency, Young and Rubicam) reported to President Eisenhower, who in turn reorganized propaganda activities and created the USIS.[7] Since its inception, USIS has grown from a tentative venture surrounded by controversy to an established instrument of U.S. foreign policy. This change is reflected in its budget. From expenditures in 1955 of $77,299,000, USIS's appropriations almost doubled in ten years, soaring to $146,832,000 in 1964. By 1969, expenses for salaries alone were $163,490,000, with a total budget of $176,000,000.[8] Thus, the continual complaints of propaganda bureaucrats that they did not have enough money were finally heeded by Congress. Any fears that conservative opposition would topple the agency evaporated when President Nixon, in his first inaugural address, endorsed the basic principles of the United States Information Agency, as it had come to be called. State-directed ideological repression became a reality, as conservative opposition melted away under the ideology of anticommunism.

The lesson to be learned from these events is that international propaganda as a policy instrument of the United States is not a "given." The decision by this country to assume on its own part a propaganda apparatus was a political decision; that is, it was designed to produce certain purposive consequences. Why was this decision reached when it was? The standard answer is that with the rise of a ruthless international Communist movement, democracy had to protect itself by stating its own side of the case. Thus, defenders of the new faith described themselves as realists trying to meet a totalitarian threat. Although most of them were liberals, they ultimately were as anti-Communist as anyone; a casual reading of their books discloses the most vituperative and conspiratorial vocabulary whenever the subject of communism arises, which is frequently.[9] Yet by now it should be clear how insufficient the standard answer is. For one thing, communism had been around for some time before the decision to create a permanent state-directed propaganda bureau was reached. More likely the existence of the Soviet Union and its allies was simply a justification for a policy designed to serve other purposes than straight anticommunism. By the end of World War II, the United States had emerged as the premier imperialistic power in the world (coinciding with overt hostility to the Soviet Union, leading to the cold war), although its imperialism did not take traditional colonial forms. Rather, its economic ties to Europe and the Third World, combined with the need for allies to enable it to remain a world power, led the United States to exercise more and more control over the internal affairs of other countries. State-directed propaganda was one attempt, among many, to provide that control.

This interpretation helps explain the current repressive policies of USIA, with its more than 200 posts in 80 different countries.[10] USIA directs its attention to winning support for the policies of the United States in those crucial countries of the Third World that are capable—as Cuba was—of someday having a socialist revolution. Private agencies were too uncoordinated to keep these countries "free," thus revealing another reason for the importance of state-directed propaganda at the time it was created. USIA promised unity, which private groups tried to achieve but could not. The need for unity was realized by one government official, who in the late 1950s argued the need for a centralized approach to the problem:

> Political communication, to be effective, has to interpret and explain the national aims of the United States and clarify our truest and fundamental objectives. The point to notice is that it should reflect *national* policy.[11]

With national coordination, an information agency could do for citizens of the world what diverse institutions do at home. That is, it could repress by promoting values compatible with "the American century" (indirect ideological repression) and by participating directly in specific events to win a favorable opinion from one side of a controversy (direct ideological repression).

For USIA the problem of indirect repression is a technical one—making sure that American media (reflecting American values) reach as many people throughout the world as possible. The distribution of American motion pictures provides an example of how this has been done. In 1959 one billion tickets to movies were sold in India alone, and new theaters in Southern Asia were opened at the rate of one a day. Altogether the American film industry grossed $300 million overseas in that year.[12] On the one hand these figures reflect a profitable outlet for the products of an important industry. But there is more to it than that. One U.S. producer of movies for export was quoted by *Variety* as saying: "The American entertainment world—particularly motion pictures and music—is doing a better job indirectly in selling democracy and America to European nations than the U.S. State Department is accomplishing directly."[13] That may be hyperbole, but it is indicative of a close cooperation between USIA and the film industry which has been described by one USIA official this way:

> In recent years both the commercial film industry and the American government have shown an increased awareness of the place of films in molding world opinion. This has resulted in closer liaison between government and the industry on the problem. USIA has taken the lead in assisting to keep producers and script writers informed on foreign events, customs, and cultural values that should be considered in the production of films. This is not censorship but rather a healthy cooperation between government and the film industry that results in products more acceptable to overseas audiences.[14]

With state aid, 210 USIA film libraries throughout the world show American movies—and the repressive values they continually convey—to 500 million non-Americans per year.[15] The same aid is provided to television and radio companies, which could not have reached their position of international influence without significant direct help from the state.

There is no way to estimate the impact these media have on shaping the values of citizens of other countries, but from a policy maker's point of view, "modernization" would surely be enhanced if "modern" values became the norm. (In the language of social science, the task becomes one of enhancing what David McClelland calls n-achievement, the promotion of entrepreneurial values.)[16] No one expects that by themselves American movies will produce new attitudes. But in conjunction with all the other instruments of repression, they certainly do not hurt—and they most likely help in the attempt to produce loyal allies for the United States without resort to violence.

When violence is used, the means of ideological repression need not remain idle; they can enter the fray directly in order to help the situation be resolved favorably. Two examples might be enough. According to one USIA official, one of his bureau's most successful moments occurred in the midst of violent repression, when the United States sent troops to Lebanon to preserve its interests in 1957.

> When the move met severe criticism in Asia and Africa, USIA posts in those areas were prepared to explain why the action was imperative to our own vital interest as well as to those of the free world in general. Many opinion leaders were persuaded by our explanations especially after the United States showed its respect for Lebanese independence by pulling out its troops on schedule.[17]

USIA also operates in a crisis brought on by the other side. When the Hungarian events of 1956 broke out, USIA took only two days to make a film on the subject after footage arrived in Washington. Within a week, twenty-four different languages were dubbed in, and the film was immediately sent overseas where it was shown throughout the world.[18]

The extent of USIA activities indicates that in the controversy over whether to make the export of ideological repression a permanent feature of American foreign policy, those who supported the idea won. But how much is ideology exported at the present time? It is impossible to answer this question, because this general task is done by both the public and the private sector within the United States. When the means of violent repression are discussed later in this chapter, we will see that violence is primarily an affair of state. Some private groups occasionally contribute to the exportation of violence, but the American government has centralized this function under its own leadership. The export of ideological repression is still carried on by private institutions, however, including the media, foundations, universities, and corporations themselves.

A brief introduction to the problem of private export starts with a story and is followed by some figures. The story is one of the increasing commercialization of world television under American leadership. For a nation that early in its history was concerned with stopping piracy on a worldwide scale (to be discussed later in this chapter), it is ironic that the major tactic for extending commercial television to the world has been through "pirate" ships. Since many, indeed most, countries did not particularly want their television networks dominated by American-type television, they passed laws preventing foreign-owned companies from broadcasting within their borders. But laws cannot stop an idea whose time has come, and the American media were convinced that commercial television on a worldwide basis was a necessity. (This was not totally an ideological conviction; the needs of American capitalism required advertising all over the globe, since Americans themselves had become saturated with products and demand was about to level off.) In order to circumvent local laws, ships could be found broadcasting American commercial television into countries from open waters nearby. These ships were called "pirate" ships because of their intentionally confusing background. For example, the ship that invaded Sweden was registered in Lichtenstein, flew a Nicaraguan flag, was piloted by Swedes, but was, of course, owned by Americans. Similar ships operated near Britain, Holland, Finland, Denmark, and Norway.[19]

As each of these countries was under considerable pressure to "Americanize" its communications industries, the pirate ship invasion was meant as a threat.[20] It was in general successful. American television is now a worldwide phenomenon. Oscar Lewis has noted its effects in Mexican villages.[21] "Wyatt Earp" became Bangkok's favorite show in 1960, while "The Untouchables" was popular in Manila and Sidney.[22] Expressed in figures, CBS, according to its company reports, broadcasts in 94 countries; RCA distributes "Bonanza" alone to 60 countries.[23] One American advertising agency (McCann-Erickson) has 70 offices in 37 different countries. Fifteen American advertising agencies have offices in Brazil. Under relentless American impact, American media have changed the language, habits, and political attitudes of people throughout the world.[24]

The television invasion, from the viewpoint of repression, is probably as important as any military invasion of any country since the end of World War II, with the exception of Indochina. The experience of the television invasion demonstrates that people will watch commercial television and learn from it. It is worthwhile to point out that when American television commercials are broadcast overseas, they are not changed, except for dubbing in a new language. The Peruvian citizen still watches two American housewives making each other envious because of the use of certain detergents. Such a situation may not be relevant to his or her life, but it is at the level of fantasy. Surely the advertising agencies know that American commercials shown overseas not only sell the product, but also encourage all those who watch them to believe in the values they represent. Such values may be in conflict with traditional norms in the countries where these commercials are shown; it will be interesting to see what happens as a result. Already the leaders of many countries have reacted rather violently to the content of American programming,[25] which puts economic considerations of American firms before the needs of the local population. Educational shows from socialist countries have increased in popularity throughout much of the world, particularly Africa. Harry Skornia's comments on this situation reflect the basic contradiction facing the rulers of this country as they extend their repressive apparatus abroad: "It is a bitter irony indeed that those allegedly profiting most from the American way unwittingly contribute most to its undoing."[26]

Lest one get the idea that the media repress intentionally only in indirect ways, through the presentation of certain themes compatible with capitalism, it is important to note the direct role played by the media in repression. Sometimes this aspect has a humorous touch; according to the *Wall Street Journal*, more than ten thousand transistor radios, manufactured so that they received only pro-American stations, were dropped into North Vietnam (and hostile parts of the South) during the war there.[27] At other times, there is little humor, such as in the various American attempts to use the Communications Satellite Corporation for purposes of foreign policy. Although there was much talk of placing COMSAT (and its international parent, INTELSAT) under effective international supervision, American interests have continually pushed their own objectives, to the point where proposals for the international use of satellites generally originate in the Pentagon.[28] There has been a push to concentrate on those frequencies that reach the southern half of the globe, where wars of national liberation are most likely to be fought. The United States has been trying to use satellites as a way of communicating rapidly with its forces in such places to put down insurgencies. To some extent, this strategy is already in practice: American bombs in Vietnam found their way to their targets through the use of weather satellites sitting in space. Nothing—or as little as possible—has been left to chance.

The communications industry is only one example of the export of ideological repression. Domestically, that type of repression was performed by institutions that ranged in size from big organizations (e.g., corporations and universities) to intimate ones (e.g., families and associations). Internationally, the latter become less important. Occasionally there are attempts to export American families overseas, people-to-people type programs and other such endeavors, but they are not politically important. Similarly, social and fraternal organizations have international affiliates, but here the only people reached are those who are sympathetic to the expansionist aims of the United States in the first place. In general, complex organizations export this type of repression, and of the various forms, a few words should be said about foundations, universities, and business corporations.

Reference has been made periodically throughout this book to the role of philanthropic foundations. It should perhaps be stated forcibly at this point that foundations are to ideological repression what the Central Intelligence Agency is to repression through violence. In other words, the work that foundations do in countries outside the United States is so important to the maintenance of American capitalism in its present form that a special set of relationships has been created between the leaders of the United States and the directors of the foundations. Domhoff has shown how the major foundations are dominated by people from the highest social circles.[29] This pattern is unchanging. It is reinforced by a series of interlocking names found on the boards of the foundations and similar institutions—public and private—that engage in other forms of repression, domestic and foreign. For example, the Ford Foundations trustees include John J. McCloy, formerly of the diplomatic corps, Donald David, chairman of the Committee for Economic Development (see chapter 3), Eugene R. Black of the International Bank for Reconstruction and Development, the directors of two newspapers, an executive of Time Inc. and the presidents of two universities, including the one (M.I.T.) most active in researching and applying its research to the Third World.[30] The president of the Ford Foundation is McGeorge Bundy, who learned the art of repression at Harvard at home and in

Vietnam abroad. (See chapter 3 for more on Bundy.) This membership reflects the fact that the work of an organization such as the Ford Foundation is so vital to the powerful in America that they trust nobody else but themselves to perform it. No attempt is made to hide the ruling-class bias of the foundations; often it is proudly proclaimed. The few exceptions, men like Dean Rusk of poor Georgia background, become such dedicated ideologues of the ruling class that they almost embarrass it. Those few times when ruling-class domination has come under serious attack have not produced much in the way of change, since the foundations' tasks made them resistant to any changes in directorship.[31]

What are those tasks? A basic policy statement of the Ford Foundation, written in 1950 and reaffirmed in 1962, gives a clue:

> The crisis in the world today requires that democracy do more than restate its principles and ideals; they must be translated into action. We must take affirmative action toward the elimination of the basic causes of war, the advancement of democracy on a broad front, and the strengthening of its institutions and processes.[32]

Little translation is needed to make sense of that statement. Democracy is obviously meant not as an ideal but as the actual practice of the United States. To translate that into action is to perpetuate the influence of the democratic state throughout the world. To strengthen its institutions is to weaken competing ones. By its own statement, the Ford Foundation sees its goal as one of repression, not through violence, but through what is in essence the same thing, the promotion of the "democratic way of life."[33]

By 1955, the Ford Foundation had decided that its program of support for economic development should be concentrated in only two parts of the world, the Near East and South and Southeast Asia.[34] Since that time the scope of its Overseas Development Program has broadened but the Asian emphasis has remained a strong one. At the same time that the U.S. government was sending police units to repress insurgency in Vietnam, Ford was experimenting on its more benign repressive techniques in the larger and ultimately more strategically important states of India and Pakistan. In India alone, by 1955 Ford had provided grants for agricultural extension projects ($1.2 million), training extension workers ($1.8 million), creating an "infrastructure" of "social education organizers" in various villages ($375,000), building agricultural colleges ($1.3 million), training project officers ($204,000), implementing small industry ($107,000), training technicians ($108,000), sponsoring teacher training ($102,000), building an institute of public administration ($350,000), and funding studies of India by American universities and research institutes ($260,000).[35]

Is this repression? One way to approach that question is to emphasize what should be readily known, that such largesse was not promoted solely by feelings of generosity. All these grants have at least two purposes in mind, and both purposes are repressive, even if they never lead to violence. One is to provide for the capitalist development of such countries as India, by encouraging capitalist methods of agriculture and light industry. Thus, behind Ford's activity is not so much the desire to prevent a country from "going Communist" as it is to keep it capitalist, i.e., available for investment by American corporations. Ultimately there is no difference between these strategies, but it should be clear that Ford's purpose is not so much the political one of winning allies for the United States as it is the economic one of industrial compatibility. The other purpose of Ford's activity is to create a local elite, sophisticated in the uses of the new technology, to govern the country with American aid. This accounts for the training and education grants. In both cases, Ford is fighting against the creation of a socialist economy in the dependent country, and in that sense, it is performing the same task—albeit in a different way—as the U.S. Army did when it fought in Vietnam.

Overseas development projects such as the one in India have increased in importance to the officials of Ford, especially as more violent forms of repression obviously become counterproductive. Consider the case of India's major rival, Pakistan. Just as the U.S. government distributed arms to both India and Pakistan which were eventually used against one another, Ford has made sure to favor neither country with its grants. A program involving the government of Pakistan, Harvard University, and the Ford Foundation was developed in 1954 to assist the Pakistan Planning Commission in its plans for internal economic development.[36] An advisory group of Harvard-related specialists, including fifty-six advisers and twenty-six consultants in various academic disciplines, went to Pakistan to provide their services. David Bell, later to head the Agency for International Development, was the first field director of the program, while the overall direction was left to the dean of Harvard's School of Public Administration, Edward F. Mason. Most of the work of Harvard and Ford was devoted to such tasks as administering various development programs, creating a technical elite, centralizing financial procedures, developing systematic statistical information ("Knowledge is power," one writer has suggested;[37] without effective data, repression would be much more haphazard), and helping the central government exercise control throughout the country.

This effort was one of the most heavily financed by Ford, because, in its own words:

> A distinctive characteristic of development in Pakistan is the role of the
> private sector. Pakistan has evolved an enterprise system combined

> with a government-formulated framework of policies and
> planning. Eighty-five percent of its output is privately produced. While
> government has protected, stimulated, financed, and guided its
> agriculture and industry, it has relied heavily on private initiative in
> its economic growth.[38]

Significant in this context is that even though Pakistan began to loosen its political ties with the United States by drawing closer to China, no substantial change ever occurred in the economic relationship that Ford built between the needs of American corporate liberalism and the ambitions of a specially trained Pakistani elite. Perhaps this is one reason why the Nixon Administration so quickly sided with Pakistan in its war with India in 1971.

The great emphasis placed on the Ford Foundation in the preceding paragraphs develops out of its premier role in international repression. But Ford is, of course, not alone. The Rockefeller Foundation budgeted $9 million for international programs in 1970, and most of that money was directed toward the creation of pro-capitalist local elites.[39] Because of the Rockefeller family interests in oil, this foundation has concentrated heavily in the one area that Ford tended to ignore, Latin America (although Ford is currently trying to remedy this deficiency). Also worthy of note is the fact, which David Horowitz has pointed out, that someone from the Rockefeller Foundation has been represented in every American Cabinet since the Truman Administration.[40] (This pattern has been continued with Carter's appointment of Rockefeller Foundation official Cyrus Vance as secretary of state.) When Rockefeller is combined with Ford, and the Carnegie Foundation is thrown in for a touch of spice, the result is a situation of monopoly capital among the foundations themselves. Together, for example, these three foundations originated and financed every single area studies research institution at elite academic institutions in the United States.[41] Compared with them, other foundations—e.g., the nouveau-riche Pew, Johnson, or Lilly foundations—pale in importance, no matter how much money they spend.[42] It is ironic, to stress a point made before in this volume, that the very instruments of repression are taking on the monopoly aspects of the society whose character they are trying to preserve.

It is through the just-mentioned area studies research institutes that the universities of America contribute their share to the internationalization of repression. Unlike the domestic situation, where nearly all universities are repressive in the sense that they are attempting to mold the students who come into contact with them, it is only the "elite" universities that make a substantial contribution to the export of repression. The degree of similarity between the way in which the major research institutes were founded (by State Department and intelligence officers), funded (by one of the big three foundations), and operated (by social scientists with similar ideologies and contacts) is quite startling, unless one begins with the assumption that the purpose of such research is not to advance learning as much as it is to contribute to the extension of the democratic state. Thus it comes as no surprise that all the work done at the area studies institutes of Columbia, Harvard-M.I.T., and Berkeley (again to mention a big three) is explicitly cold war in direction. For those in doubt, there is the experience of one institute that became critical of the direction of U.S. foreign policy and as a result lost all its foundation support and status within its university.[43] The functions of these institutes—providing knowledge about a country to make U.S. control over its destiny more successful and creating alliances with local elites who can be trained in America—means, once again, that the myth of disinterested scholarship is suspended when it interferes with the business for which the institutions were created.

There would seem, from this discussion, to be a number of institutions working for the interests of American corporations overseas. That does not mean that the corporations themselves have been idle. In fact, the international activity of American corporations is a huge subject that cannot be explored at any length here.[44] It is enough to say that corporations directly provide their own aid to "economic development" in a variety of countries, and that they engage themselves directly in training programs as well. This follows from the investment policies of American companies, for if capital is to be exported somewhere, there had better be ways to guarantee its safety, which is why the International Telephone & Telegraph Company tried to interfere in the internal politics of Chile. Recent years have seen a dramatic increase in the size and scope of multinational corporations; and the more multinational the firm, the longer its potentially repressive reach. Certainly a major shift to international business can be detected. *Fortune* described it this way:

> What is taking shape, slowly and tentatively but nonetheless
> unmistakably is "one world" of business, a world in which business
> will truly know no frontiers, in which the paramount rule governing
> the movement and goods and money will be the rule of
> the market.[45]

To an extent, the abolition of frontiers has already occurred. It no longer matters to an American corporation in what country the citizens it deals with happen to live. Wherever they live, they can be made to understand the importance of free enterprise to their own freedom; they can, in short, be repressed regardless of country of origin.

Exporting Violence

Violent repression, when practiced domestically, consists of three general forms: the use of laws, political intelligence, and military or police force. All three have their international counterparts.

Legal repression is the form least likely to be used for export, not because it is unprofitable, but because there is so little international law. A few examples of the phenomenon do exist, however, and they are worth mentioning because they serve their purpose. Of the various kinds of laws used for purposes of domestic repression, the one most common to the international situation is the *inclusion* law, that which defines certain people as members of the society and others as pariahs. Most writers on international law specify two conditions for any codification to exist, a balance-of-power situation and a commonality of interest among the parties.[46] It is easy to see how these two can be combined to exclude nations that deviate from methods to which stronger powers give their sanction. If a country, particularly a small one, has a revolution establishing a government hostile to the existence of world capitalism, so long as its leaders adhere to their socialist aims, the stronger powers will combine forces to declare the country "a threat to international law and order," "not deserving membership in the community of nations." The purpose is obviously to exclude the country from contact with its neighbors, isolating it, making it substantially weaker and ultimately repressing it.

To Woodrow Wilson, a belief in the importance of the League of Nations grew out of the same motivation as his hostility to the Russian Revolution. The program of the League, wrote Williams, "amounted to a direct and almost literal application of the principles of domestic liberalism to the world at large."[47] Since, as we have seen, Wilson's domestic liberalism included both the violent repression of the IWW and the development of state-directed ideological repression through the Committee on Public Information, it is not surprising that Wilson realized how essential to worldwide repression an international organization could be once revolutions became a reality. Direct intervention after revolutions, as in Russia, was a negative approach; defining acceptable international behavior through the League of Nations was positive. Both were repressive.

This approach to foreign policy has characterized post–World War II diplomacy. Since the beginnings of the United Nations, the United States has used that organization to define certain nations out of existence, so as to limit their international effects, so as, in other words, to define acceptable definitions of international conduct. Because the Russians had shown their dependability to some extent by winning the war for the Allies, or at least making the heaviest contribution, they could be trusted

to be members of this new body. But other socialist governments, particularly those emerging in Asia, were excluded. In order to do this, it was
necessary also to exclude some American allies, but they could easily be
protected in other ways. Thus, when the Korean war broke out between
two countries, neither of which belonged to the United Nations, one of
them was called by the American secretary of state a "Soviet puppet,"
which constituted "an open, undisguised challenge to our internationally
accepted position as the protector of South Korea."[48]

U.S. "protection" is humanitarian and therefore within the scope of
international law, while the puppet-string pullers of world socialism are
"totalitarian" and therefore outside accepted canons of behavior. An identical type of situation, almost a reflex action, has taken place whenever a
socialist revolution occurs. The best examples concern the attempts by
American statesmen to exclude Cuba from all regional organizations once
its revolution could no longer be controlled and the attempt to create a
fictitious China because of a dislike for the politics of the real one. Fortunately for the world's sanity, fictions like these are no longer maintained, Nixon ended the U.S. isolation vis-à-vis China, and Carter has let
it be known that he will not oppose the admission of a united Vietnam to
the United Nations.

Violent repression through infiltration and espionage is much more
popular than the use of international law since it is so much more flexible
in the relatively anarchic international situation. The use of espionage is a
recognized tactic of all states in the international arena, and it is not
very insightful to point out its existence. Nonetheless, there are some
interesting aspects to the espionage practices of the United States. The
most interesting is that not all infiltration is state-directed; private groups
still play a role in this form of repression, even in the international sphere.
Foundations, corporations, universities, and labor unions—none of them
formally part of the state—have all worked for the United States in
subverting revolutionary consciousness abroad, thereby winning forcible
support for the aims and policies of American expansionism.

Most "private" repression of this sort is devoted to the training of a
political elite that will be receptive to American interests. This is a practice engaged in not only by foundations, but by other groups as well.
Universities do this frequently, bringing potential leaders of other countries to the United States for their education. Clubs, business corporations, and fraternal organizations sponsor similar programs. One should
not, however, get the idea that the only form of leadership replacement
engaged in by private groups is a relatively benign sort. The American
Federation of Labor, for one, has a full-scale espionage program that
rivals that of the Central Intelligence Agency. Directed by Jay Lovestone
(a former Communist who became vehemently anti-Communist) this

program works throughout Latin America, engaging in violence against some labor leaders and encouraging the success of others. It is a semisecret world, but enough has been written elsewhere to convey a sense of the scope and importance of such exporting of repression by nonstate institutions within the United States.[49]

But the use of intelligence by private groups is an amateurish effort when contrasted with the role that the state plays directly in exporting this form of repression. Indeed, in no other form of repression described anywhere in this book is the state more actively involved in repression than in international espionage. In the late 1950s, one student of the subject concluded that as many people were employed by the American government in intelligence functions as worked in the Department of State.[50] A few years later the same writer concluded that the Central Intelligence Agency alone employed some 15,000 persons and spent about $750 million a year.[51] And the CIA was only one intelligence bureaucracy; to it should be added the National Security Agency, the Defense Intelligence Agency, the State Department's Bureau of Intelligence and Research, and units in the Atomic Energy Commission, the Federal Bureau of Investigation, the Library of Congress, the Department of Commerce, and the Post Office Department.[52] Of course, not all this intelligence gathering is related to repression. Or is it? To argue that any society needs intelligence about other countries is to raise the question why. And in the case of the United States, intelligence is not valued for its own sake. (If it were, with all the money spent, Americans would be among the most intelligent of peoples.) Intelligence is used basically to control, sometimes *only* to control. Thus there is ground for believing that ultimately the function of all intelligence operations is repression. The point, however, is not of great importance. Even if the security apparatus of this society is not totally repressive, so much of it is—as innumerable examples could show—that the question of percentages begins to evaporate.

It is scarcely necessary to point out that the Central Intelligence Agency is involved in the domestic affairs of other countries, and that the involvement takes the form of being antagonistic to those interests that threaten the triumph of world capitalism. The CIA's role in Iran, Guatemala, Cuba, and Vietnam is too well known to bear retelling here.[53] What does need emphasis is a proper political understanding of the role of international intelligence. This is especially the case because so much of what is written on intelligence emphasizes the mistakes made and not the underlying questions raised. For example, Roger Hilsman points out how the CIA became something more than even its creators hoped. By the time Kennedy became president, according to Hilsman, the CIA was an independent political force that responded very little to presidential leadership.[54] In his account, the CIA takes on a mystical character constantly expanding against the wishes of most policy makers. Thus we are led to believe that much of the CIA's activities are unintended; a proper rearranging of government can make intelligence more "respectable." In short, writers such as Hilsman accept the propriety of international repression; they wish only to reform it in order to make it accomplish its goals better. In the end, there is little difference in goals between Hilsman-type liberals and conservatives such as Allen Dulles. In Hilsman's words:

> So long as the Communists themselves are openly antagonistic to the
> rest of the world, as they openly and avowedly are, and so long
> as they use the techniques of subversion to bring down governments,
> which they do and which they openly and avowedly advocate
> doing, then the countries to which they are so hostile have both a
> right and a duty to use the methods of secret intelligence to protect
> and defend themselves—where those methods are effective and
> appropriate and for which there is no effective and appropriate
> alternative.[55]

The anti-Communist consensus surrounding the work of international intelligence is a clue to how the CIA grew in size against the wishes of Presidents Truman and Kennedy. The answer is that its constituency lay elsewhere than in the executive branch. Central intelligence is more vital to economically powerful members of the ruling class than it is to the less powerful members of the politically governing class. The CIA, particularly under Dulles but under its later leadership as well, could ignore presidential leadership because more powerful interests were involved. In specific cases, these interests might be Standard Oil, United Fruit, or the New York law firm of Sullivan and Cromwell. That is why the CIA has been dominated directly by ruling-class families such as the Dulleses (or men like Kermit Roosevelt and—the name is almost a parody of aristocratic pretensions—General Cortland Van Rensselaer Schuyler),[56] contrasted to the FBI, where many of the chief officials are middle class, Catholic, and "ethnic." It is this bias of the intelligence function that explains its policies. Contrary to popular belief, the role of the CIA is not to protect America from its enemies; it is to protect America's leaders from their enemies. In most cases, this will amount to the same thing. But understanding its role properly shows that, in the international class struggle, the CIA is less concerned with national security than it is in protecting vested interests. It is an agency of repression, not war.

In the 1970s, the cover that had been clamped tightly on the CIA lifted somewhat. First, a former agent named Philip Agee published a diary that indicated that repression of local activists in Latin America was a major concern of "the company." Then the *New York Times* published stories documenting the domestic aspects of agency work. In response, two congressional committees investigated the CIA, as did a presidential commission chaired by then Vice-President Rockefeller. This flurry of activity made Americans more conscious of actions taken in their name than ever before. Its back to the wall, the CIA counterattacked. It helped defeat Theodore Sorenson's bid for nomination as head of the agency. It is trying to portray itself as a responsible organization that makes policy and does not engage in war, a process that may be facilitated by a military chief, Admiral Stansfield Turner. But even Turner was unable to suppress a recent critical look at the agency by ex-CIA man Frank Snepp.

Nonetheless, war often does follow where the CIA has feared to tread. It becomes difficult to say where intelligence leaves off and actual military repression begins. But for purposes of clarity, some discussion of military and police force is necessary to close this discussion of the types of violent repression used internationally by the United States.

The direct use of troops for purposes of political repression against citizens of other countries has had a continuous history in the United States, much like the use of the National Guard and militia in domestic disturbances. This does not refer only to wars, when a declaration from Congress was made and formal fighting took place. Rather, it includes those instances in which troops were dispatched, without congressional approval, to other countries for purposes of keeping the citizens of that country loyal to whatever the American interest happened to be. Early in American history, there were instances of troop use, but with minor repressive purposes in mind. There were direct wars, like the War of 1812 and the war against Mexico. There were a series of boundary disputes, particularly with Spain over the Florida territory. Troops were used against pirates, frequently in the Caribbean around Cuba. In other instances, American sailors could be found off the coast of Africa, disrupting the slave trade. But around 1830 the nature of troop use began to change. More and more the purpose of using troops became politically repressive, in ways that can be categorized.

Between 1789 and the outbreak of World War II, American troops— without authorization from Congress—were sent to foreign countries 145 times.[57] In most cases, especially as time passed, a repressive motive became dominant. For example, inhabitants of places where American ships went exploring showed their resentment against the invader by such actions as burning ships and kidnaping sailors, most of which were provoked by Americans being far from home. American troops would then be sent to punish the natives for their deeds. These happenings were frequent (Sumatra, 1832; Sumatra, 1838; Drummond Islands, 1841; Samoa, 1841; Africa, 1843; Smyrna, 1849; Johanna Island, 1851;

Nicaragua, 1854; Fiji Islands, 1855, 1858; China, 1856; Paraguay, 1859; Angola, 1860; Japan, 1863; Formosa, 1867; Korea, 1871; etc.). These were not simple cases of international hostility. All took place outside the United States, in countries where Americans were not wanted. In all cases troops were sent to make further colonization of these areas easier and to demonstrate (by word of mouth) the futility of trying to resist the American presence. As in police raids on domestic political groups, there is a motive here much more important than simple "punishment" for "crime."

Another form of international repression that characterized nineteenth-century American diplomacy was the intervention into situations of foreign unrest to protect American property, lives, or both. What makes these significant is that most of them happened in South America, which America had claimed as its special area in which to practice its arts of control. Whenever an outbreak of nationalist revolutionary activity occurred (Argentina, 1833; Peru, 1835; Argentina, 1852; Nicaragua, 1853; Uruguay, 1855, 1858; Colombia, 1860; Panama, 1865, 1885; Hawaii, 1889; Chile, 1891; Nicaragua, 1894), or a state of insurrection such as a serious riot with political overtones (Panama, 1856; Angola, 1860; Uruguay, 1868; Colombia, 1868; Haiti, 1891; Nicaragua, 1899), or a civil war in which the United States had an interest (China, 1854, 1855; Japan, 1868; Samoa, 1888; Brazil, 1894), or a coup or an attempted coup (Nicaragua, 1857; Samoa, 1899), or a war between two powers in which the United States expressed an interest (China vs. Britain, 1856; Sino-Japanese War, 1894), the intervention of American troops changed the nature of the political activity. Far from simply restoring order or neutrally preserving property, troop activity was similar to the use of National Guard troops in domestic disputes. Force inevitably benefited the stronger interest, which also inevitably turned out to be the one that American policy makers favored. Sometimes these incidents reached ludicrous proportions. In early 1893 American troops were sent to restore order and protect property in Hawaii after a revolution, but the actual result was to establish a government controlled by the Dole Pineapple Company.[58] Here the political bias was so blatant that the United States eventually repudiated its own actions, but most of the situations cited in this paragraph differed from the Hawaii situation only in degree.

In the chapter on domestic violent repression, the importance of symbolic shows of strength by the state was emphasized. Occasionally the show of force dispels any need for its use. This is clearly the case with another form of international use of troops, involving a demonstration of troop strength to the weaker country whose citizens are being repressed. The most famous instance of this was when President Theodore Roosevelt paraded American ships around the world to impress Japan in 1907.

But that was not the only instance of repressive troop demonstration. Actually such maneuvers have been frequent (Turkey, 1851; Ryukyu and Bonin Islands, 1858; Turkey, 1858; Morocco, 1904). In each case, the show of strength accomplished its goals, but if the country had been stronger, then a symbolic sending of forces obviously would not have been carried out.

On the surface, these examples of various types of military repression seem to challenge the widely held notion that the United States did not become an internationally oriented country until late in the nineteenth century. There were, in fact, more uses of troops in international situations in the last half of the nineteenth century than in the first half of the twentieth. This might indicate a declining reliance on military force as a device in international affairs, to be replaced by an increasing emphasis on intelligence, international law, and ideological repression. In part this is probably true, but also important is the fact that the nature of American intervention into the affairs of other countries for purposes of repression has changed in more recent years. Intervention became more selective. It was when a serious revolutionary situation developed that American troops were used, such as after the Russian Revolution and for a long period in China before its revolution. Things calmed down to such an extent that when old-fashioned intervention was resorted to in the Dominican Republic in 1965, it brought cries of protest from American citizens.

The U.S. role in Vietnam indicated that the use of violence for international repression has not disappeared. That particular situation, in fact, revealed much about how repression is exported. There have been many attempts to account for and explain Vietnam, but none of them seems to work. The war was obviously not being fought for domestic economic purposes, since it did not hurt the economy. It was also not a territorial war, in view of a decline in the importance of territory for strategic purposes. Moreover, the war was fought in spite of enormous opposition to it within the American ruling class, as one after another influential American who helped plan the war came out against continuing it. In the absence of any explanation that makes sense, many have concluded that Vietnam was an irrationality, an escapade that was a mistake and which continually compounded itself. Is there any other way to explain the phenomenon?

There is another way, and it begins by rejecting the appellation "war" for the fighting that took place in Vietnam was not a war in any meaningful sense of the term. Rather, the American presence in Vietnam was political repression, and it becomes rational once we understand the importance of Vietnam—not strategically but politically. In the entire history of the exportation of repression by the United States, few groups—at home or abroad—have resisted the violence of the state as doggedly as the Vietnamese. By their example, they proved that violent repression need not work, if there is a common consciousness in opposition to it. In short, the Vietnamese attacked the very basis of the democratic state, its ability to control its opposition by the use of force or the threat of force. Those who make political decisions in America were divided about what to do in the face of this resistance, since the concept of determined resistance to the repression of American foreign policy was so novel. This is not surprising; American leaders have continually disagreed over the proper repressive tactics in many situations. One group was willing to allow the Vietnamese to "win," hoping to isolate the example and refusing to overextend the repressive apparatus, in fear of making revolt against it successful elsewhere. Another group, the one that controlled the policy through many administrations, refused to allow even one successful challenge, fearing the example that might be set. (There really is a domino theory.) Expressed in that fashion, it is clear that the second policy was as rational as the first. It *did* make sense for the United States to continue the fighting, whatever the cost. Thus, the United States continued to fight until it could sign a peace agreement which it felt maintained the legitimacy of its repressive apparatus. Neither tragic mistake nor Kafkaesque confusion, Vietnam was the culmination of a long policy of exporting repression. The "confusion" of the situation stemmed only from the resistance.

Support for the notion that the Vietnam situation was repression and not war (civil or otherwise) comes from the history of American involvement. To summarize or even fully refer to that history is not possible here, but a look at official pronouncements and actual activities reveals the repressive motivation. The most intelligent policy maker, and the man generally considered to be the "architect" of violent repression against the Vietnamese, is Walt W. Rostow, special assistant to Presidents Kennedy and Johnson. In his speech to the 1961 graduating class in special warfare at Fort Bragg, Rostow pointed out that "to understand this problem . . . one must begin with the great revolutionary process that is going forward in the southern half of the world."[59] This is the revolution of modernization. According to Rostow, it is the aim of international Communists to exploit this revolution for their own purposes. They, "the scavengers of the modernization process," purposely pick on the weakest governments to practice their "conspiratorial" and "disciplined" cadre organization. A sign of their nefarious aims is the choice of guerrilla warfare, but as we think about it, we should not get upset by this. "My point is that we are up against a form of warfare which is powerful and effective only when we do not put our minds to work on how to deal with it." Once we do that, we realize the importance of counterinsurgency, or, in terms of this book, repression. Now speaking directly to the soldiers (often called "green berets"), Rostow told them, "You are not merely soldiers in the old sense." Rather, these men symbolized the new approach that the United States took in Vietnam, "not merely the proper military program of deterrence but programs of village development, communications, and indoctrination." In short, in Vietnam, soldiers were professionals, devoted to protecting the country from an insidious force, internal in appearance, but external in direction. Soldiers have thus joined a wide variety of people engaged in upholding the existing system of political and economic relationships:

> I salute you as I would a group of doctors, teachers, economic planners, agricultural experts, civil servants, or those others who are now leading the way in the whole southern half of the globe in fashioning new nations and societies that will stand up straight and assume in time their rightful place of dignity and responsibility in the world community; for this is our common mission.[60]

That a policy maker could salute a group of soldiers in such a way indicates that they are going off to fight in something other than a typical war.

One speech does not a policy make. But Rostow's conception of Vietnam as something other than a mere war is brought out by the actual activities of the United States in Vietnam before Rostow's speech and after. The first activities undertaken by the United States in Vietnam were explicitly *police* actions, based on the idea that repression, not war, was the goal. Michigan State University established its program in police administration, in cooperation with the Diem regime, and academic specialists from the United States began to contribute their expertise to Diem in suppressing domestic insurgency.[61] These actions took place five years before any substantial troop commitment was made. To buttress the MSU mission, the American government began deploying police intelligence to Vietnam as early as 1955. These activities escalated even faster than troop deployments would later escalate.

Under the direction of the Office of Public Safety of the Agency for International Development—an important cog in the Rostowian conception of counterinsurgency—225 American police officials were in Vietnam, fostering, in AID's own words, "an atmosphere of confidence in law and order."[62] The Public Safety Program did in Vietnam what any good repressive apparatus would do at home; it kept tabs on everyone perceived as a threat to stability, it spied some (not as much as the CIA), and it operated political prisons, at least one of which (Con Son) has become notorious because of its inhumane qualities. Again as in domestic repression, AID's activities resulted not so much in controlling Com-

munists as it did in maintaining control over loyal opponents to the Thieu-
Ky regime, political descendants of Diem. In short, the role of police
operations in other countries adheres to the notions expressed by AID
director Bell in 1965:

> Plainly, the United States has very great interests in the creation and
> maintenance of an atmosphere of law and order under humane,
> civil concepts and control. When there is a need, technical assistance
> to the police of developing nations to meet their responsibilities
> promotes and protects these interests.[63]

Bell's reference to "nations" indicates that police repression existed
in more places than in Vietnam. Indeed it does. According to the only
information available—an operations report submitted to Congress once
a year—$29 million of the total budget of $35 million of OPS was spent
in Asia. The remainder was used in countries of high economic importance to the United States, particularly Brazil, the Dominican
Republic, Venezuela, Colombia, Guatemala, The Congo, Liberia, and
Ethiopia.[64] AID funds seem to have been used to repress antigovern-
ment riots in South Korea, help anti-Communists win elections in
Colombia and the Dominican Republic, supply Venezuelan police with
up-to-date police equipment, suppress labor agitation at Goodyear and
Gulf and Western plantations in the Dominican Republic, and pay for
the training of Firestone Rubber's security police in Liberia.[65] Here is the
internationalization of police repression in its most blatant form. When it
is supplemented by the presence of American soldiers around the globe—
in at least sixty-four countries in the early 1970s—the result is a most
extensive apparatus for violent repression. And the force is used. Between
1961 and mid-1966, the United States was directly involved in ten distinct
political situations in other countries, and indirectly involved in twenty-
seven others.[66]

The Weakness of Force

While repression at home is more often manipulative than violent,
repression abroad has an extensive violent side to it. This is in part
because such violence is less likely to backfire against American leaders.
As in domestic repression the ruling class did not carry out violent repression itself but contracted out that work to its own agents, in the international sphere repression is often carried out by local leaders, with American aid—though significant—covert and indirect. In such cases, any reac-
tions to violence will punish the local leaders and not the Americans, who
have covert contacts with alternative sets of leaders in most situations
anyway. Another American safety feature results from the geographical

distance of the population of the country in question from the United States. While the United States can reach these people, they have a hard time reaching the United States.

These considerations shed light on what is to some a puzzling aspect of American diplomacy. Enlightened liberal statesmen continually urge the United States to drop its flirtation with the reactionary and repressive anti-Communists and in turn support progressive social democrats. In the long run such a policy might be the best bulwark against world socialism, but there are very real reasons why it is not followed. The advantages of pursuing a policy of violent repression are simply too great. It is the short run in which political leaders are elected and policy makers promoted. Since resistance to violence requires extensive patience and organization, violence may produce spectacular short-run victories. *The resulting appearance of stability, combined with the isolation of American policy makers from reprisals, makes the use of violence against foreign threats to the democratic state too vital ever to be ignored.* To call for the United States to end its support of violence and repression overseas is to misunderstand the integral nature of that repression to the maintenance of a worldwide system of control, and hence continued rule at home.

Too often, there is a tendency to confuse force with influence. The United States has control over much force; in spite of its repeated appeals to an "antimilitaristic" heritage, it now commands the largest collection of violent instruments ever assembled by any country in the history of the world. But in spite of all that force, the ruling class cannot always realize its objectives. Matters have reached the point where the additional use of that force brings about less influence, not more.

There are limits, in other words, to the amount of repression in which a society can engage. Mostly, these limits are political; the Vietnamese simply refused to allow themselves to be repressed, and in so doing they made fools of Nixon and Kissinger and the strategy of saturation bombing. The way the war in Vietnam ended is proof that repression need not always work. The limits are also technological. That is, a society can use force only when it has sufficient means to do so. This can still be a problem for policy makers. When Vietnam was at its highest point of escalation, one policy maker recalled "the reluctance of certain governors to see their National Guard units federalized and shipped out of the state, for they were seriously concerned at the prospect of further urban rioting in the coming summer."[67] But this lack of resources is presumably temporary. It would not be that much of a problem for American leaders to build up a sufficiently efficient repressive force that could be used both home and abroad, though the cost would be enormous.

The real limits to repression lie not with the policy makers but with those whom they try to repress. Repression is designed to prevent people from developing their own politics, from realizing their own potential as citizens. This quest for a better political world can be temporarily halted by repression, but it can never be finally stopped, because freedom means to much to the unfree. So long as power is as inequitably distributed in the world as it is today, some people will always be trying to correct the balance. What do weapons and broadcasting mean in the face of that?

part three ☆ the future of repression

chapter
eight ☆
repression
and the
liberal state

Has Repression Been Increasing?

In his usual controversial way, Bertrand Russell said in 1956 that "There is, on the whole, much less liberty in the world now than there was a hundred years ago."[1] In doing so, he was taking part in a debate that has gone on for some time and contains a number of questions of interest to this discussion.

America is a liberal society, and from the point of view of liberalism, it would hardly be appropriate to admit to Russell's charge. Most liberals would be much more optimistic, noting that things are not perfect, of course, but that they have been getting better all the time. Milton Konvitz, for example, replies to Russell in this way:

I do not see that [Russell's proposition] at all. And certainly in the
United States, which Russell often has in mind when he lets loose his
poisoned barbs, there has been a progressive development of
human potentialities and values. . . . In the United States, in the
last twenty-five years, progress in civil liberties and civil rights
has been made at an unprecedented pace.[2]

Since liberty is being continually enhanced, it follows that one should
give his loyalty to the existing form of society and work to make it even
better.

Radicals are much more likely to support Russell. Liberty is on the
decline, they would maintain, because repression is continually on the
increase. Here is one radical, Tom Hayden, commenting on his Chicago
Eight trial of 1969: "The trial . . . symbolized the beginning of full-scale
repression in the United States. . . . Future histories will locate the sixties as the time when America's famous democratic pragmatism began
hardening into an inflexible fascist core."[3] Given that kind of repression,
it is foolish to work to improve the present democratic state. One must
instead work to overthrow it and replace it by something else.

Since the subject matter of this book is the very phenomenon Russell,
Konvitz, and Hayden are talking about, we should be able to contribute
to the debate in some fashion. Putting together everything that has been
said so far, has repression been increasing in America? The answer is that
neither Konvitz, Russell, nor Hayden is correct, that the question has
been asked in the wrong way, and that before an intelligent answer can
be given, the question must be revised.

Both Konvitz and Hayden talk about civil liberty, or its opposite, repression, as if these were elements that materialized out of thin air.
Causes are forgotten about. Hayden, for example, is so absorbed in his
own experience that he must consider it unique, yet there was nothing
startlingly new about his trial in Chicago. Judge Hoffman was no more
notoriously idiosyncratic than the man who tried the IWW in 1919 (also
in Chicago and also on a conspiracy charge), Judge (later Baseball Commissioner) Kenesaw Mountain Landis. Nor was Judge Hoffman more
severe; sentences for the IWW defendants were much higher. Nor was
the reaction of the defendants all that different. Some fled the country
(just as some of those prosecuted in the Smith Act cases did, after their
experience with another egocentrically repressive judge, Harold
Medina), while others went on to further radical activity. If repression is
basic to the society, certain methods, once found to work, will be used
repeatedly. The Chicago trial was such a method. Far from being a
unique event, it was part of a show that had a long run.

If Hayden suffers from a lack of historical perspective in his claims,

Konvitz fails to place civil liberties into a valid political perspective. His notion that freedom has made great gains since World War II is based upon the liberalism of the Supreme Court under Chief Justice Warren, when the Court invalidated a number of highly repressive acts and practices. Konvitz, however, was premature; the Warren Court by 1972 was a thing of the past, and the Court subsequently acquired a repressive majority. But even if that were not the case, he would be wrong. In order for the Supreme Court to declare a law unconstitutional, the law has to exist in the first place. One reason the Warren Court could invalidate repressive laws was because there were so many of them to invalidate. The activity of that Court could then be seen as a response to great encroachments on civil liberty rather than as something enhancing liberty.

Clearly, then, if this question about increasing repression is to be answered at all, it needs a little more thought than is usually given. It is essential to examine the reasons why the state engages in repression. For that, we already have an answer. In capitalist society, repression will continually be needed to reproduce existing power relationships. Since those relationships are based on inequality, on the exploitation of a majority of the population by a minority, some form of repression will always be needed, whether it be the manipulation of ideology or the use of state violence. Repression, in other words, is a constant, given the existence of capitalism (or any other form of class society). It will always be present; it will always be heavy. What varies over time, therefore, is not the amount of repression but the form repression takes.

It is difficult, if not impossible, to measure repression, for then every instance of it would have to be collected, given a weight, and thrown into a mixture resulting in some kind of formula. It would be more helpful to advance the notion that the amount of repression is a function of governmental output—that is, the more the state is called upon to do, the more repression there will be, because that is one of the things it does. What has to be traced over time is the changing nature of the state in capitalist society. As capitalism changed from one form to another, the kind of repression that was practiced changed as well. What is important is not to try to count the amount of repression, but to understand the different forms repression has taken in different eras.

The most striking quality of repression in the nineteenth century was its decentralized and amateurish nature. For one thing, almost no systematic ideological repression was taking place. At a time when capitalism was becoming fully developed, it did not have the verbal allegiance among groups harmed by it that it does now. One result was that a wide variety of anticapitalist movements flourished. The Populist party, while not socialist as some have claimed, contained elements highly critical of capitalism.⁴ There was also a native American socialist movement, which was to reach its highest influence in the early part of the twentieth century.

With nineteenth-century consciousness against capitalism fairly high, because there was no attempt to repress it, the last defense against dissent, violence, was used fairly heavily. But here again no systematic and coordinated campaign was undertaken. When the government acted at all, it was usually through local police forces, which were often inefficient and rank with corruption. There was at that time no federal police agency, and even state police bureaus were the creation of reformers who wanted to professionalize these matters, so that opposition existed to the idea that the states should engage in that kind of repression.⁵ When strikes needed breaking, or when disturbances needed stopping, businessmen, especially conservative ones, wished to rely either on their own private police or on detective agencies hired for specific tasks. One businessman, the notorious George Pullman, went so far as to have his company assume all the functions of government, even including those that the government itself stayed away from, such as religion.⁶ The town of Pullman, Illinois, was a society in miniature, all in private hands, and though it is an exaggerated development, it is a metaphor for the lack of state activity in this area through the latter part of the nineteenth century.

If conservative businessmen, particularly smaller manufacturing interests in the Midwest with parochial perspectives organized into the National Association of Manufacturers, opposed the creation of a coordinated state-directed repressive agency, it was their more liberal counterparts who advocated it. This is a crucial point that often is not understood. *The creation of a modern repressive state was the work of reformers*, liberals who had to fight vested interests in order to get what they wanted. Just as the first major wave of reform in the nineteenth century turned to state legislatures to regulate railroads and other industries, so these repressive reformers turned to the states to create state police agencies. Then, during the Wilson Administration, when reform of the economy meant federal regulatory action, the same kind of people supported federal repressive action. The modern repressive state did not just happen; it was brought into being, and those who worked to give it birth were cosmopolitan, liberal reformers who thought of themselves as progressives. This explains why a man who trained a whole generation of progressives to aid the state in extending its welfare privileges, Felix Frankfurter, could also be credited, as Melvyn Dubofsky shows, with developing the means for the destruction, through violent repression, of the Industrial Workers of the World (see chapter 1).⁷ It also explains why George Creel, one of Wilson's most liberal supporters, was also one of his most repressive (see chapter 5).⁸ Finally, it may also shed light on the fact that a number of progressives who were influential in the Wilson Administration were sympathetic to Mussolini's attempts to provide social control.[9]

In any case it is clear that the time period in which repression changed from being uncentralized and uncoordinated to professionalization were the years from 1912 to 1920. This was the time when, as James Weinstein has shown, a new corporate order emerged in the United States.[10] Groups such as the National Civic Federation were opposed to the twin "dangers" of Social Darwinism on the Right and socialism on the Left. They wished to fashion a new corporate order in which the state would play a major role, upholding the interests of capitalists as a class (rather than the selfish interests of any one particular capitalist), rationalizing the economy to make it run more smoothly, and providing welfare benefits to cut off potential revolutionary movements. This meant a highly expanded role for the state to play, one that challenged laissez faire directly, and one that corporate liberals were willing to concede. Capitalism was becoming too important to be left to the capitalists.

At the same time, the anticapitalist movements of the previous century were still strong. By 1912, it has been shown, there were 118,000 members of the Socialist party reading 323 different English and foreign-language publications. The election of socialist Meyer London to Congress in 1916 was icing on an electoral cake; actually, the SP held 1,200 offices in 340 cities, including 79 mayors in 24 different states, and, by 1918, 32 legislators throughout the country.[11] While the Socialist party was not overly militant in its opposition to capitalism, it was perceived by many in and out of power as if it were. In addition, it was not alone. The IWW, which represented a syndicalist alternative to capitalism, was strong through these years.[12] When, in 1917, a revolutionary government took power in Russia, it was supported by many in this country, and its emergence led eventually to the formation of two Communist parties to carry on the work here.[13]

The clash of these two forces—movements by reformers to change the nature of capitalism and the existence of a strong anticapitalist alternative—combined to produce the modern repressive state. It was formed at the same time that the modern corporate state was formed, during the presidency of Woodrow Wilson. Consider some of the unique "firsts" of the Wilson Administration. There was the appointment of George Creel to head the first important state propaganda machine in the United States, a major step to remedy the lack of any ideological repression. But Wilson's second term also saw the following developments in the area of violent repression: the appointment of J. Edgar Hoover to head the Radical Division of the Justice Department;[14] the first extensive use of deportation as a political weapon;[15] the first use of systematic, nationally

planned raids on the offices of local political groups;[16] the first use of the
Selective Service System (and the first arrests, like that of Eugene Debs,
for interfering with its functioning);[17] the first important racial pogroms
of the twentieth century (Omaha and Chicago) and the first coordinated
effort by police to develop a strategy for controlling them, including
systematic police work and the publication of riot-control manuals;[18] the
first intervention into the affairs of another country for purposes of containing an explicitly socialist revolution (because it was the first country
to have an explicitly socialist revolution);[19] the first attempt by the government to take over the hiring of undercover agents to report on "subversive activity" (such as Francis Morrow, who became the agent who
revealed the location of the Communist party's Bridgman, Michigan,
meeting, leading to one of the largest political raids in American history);[20] the first extensive recruiting of labor leaders by the state to work
directly in repressing their own memberships;[21] the creation of a Militia
Bureau to centralize somewhat the use of state and federal troops (the
Militia Bureau later became the National Guard);[22] and the first ruling
by the Supreme Court interpreting the First Amendment in such a way as
to provide a justification for governmental repression.[23] In addition, the
same period saw the federal trials of the IWW and the first general strike
in American history.

That is quite a record for one administration, especially one considered to be among the most liberal and progressive in American history.
It is not enough to suggest that it was the work of evil men, such as
Attorney General Palmer, or the result of the stresses induced by the first
World War. Neither of these explanations works, because the repressive
state was never dismantled after 1920. Although there were changes, and
although different presidents have approached repression in different
ways, the idea that the state should play the major role in repression has
not been challenged since those years. As chapter 4 has shown, some kind
of systematic repression has taken place in every decade since 1910,
under all kinds of administrations. This reaffirms the point made earlier
in this chapter that, ultimately, the question whether repression has been
increasing is unimportant. So long as the state plays a role in preserving
capitalism as an economic system, it will also play a role in preserving it
as a political system, and that role will be a repressive one.

Repression and Public Policy

Although the existence of repression has been a constant in American
history, we have at all times through this book made a distinction between ideological and violent repression. Would it not follow that what

does change over time is the relative proportion of one or the other? Are there some periods when violent repression is on the upswing and ideological repression is less important, and vice versa? These are much more fruitful questions when trying to account for changes in repression over time. They pose the problem of whether the types of repression are a matter of public policy, whether they can be changed from time to time. Since the use of state violence is the kind of repression that most people associate with the term, we can ask the question of what causes the amount of state violence to change.

One answer, particularly popular among newspaper columnists and among those in power, is that the tactics of dissenting groups "cause" violent repression. This point of view holds that as groups escalate the militancy of their tactics, they force the state to respond in turn. We have here a "backlash" theory. If groups would only behave in a civil fashion, there would be no violent repression; they are therefore urged not to engage in disruptive and militant activities because that will bring down the full power of the state not only against them but all right-thinking people as well. In one sense this argument is correct, for if there were no obvious and visible dissent, there would be no need for violent repression. But it is not an argument based on either the empirical evidence concerning the use of repression or the logic of the situation, as a few examples might make clear.

It has most often been the case that groups have been violently repressed, not when they have made their activities more militant and terroristic, but when they have softened their rhetoric and pursued mass-organizing techniques. The IWW, for example, was put on trial and raided at the point when it stopped talking about armed self-defense and began to stress its nonviolent aspects.[24] There is a logic to this. The continued escalation of rhetoric often comes about when a group has little mass support; revolutionary rhetoric then serves as a surrogate for the lack of anything else. Since little support exists, there is no real reason to repress because there is no real danger. In those periods, the role of the state is actually the opposite of trying to repress revolutionary rhetoric out of existence; in fact, through its undercover agents, *the state seeks to encourage the group to engage in more terroristic words*, not, as most people hold, in order to repress it later, but to isolate it from a mass base. If a group gets through that period and does begin to organize, then its rhetoric and tactics will become decidedly less militant and terroristic, as if almost by law. But it is at this point, when the state's policy of encouraging more militancy breaks down, that the use of violence by the state is substituted as a form of repression, because that is when the group is most dangerous. It is interesting that the most severe repression of the Black Panther party came, not after it carried guns into the California legislature, but after it instituted a program of free breakfasts, as it tried to build a mass base.

It should also be pointed out that there are times when the tactics of dissenting groups have nothing at all to do with repression. Because of its ties to the Soviet Union, the U.S. Communist party was continually under siege by the government of the United States. After the Second World War the government moved to destroy the party, and whether the CP adopted a popular-front line or an ultraleftist line was irrelevant. Thus, even in situations like this, the point holds that the state's decision to use repression is not determined by a dissenting group's tactics but by the state itself.

If the choice of tactics is not the cause of repression, if the cause lies with the state, then a second notion could be advanced to account for repression: that it is a matter of public policy. Different political parties—this argument would hold—have different attitudes toward the question of repression. While both Democrats and Republicans might be repressive, there is a real difference between them (the idea continues), and—unless one wishes to follow the disastrous policy of supporting quasi-fascistic leaders to make things worse so that they might get better—one should see this difference in degree as vitally important. Such an argument holds or implies that liberal Democrats will place more of their faith in ideological repression and long-term repressive strategies, while conservative Republicans are more likely to use the police and the military ("law and order") to get their way. Since the latter policy involves greater threats to human life, while the former presents more contradictions which can be exploited, Republicans will "cause" more violent repression to take place, so that their administrations should be avoided.

This is an interesting argument, which many people believe in, but it has flaws and, like the previous explanation, it falls apart on close examination. It is important here to stress that in one sense, repression is definitely *not* a question of public policy. No administration, whether Democratic or Republican, can ever end it; part of what it means to hold power in America is to be repressive. This point needs emphasis because the feeling is often expressed that a political leader like Nixon is "worse" than someone like Kennedy on the repression "issue." This is a variation of the theme of such liberals as Richard Harris, who argue that John Mitchell, Nixon's former attorney general, inaugurated a new era of repression, turning his back on the liberal tolerance of his predecessor, Ramsey Clark.[25] There is some truth to this argument; Nixon's administration was as repressive as they come, culminating in a governmental scandal of major proportions. But the Democrats, including Ramsey

Clark when he was attorney general, should not be forgiven their own repressive inclinations, including political trials they began.[26]

With the important exception of Richard Nixon, *the presidents most inclined to use the instruments of state violence for purposes of repression in this century have been liberal Democrats, not Republicans.* Why, to cite one rather typical yet good example, did Woodrow Wilson spend so much time sending Eugene Debs to jail, and why was it Warren Harding who freed him? The usual answer sees the repressive character of the Wilson Administration as irrelevant to Wilson himself, rather as the fault of men like his attorney general, A. Mitchell Palmer. Yet Wilson was quite aware of what his administration was doing. A much more likely explanation will result from a look more specifically at liberalism itself.

As has been mentioned, liberals are much more likely to use the state as an instrument of corporate rule, playing a "progressive" role in helping the economy resolve, at least temporarily, some of its contradictions. As the state takes on a more positive role in the affairs of the citizenry, it is only a small step to make the repressive role of the state more positive as well. Repression, particularly violent repression, is an aspect of liberalism, not something alien to it. A relationship exists between the party in power and the amount of violent repression, but it is the opposite of the one usually advanced, for as just noted, it is under the most liberal presidents that the most violent repression has taken place. No wonder liberal thinkers and politicians have such a difficult time understanding repression; they themselves are the "problem" they are trying to find.[27]

It follows that conservatives, who tend—at least in rhetoric, but also to some extent in practice—to rely on "individual initiative" rather than the state, will be reluctant to see the means of repression centralized in a federal bureaucracy in Washington. By and large this has been true. Eisenhower, for example, did not contribute as much to the growth of the FBI as John F. Kennedy (Robert Kennedy's objections to the FBI, by the way, were not that it was repressive, but that he was unable to control its repressive function; he wanted to be in charge of repression). And even though Eisenhower's attitude toward Senator Joseph McCarthy was characterized by inconsistencies, who among the liberal Democrats at the time was an outspoken opponent of that form of repression? (John Kennedy was in the hospital at the time of McCarthy's censure, conveniently writing *Profiles in Courage.*)

The general conservative reluctance to use the state as an instrument of repression was candidly discussed by one of the men most responsible for repression in the Nixon Administration, former Attorney General Richard Kleindienst. Asked if he felt that the liberal government of Pierre

Trudeau in Canada had overreacted to political kidnapings by invoking an Emergency Powers Law, Kleindienst replied:

> We conservatives would not have reacted that way. Cool-headed
> Wall Street types—like Nixon, Mitchell, and me—would never respond
> emotionally. We would be conservative in invoking extraordinary
> powers. You liberals, on the other hand, you don't anticipate crises; you
> worry about upsetting constituencies. When you do act, things
> have gotten so far out of hand that you have to overreact. That's why
> liberals are more likely to invoke emergency powers than
> conservatives.[28]

Granted that mere words do not a policy make, Kleindienst's point is definitely worth serious consideration.

Thus, we may have finally arrived at a valid explanation for changes in the amount of violent repression. There is an association between liberals in power and the amount of repression, but the existence of liberals in power does not cause it. The cause lies with something that happens when liberals are in power: it is during liberal administrations that hopes are raised, that people feel change can take place, that political struggles to make this a better world take place. Kleindienst is right; liberals raise expectations the political system cannot satisfy. When people expect those hopes to be translated into reality, and when they are not, people get angry and take to the streets. It is at that point that the violence of the state is brought against them. Kennedy's war on poverty program is the perfect example. It called for the "maximum feasible participation of the poor," encouraging the notion that real change might be possible. That hope ran squarely into entrenched power interests, and when the conflict became acute, the vested interests were listened to, not the poor. Is it any wonder that tremendous civil disorder followed in city after city, disorder that was met with the full police power of the state, with the dispatch of troops who used real bullets? Interestingly enough, after Nixon became president, the use of the National Guard once again declined decisively.

Violent repression is caused, then, by the amount of dissent, not by the tactics of the dissenters. And dissent takes place, by definition, when ideological repression no longer works, for if it were working, there would be no dissent. Once again, it is not the amount of repression that changes but the form. Repression of one sort or another always exists.

If it is true that there will be less violent repression under conservative Republicans, it does not follow that one should seek their election in order to hold down the amount of violent repression. Such a tactic would not reduce the amount of repression; it would simply shift the form. But much more important, such a tactic presupposes that violent repression is a "bad" thing that should be avoided. On the contrary, the use of state violence is neither "good" nor "bad" but a response to a situation. The situation is one of visible dissent. When the state meets dissent with repression, it is not showing its strength but its weakness; it reveals that it has been unable to convince people that this is the best of all possible worlds. False consciousness has broken down and people are seeking better lives for themselves. This is the importance of violent repression. If there are any tactical conclusions to be made from this analysis, they are that it is much preferable to seek the election of liberals, for then organizing and struggle can take place. When those attempts are met by violent repression, if one is prepared for such repression in advance, one can use the repression of the state to engage in further organizing. That is a difficult, sometimes impossible, action to carry out (the notion that repression helps the movement by radicalizing people is simply not true), but it is less difficult than trying to bring about change under conservative Republicans, when less violent repression exists, but so does less political interest, less activity, less excitement, and fewer visions of a better life.

Liberalism and Fascism

To point out a link between liberalism and violent repression is not to do something totally new. The relationship has been realized before; in fact, some have gone so far as to suggest that since liberals engage in state violence so much that there is a relationship between liberalism and fascism, which is the most repressive form of capitalism possible. Earlier in this chapter, we saw how Tom Hayden thought his trial revealed a "fascist core" in American democracy. He goes on to state that "the pursuit of imperialism created a necessity for repression, even fascism, to stabilize the home front."[29] Nor is Hayden the only person who uses the term with respect to America, as we shall see. The thought that American liberalism is repressive enough to contain a fascist potential is an interesting idea that should be summarized in detail, for it is an incorrect notion, as well as a dangerous one, and if the proper relationship between liberalism and repression is to be understood, this notion must be dealt with directly.

Interestingly enough, it was in Germany that the first important statement of this problem was made. During Hitler's rise to power, the so-called Frankfurt school had addressed itself to the question of fascism. In 1934, for example, Herbert Marcuse published an essay in which he dealt with philosophical fascism's opposition to liberalism.[30] Marcuse was puzzled by this opposition, for, he claimed, if one looked at liberalism in practice rather than the ideals of 1789, there was very little difference between liberalism and the new ideology of totalitarianism. Did fascism believe in a strong nation? So did liberalism. Was the new ideology against Marxism? So was liberalism. Both, moreover, believed in "eternal natural laws of social life." Finally, just as fascism worshiped leadership, "The idea of dictatorship and of authoritarian direction of the state is . . . not at all foreign to liberalism." According to Marcuse, liberalism was the ideology of developing capitalism. As capitalism reached the monopoly stage, it needed stability, a strong state. Hence fascism grows out of liberalism and is not something alien to it. "It is liberalism that 'produces' the total-authoritarian state out of itself, as its own consummation at a more advanced stage of development."[31]

Marcuse was not alone in these views. His colleagues Max Horkheimer and T. W. Adorno shared them as well. Though published some time ago, thoughts such as these have been influential among left-wing intellectuals since the rise of Hitler. Yet there is a problem here. Germany was not a liberal society; the development of capitalism there was quite different from what it was in England and the United States.[32] And, in addition, the philosophers of the Frankfurt school were writing about other philosophers, not politicians. Marcuse's critique never mentions Hitler, for example. Thus, Göran Therborn is probably correct when he points out that Marcuse, Horkheimer, and Adorno had little practical understanding of actual politics and therefore understood the fascist experience poorly at best.[33] The questions of the relationship between liberalism and fascism were not settled by these men at that time.

Closer to home, charges of fascism have been made periodically, both by political activist groups and by various intellectual commentators. During the 1930s, the idea that fascism was a real possibility generally referred not to the liberalism, which was then in power (with few exceptions, the American Left supported a liberal administration during the New Deal), but to the extreme Right and the various neopopulist movements that contained strong elements of anti-Semitism. From Sinclair Lewis's *It Can't Happen Here* to Arthur Schlesinger, Jr.,'s popular history of the period, fascism was a threat, but it was liberalism itself that was the greatest defense against it.[34]

This pattern began to change in the 1960s. The Black Panther party, for example, frequently made the charge that its members lived in a fascist society—a charge made while the Democratic party was in power, led by a man who had been shaped and promoted by the New Deal. Student groups, too, threw the term "fascist" about fairly loosely, and instead of replying to them in a rational way, many conservative adults instead threw the term back at them. The students themselves, the charge went, were "left-wing fascists" because they were trying to deny free speech to others by shouting them down and obstructing their freedom.[35] By 1968, the word fascism was again popular in American political discourse.

A different approach to the question of liberalism and fascism came out of a provocatively titled essay by Bertram Gross called "Friendly Fascism: A Model for America."[36] Gross argued that the welfare state, one of liberalism's proudest contributions to the art of governance, contained the potential for a fascist society. But, according to Gross, this would come about, not through violence, since that seemed to be on the wane, but through the social control mechanisms that the welfare state had created. Thus, this fascism would be "friendly"; through the rhetoric of beneficence, it would impose order, controlling people through the provision (or nonprovision) of the rewards that the welfare state could hand out. And it would also be liberal, for the threat would come, not from reactionaries sending in the police, but from social engineers who would in all likelihood be members of the Democratic party, if they had any politics at all.

Given all these points of view, the first task in trying to make sense out of this problem is to define what fascism is. This is not easy, for the term has so many polemical connotations that a variety of vested interests have grown up around various definitions. Socialists, for example, generally see in fascism a capitalism run rampant. The Communist International in 1933 expressed it this way: "Fascism is the unconcealed terrorist dictatorship of the most reactionary, chauvinistic, and imperialistic elements of finance capital."[37] Conservatives have an alternate view: fascism is the triumph of the vulgar masses against the finer values of civilization, a continuation of the French Revolution by other means, an expression of the baseness of mass society.[38] Not surprisingly, liberals have defined the term their way as well. Fascism to them is the denial of the liberal ethic: due process, parliamentarianism, free speech, pluralism, the multiparty system.[39] It should be clear, then, that *fascism serves an important political purpose; it permits each major ideology of the twentieth century to define itself by establishing fascism as its antithesis.* We are the opposite of fascism, all seem to be saying. In actuality, none of them is totally right and none totally wrong. Fascism is a hybrid form of polity, borrowing freely from the liberal, conservative, and social traditions. But an examination of its key characteristics reveals that it has borrowed most from conservatism and liberalism, least from socialism. That is why Marcuse is partially correct; there does seem to be a relationship between liberalism and fascism. They do have elements in common. But it is a mistake to conclude from these common elements that the one will evolve into the other.

The most important characteristics of European fascism, the elements that tie together the Italian and German experience, are four in number: a heightened antiradicalism, an excessive reliance on means of controlling the population, a state-directed though private (capitalist) economy, and an emphasis on the lack of dogma, leading to a worship of the spontaneous and the irrational.

Antiradicalism is the basis of all fascism, its reason for existence. It goes far to explain anti-Semitism in Germany, because of Hitler's identification of Jews with radicals. Fascism is explicitly counterrevolutionary, especially when it is a movement, before it takes state power. Both Mussolini's and Hitler's movements rose to prominence because of a general antipathy to Marxism on the part of a number of well-off Italians and Germans who were afraid to express their prejudices as vividly. Nolte is correct when he says that ". . . without Marxism there is no fascism . . . ,"[40] for the one naturally precedes the other. But fascism did not invent anticommunism; it borrowed it, both from liberals and conservatives, to win its way to power. Thus, Dante Germino notes that in the struggle between Mussolini and the Italian Communists,

> . . . support came to the Fascists from certain industrialists and wealthy landowners, who viewed Fascism as the last bulwark against Communism. Not a few liberals were content, also, for the state to sit back and let the Fascists teach left-wing radicals a lesson.[41]

The difference is one of degree. Fascism was much more vehement in its antiradicalism than the traditions it was borrowing from, more willing to take extralegal and illegal action to accomplish the same end. But the end was the same, and that is something often overlooked, which should not be.

Second, fascism means an intensification of the means by which the population is controlled. This is recognized by all writers on "totalitarianism" as central to their definition, and the notion finds its complete expression in the monumental work of Hannah Arendt.[42] To her, however, the control is not all one-sided; the "masses" seek to be controlled because it gives their lives meaning and purpose. At this point precise analysis becomes impossible; who can tell whether the chanting mob is expressing its own opinion or simply being manipulated? In either case, however, there is a strong dose of false consciousness. The essence of fascism is to produce as much false consciousness as possible. In the perfect fascist system, the great mass of people come to believe so firmly in the antiradical policies of the government that they take much law enforcement upon themselves; they spy on each other, become informers, and engage in violent vigilante actions. They are encouraged in this by all the repressive instruments that the state can manage, but particularly by more intensive variants of the kinds of activities described in this book. Ideological and violent repression are relied on so heavily that the result is what many writers call "terror," systematic attempts to coerce the population into its false consciousness.

The third feature necessary for a fascist order is a private enterprise economy under some form of state direction. Though fascism had some historical associations with socialism (Mussolini was editor of *Avanti* and the German party did include the word socialist in its title), in actual practice, both types of fascism relied upon capitalism. True, fascism was far removed from the conservative tradition (the original liberal tradition) of atomized units operating without central control. There is no question but that in all fascist states private economic decisions are tempered by considerations of the state. But, then, so is modern liberalism, where state intervention is also expected and rationalized. Reviewing all the books on the subject, it is hard to dispute Franz Neumann's, one of the earliest, which documented the extensive series of relationships that existed between Hitler's movement, huge corporations, and the needs of private capital.[43] The monopoly exercised by the fascists in the political sphere was related to monopoly control of the economy by a few important private firms.

The final characteristic of fascism is a deemphasis on dogma, leading to a worship of the spontaneous and the irrational. Mussolini said it well: "No Dogma! Discipline suffices." Or, "My program is action, not thought." Or, "We think with our blood."[44] Similarly, as Neumann points out, leaders of Hitler's Germany continually sacrificed ideology to practice. Neumann in fact goes further by claiming that National Socialism was guided by no political thought at all. Mussolini, he suggests, at least had a tradition of pragmatism to fall back upon, while the German fascists did not even have that. "No known absolutistic or counterrevolutionary theory fits National Socialism, because . . . it has no theory of society."[45]

If these four characteristics are the common elements in the two major fascist experiences, it is easy to see why the claim that liberalism has much in common with fascism developed. Both the liberal and conservative traditions share all four elements. Both are antiradical, specifically anti-Communist, and in practice often try to outdo each other in asserting their hostility to the revolutionary Left. Both are ideologies that have been associated with the holding of political power; therefore, both have had to rationalize the importance of control mechanisms, including ideological and violent repression. Both are associated with different forms of capitalism, and each in its own way has recognized the necessity for state intervention, though here the liberal tradition more resembles the fascist experience than the conservative. Finally, liberalism is clearly associated with a lack of dogma and a belief in pragmatism (hence, as mentioned above, the identification many pragmatic liberals had with

Mussolini in his early years of rule[46]) and the conservative tradition has contributed much to the ideology of the irrational. Thus, although fascism borrowed from Sorel, an irrationalist who grew out of the Marxist tradition, it also was inspired, at least in part, by others whose irrationalism was more clearly within a conservative purview: Rousseau, Nietzsche, Pareto, Junger, Bonald, and others.[47]

Fascism has elements in common with both liberalism and conservatism because they are all political forms of capitalism. It is because all three ideologies rationalize societies that allow wealth and power to be concentrated into the hands of few that antiradicalism becomes policy, that social control over the majority of the population is needed, that the economy remains in private hands, and that systemic modes of thinking are discredited. But there are differences. Conservatism is associated with a form of capitalism that no longer exists. Liberalism is associated with a state capitalism that developed in countries with a tradition of representative democracy. Fascism, then, is caused, not as Marcuse said, because of the needs of monopoly capitalism, but because of the needs of monopoly capitalism in specific countries with specific (antiliberal) traditions. It is quite possible to have monopoly capitalism without fascism, as in England, Sweden, and the United States. There will, in those countries, be antiradicalism, social control, and the other elements of fascism, but there is no reason why there need be fascism itself.

This is what finally discredits the notion that liberal societies will evolve into fascist ones. That correlation has simply never worked out in practice. Fascism has developed where the liberal tradition was weakest. It is poor social and historical analysis that transposes from one country's experience to another's and ignores the traditions that shaped the experience in each instance. What happened in Germany was due to particular German conditions: the delayed nationalism; the Junker domination of the country until relatively late; the defeats in wars; the particular intellectual traditions. But the primary point of difference is that Germany did not have a tradition of liberalism that affected the development of its form of capitalism. When a severe capitalist crisis emerged, there were few checks upon the emergence of fascism.

There is another reason to question the notion that liberal societies will turn themselves into fascist ones. Although that hypothesis sounds like a particularly "militant" one, those who have advanced it have not always been political activists. This was true of the intellectuals in the Frankfurt school, for example. There is a very good reason that the fascism hypothesis is often associated with those who are not engaged in active work seeking political change. If one believes that one's country is going to turn fascist, there is little reason to do anything about it. Fascism is a force of such power that one might as well not try to head it off, since one's efforts are bound to be fruitless. Thus, the fascist hypothesis becomes extremely self-defeating, a rationalization for inaction, ultimately, a means of quiescence. Those who are active in the anticapitalist struggle must believe that their efforts will produce real change, and that belief is incompatible with the notion of an emerging fascism. Put another way, those who see fascsim as inevitably coming out of the repressive potential of the liberal democratic state give more time to the rulers of that state than they actually have; they give them more credit than they deserve. It is true that there are similarities between the fascist experience in Europe and what has occurred in the United States, but it is just as true that anticapitalist movements have the potential to prevent anything like that from happening. Why assume that one side will win and not the other? Those who are disillusioned by the amount of state violence in the United States are those who had illusions about the democratic state in the first place. If we understand the causes of repression, particularly that it is used out of desperation, we are one step closer to understanding how a nonrepressive society can be built.

The Uniqueness of Repressive Liberalism

If liberalism is not a prelude to fascism, it is, as most of this book has tried to show, a repressive system in its own way. Liberalism is very much an ideology of social control and repression, and for those who are the victims of repression, it matters little whether the guns that shoot at them are in liberal or fascist hands. But a proper understanding of repression in America means that liberalism must be understood on its own terms and not be continually compared to something quite alien to it.

Those who see a fascist potential in the liberal state are perhaps suggesting that American liberalism will reach the point where it will become so repressive that a qualitative change in the nature of the society will take place. The instruments of violence will come to be relied on so much that a "police state" will result in which the usual liberties associated with democracy will become totally suspended.[48] This is a different, and much more valid, argument than the previous one. It asks whether capitalism is going through changes that require ever more social control, whether in the face of the delegitimizing of its institutions it becomes increasingly forced to reveal the violent potential that holds it together.[49] In order to deal with such ideas, it is necessary to talk briefly about the uniqueness of liberalism as a form of social control.

There are many competing definitions of liberalism and of the liberal state, but the essence of all of them eventually comes down to two phenomena. A liberal society is one in which equality is upheld to be a general ideal and an attempt is made to assert that there are certain areas of freedom with which the government is not supposed to tamper (areas that change from one period to another). Viewed in the context of a revolutionary change from feudalism to capitalism, it is easy to see how liberalism was an almost natural ideology for the new order. As Max Weber noted:

> The modern capitalist concern is based inwardly above all on calculation. It requires for its survival a system of justice whose workings can be rationally calculated, at least in principle, according to fixed general laws. . . . Judicial formalism enables the legal system to operate like a technically rational machine. Thus it guarantees to individuals and groups within the system a relative maximization of freedom, and greatly increases for them the possibility of predicting the legal consequences of their actions.[50]

Equality thus came to mean that anyone with the right skills could become a capitalist, and freedom was defined as the enterprise of making money.

But there was a problem. Liberalism was more than an ideology; it was also a political system with very real class differences. Liberal society worked best when only the class in power received its benefits. As Andrew Hacker pointed out, the notion of freedom was freely granted to dissenting members of the upper class, to "the Harvard atheist of good family, the transcendental rebel with manners and breeding, the Utopian socialist who paid heed to the rules of gentlemanly intercourse." But when claims for freedom came from others in the society, particularly from the downtrodden, freedom easily became repression:

> The civil liberties of the trade union organizer in Colorado, of the Negro in Alabama, of the disabled factory worker in Pennsylvania or the nonconformist professor of economics in a small Midwestern college—these persons were not considered proper material for defense. Had the ruling class sought, say, to put its power behind the radicals of the I.W.W. it would have so endangered its foundation of deference that the existence of the class itself would come into question.[51]

The history of liberalism has been a struggle between those who controlled the society and found the tenets of a limited liberal state perfectly to their liking and those who wished to share in the blessings of liberal society but were not allowed to do so (or were permitted to do so only after a struggle) because they had no base of private property from which to act. For this reason, many of the victories of liberal society were won through the martyrdom of groups that were not liberal. The IWW, for example, a syndicalist and socialist organization, did more to establish the right to speak freely on a street corner than any other group in

American history, and in so doing, it contributed to the development of a society with which it was at war. The same is true for a variety of other groups, from the early CIO to the Student Nonviolent Coordinating Committee (SNCC). Before being able to engage in the struggle for their goals (higher wages, an elimination of segregation) they first had to establish the right to organize, a right that those who held power in liberal society always had.

These convulsions shook liberal society to its roots, for liberal society worked best when no demands were made on it. As Hacker perceptively has noted, "The basis of power in liberal democracy has traditionally been deference to a ruling class."[52] Deference, however, is an adjustment to powerlessness, nothing else. When people choose to remain powerless, they refuse to claim the benefits of liberal society for themselves. But what happens when oppression is no longer accepted, when the demands are made? Then the fundamental contradiction of liberal society asserts itself. Liberalism can work only by being restrictive, particularly to those in power. Each attempt to extend the principles of liberalism to a power-less group has been convulsive. *Liberalism, in other words, works only when it does not work and does not work only when it works.*

Often groups have made very real gains from these convulsions, though only after long battles with many casualties. The right to speak on a corner in San Diego is now assured (so long as not too many are doing it and they are willing to obey police regulations), unions can organize in the plant and can push for higher wages, formal segregation has come to an end, and black people have a legal right to eat and sleep in any business establishment. These were important victories that should not be denigrated, but they all fell short of creating any basic change in the society. In all cases, those who held power were willing to concede on specific issues in order that they could hold onto what was most dear to them: the very power to concede. For having the power to concede implies having the power *not* to, and it is power that is the most scarce resource for most people in liberal society and the most precious resource for a few.

Repression and power are intimately related. So long as a group demands something that does not involve changes in the distribution of power, bargaining and cooperation can take place. But when a demand is for power itself, those who have power will give some of it up only with the greatest reluctance, only when not relinquishing some of it will pro-duce even worse consequences. Repression, then, will exist in liberal society as long as power is not equitably distributed. If those who do not have power make no demands for it, ideological repression is working well. When they do make demands, violent repression is the likely prompt response. Therefore, the question of whether or not a new repressive stage in the history of liberal society has been reached is really a question involving the demands that people are making.

It is true, then, that liberal society has reached a period of crisis, but only because liberalism is always in a period of crisis. It is a compromise system, filled with so many difficulties that it cannot possibly work without trouble. Liberalism is based on an agreement between those in power and those who are not. The powerless agree to allow control of the society to remain in the hands of those who have access to the crucial economic positions, in return for being granted (1) the appearance of power, through elections and other symbols of popular control and participation; (2) actual power over some of the less important aspects of the society, such as city politics (as long as the decision makers at that level make their decisions within the framework of liberal democracy); and (3) certain benefits, such as highways, welfare, housing, designed to "prove" that the system really does work in people's interests after all. For a time the compromise can work. As long as things move along well, without fiscal crises, inflation, higher taxes, wars, people can accept their lack of power, since they feel that they are getting quite a bit for it, anyway.

But things do not always move along well. The fact is that most people are powerless and know it full well. Let a crisis emerge and unhappiness rises to the surface quickly, often expressing itself in the form of reactionary or racist movements, but also as populist and sometimes even leftist movements. It is at those times when the institutions of power in liberal society, unable to meet the demands made upon them, which are usually that they share some of their power, respond instead repressively. When they do—when the university calls in the troops, the hospital director refuses to deal with the neighborhood, the day-care center turns people away—then the process of delegitimization sets in. The institution no longer can claim neutrality, that it only serves its clients. It is revealed as part of a system of power, as serving those in power and not those out of it. The stage is set for institutional confrontation on the one hand and more repression on the other.

Since this process of increasing delegitimization was intense throughout the 1960s, it has led many people to ask whether the United States must inevitably become a police state, since the response to institutional confrontation so often involves force. We are now in a position to answer such a question. It is really a question about the strength of the dissenting movement, for if that is strong, the police will be called out to quash it. If it is not strong, there will be no need for the police. But we have already seen that movements are weakest when ideological repression is strongest. Therefore, what is often forgotten, but must be kept in mind, is that *the most repressive system possible in America would not be a police state but its very opposite, one in which there were no police because there was nothing to police,* everybody having the same lack of ideas. Fortunately, that has not occurred. Dissent has been visible, and when it is, the state responds with force. But that does not mean that a police state will arise. It means that challenges are being made.

If the movement becomes so strong that a situation of revolutionary ferment appears possible, the dosage of force needed to put down the dissatisfaction will increase to where it could be called a police state. But this will never be permanent. Either the dissenting forces will win or they will go back to being quiet for a while. But the use of force by the state is a response, and it is important to keep in mind what provokes it.

This kind of analysis gives a good deal of attention to the role of dissenting groups, for it is they who eventually determine the amount of violent repression. It also suggests that a more pertinent question than whether a police state will emerge is whether a nonrepressive society can be built. That question, like the other one, will be answered by those who are trying to change American society into something better than it is now.

chapter
nine ☆
building a
nonrepressive
society

Obviously, to accept the analysis presented in this book is to come away fairly disquieted about the nature of American democracy. It is not easy to accept the conclusion that one lives in a repressive society. Those who do not accept this have two options. One is to deny that America is as repressive as this account has made it out to be. But to do that means to account somehow for all the examples of repression that have existed in the United States—and that is not an easy thing to do. One could claim that they were "accidental," not the essence of the "real" America. But explanations based on accident do not take us far, expecially when there have been so many accidents. Repression, as the first seven chapters of this book have tried to show, is very "real," an important aspect of liberal society that most political scientists have chosen to ignore.

Completing the Liberal-Democratic Revolution

Liberalism, as chapter 1 suggested, was at one time both a revolutionary and a reactionary doctrine, depending upon whether one wished to emphasize its liberating or repressive component. Those who were challenging the old order around them used the language of freedom to engage in their revolution. Once they reached power, they used the language of order to keep themselves there. Both languages were part of liberalism, hence its contradictory character. Since that time, the needs of order have continually taken precedence over the needs of freedom as groups have tried to share power in the liberal state. The question then arises of whether it is possible for liberalism to recapture its revolutionary character; whether the ideals of freedom and equality could again take precedence over the ideals of order and stability. Can the liberal revolution be completed? Is genuine liberalism (free thought and expression, a true nonrepressive society) possible within liberal society? Is democracy possible in a democracy?

For answers to these questions, we must go back to the origins of liberal society, where an analysis that has been made by C. B. MacPherson is extremely helpful. MacPherson shows that liberalism and democracy were originally very different things. A liberal society was one that was governed by the idea of the marketplace, where the principle of freedom of choice was made the basis of the ideology. This society was not democratic. In fact, the majority of the people living in liberal societies such as England did not participate with free choice in the market. Even as late as John Stuart Mill, there was a fear of democracy, as Mill took steps to protect the rights of the powerful from the masses of people. But once the notion of free choice was introduced, it became apparent that the democratic state—defined as one in which all the people, even the poorest, participate—would be demanded. When the demand came, some interesting things happened. Democracy did not have to come about within the liberal state. Any kind of state can have mass participation. But democrats used the rhetoric of liberalism, free choice, to demand democracy. As MacPherson put it:

> . . . democracy was demanded, and was admitted, on competitive liberal grounds. Democracy was demanded, and admitted, on the ground that it was unfair not to have it in a competitive society. . . . Democracy had been transformed. From a threat to the liberal state it had become the fulfillment of the liberal state. . . . The liberal state fulfilled its own logic. In so doing, it neither destroyed democracy nor weakened itself; it strengthened both itself and the market society. It liberalized democracy while democratizing liberalism.[1]

This is an extremely important point, because it suggests that liberalism and democracy need not go together.

It is quite possible to argue that those who sought to extend participation (democracy) in a system based upon the marketplace (liberalism) have now been proved incorrect. Each time there has been a confrontation between genuine democratic sentiment and the needs of order and stability, the latter have triumphed over the former. Struggles to extend participation have won the right to vote (though not without a struggle), resulting in one form of participation. But as masses of people have sought to extend their participation to institutions that dominate their lives—to their schools and hospitals, to the marketplace itself, to corporations and foundations, to the making of foreign policy—they have been stymied by the very ideology of liberal society. Here is former Yale University President Kingman Brewster responding to student demands: "Perhaps the greatest contribution we can make is to reaffirm in the face of those who would seek to coerce conformity that practical progress relies most of all on the evolution of the better by the survival of the fittest among ideas tossed in the blanket of debate, dispute and disagreement."[2] (Brewster is currently U.S. Ambassador to Great Britain.) Thus, Social Darwinism returned to Yale, only this time it was in the realm of ideas, not economic forces. The point, however, was the same: the analogy was designed to give legitimacy to certain ideas by discrediting others, the former being the ones that were able to drive the latter out of existence. By using the principles of liberalism to nullify the principles of democracy (student participation in defining their own lives), Brewster indicated the tension that still exists between these ideals.

In American society at the present time, the demands of democracy and of liberalism are incompatible. If people were able to participate in the institutions that affect their lives, the marketplace criterion that key decisions are to be left in private hands would have to be abolished. Genuine democracy requires control and power, and these are withheld from the majority of people in liberal society. In those activities called "public," there is the right to vote. But this right is not freely exercised because of the tremendous ideological repression associated with making the vote turn out acceptably to those in power. In those activities called "private," there is not even the pretense of control. Institutions of private power in the United States are based on the notion that those who have contact with them will have little or no power in determining how they are run. From this fact stems repression, because repression is a mechanism designed to prevent people from exercising control over the institutions that affect their lives.

It follows from this that the way to complete the democratic revolution is to go beyond liberalism. A genuine, popularly based democratic system can take place only when no centers of private power are consciously removed from popular control. Guaranteeing democracy means the creation of a popular, democratically run, socialist society, one in which the idea of democracy would be extended from the political realm to the economic, and established in such a way that a meaningful choice will exist. It is not that one has to choose between liberalism and democracy (or socialism), that in order to obtain equality and popular control it is necessary to sacrifice the civil liberties associated with liberalism. That is not a false dichotomy: it is a backward one. It actually works the other way around. Civil liberty and genuine choice and control presuppose a democratic socialism. Because it does not have such a system, American liberalism is continually forced to deny its libertarian heritage and engage in repression. Socialism, then, will not only complete the democratic revolution; it will also complete the liberal one. If it gives popular participation, it will also give civil liberty, for the social conditions of repression will no longer exist. There will be nothing to repress because the system will be made to accept popular control, not to destroy it.

A Nonrepressive America?

One cannot sit around and wait for a nonrepressive America to come into being. It has to be built, and it will take a political movement to do the building. Whether such a movement is in existence at this time capable of doing that building is a huge question that cannot be satisfactorily dealt with here. What it is possible to do, in closing this book, is to indicate what such a movement is *not*, where such a movement might develop, and what such a movement might accomplish.

In order to build a nonrepressive society, it is necessary to have a nonrepressive movement. Marxist-Leninist parties, based on either sectarian schism, loyalty to a socialist country somewhere else, the personality of a leader, or extreme hierarchical organization, cannot bring about a participatory socialism, because they are not participatory themselves. A Leninist model, however modified, is not the place to look for the seeds of a nonrepressive society. Those movements have taken on many of the characteristics of the society they are trying to change, and it is quite plausible, therefore, to be skeptical of their ability to do it.

Instead we must look, not at the traditional left-wing parties, but at the struggles of masses of people engaged in obtaining for themselves some control over their own lives.[3] This is particularly important; since repression is a method of preventing people from gaining power, those who are trying to do so constitute the logical place to begin the search for the origins of a nonrepressive society. Nor is this an impossible task, for the last few years have seen tremendous amounts of dissatisfaction among Americans with their powerlessness. Whether it be middle-class youth looking to arts and crafts in order to create community, Black Panthers trying to start breakfast programs, welfare recipients organizing to abolish or change the welfare system, lawyers building law communes, doctors allying with neighborhood residents to push for control of health care, parents opening up locked schools in an effort to obtain education for their children, mothers demonstrating for day-care centers, students building counter-educational institutions, or native Americans taking over unused islands, the dissatisfaction with a society that leaves most of its members powerless has become reasonably acute. *It is in these attempts by people to win back for themselves the power that they should have had as human beings that the possibility of a nonrepressive society most clearly asserts itself.* Although highly publicized demonstrations declined during the 1970s, less visible attempts to challenge the system probably increased, as more and more people realized that the business of building a nonrepressive society is serious and long-term.

What is taking place, to give it a name, because it deserves one, can be characterized as institutional illegitimacy. To increasingly large sectors of the American population, institutions that were previously accepted as normal and inevitable are being subjected to fairly severe inspection and are being found wanting. Out of that dissatisfaction have come two general responses, each important in the building of a nonrepressive society.

One response is the creation of counterinstitutions, involving a group of people who "drop out" and establish their own methods of obtaining a goal. Free schools, communes, and the renewed emphasis on arts and crafts are examples of this trend. Because a certain amount of personal choice is required in order to engage in this type of response, such activity can be afforded only by people from relatively comfortable backgrounds. Therefore, the creation of alternative institutions has had a middle-class bias from the beginning, which makes it relatively easy for movements of this sort to be rendered harmless through cooption. Nonetheless, the existence of alternative institutions throughout the country is an indication of how much even relatively well-off people find oppressive their lack of power and lack of self in the society.

A second response to institutional illegitimacy, more often associated with poorer groups, occurs when a group organizes within the institution to press for its goals through political confrontation, hoping to demonstrate the institution's illegitimacy to others. Community-control struggles, whether over education, health, or day care, are examples of this trend. Here, too, are difficulties. If the dissatisfied people ask for too much, they remain utopian and cannot deliver anything to relieve the unhappiness, thereby finding themselves isolated from the needs of their community. If they ask for too little, they may be able to deliver, but only as reformists who postpone dissatisfaction for a while but do nothing to relieve it. The existence, then, of institutional confrontation does not guarantee success, but it does mean that people who have gotten very little out of the society are no longer prepared to accept being treated as clients and want to determine for themselves what will happen to them and their children.

A consequence of these two responses is that people are questioning the nature of capitalist society. "Socialism" is no longer the dirty word it was; even an occasional member of Congress is willing to apply the label. Critiques of the capitalist mode of production and its costs come in increasing numbers from academia and the media.[4] A general sense exists—not only in America but throughout the world—that the old clichés have been bypassed and that new solutions must be developed to meet the contradictions of advanced capitalist societies. In this atmosphere, the question of whether a nonrepressive society can be built becomes askable.

Why have American institutions become illegitimate to so many in recent years, even cutting across class lines? The answer lies in the serious lag between the performance of these institutions and the expectations people bring to them, and because of the general rapidity of change, which continually outstrips any erstwhile balance effected between them. Gaps between expectations and performance are produced in part by economic fluctuations, because in periods of recession there is a "fiscal crisis of the state," leading to the retraction of benefits that were once promised. But there is more to it than that, for even in periods of prosperity, American capitalism cannot deliver what it promises, because there are manifest contradictions between professed goals (equality, freedom, democracy, community) and vested interests (racism, class stratification, private power, profit making, bureaucratic decision making). A society that stimulates certain desires and constantly fails to satisfy them is one that will permanently have to deal with institutional illegitimacy and the resulting responses to it.

Given both a capitalist economy that results in economic cycles and a government unable to confront private power satisfactorily, illegitimacy is a relatively permanent feature of American politics. It is not illegitimacy that has gone up and down over time, but its opposite. In other words, the only thing that changes is the consciousness of the population, not the nature of the institutions. Periods of seeming health, then, when people accept and are satisfied with their institutions, are not really healthy at all, but are periods of less-than-overt repression and of promises that are believed.

Thus, we reach an ironic conclusion. *The very facts that cause repression—the nature of class society and the gaps between what people are told and what they actually experience—contain within them the seeds for overcoming repression.* A nonrepressive society will necessarily have to grow out of a repressive one. There would be no dissatisfaction with capitalism if capitalism satisfied everyone. This does not, however, mean that the existence of dissatisfaction guarantees the eventual victory of a new popular consciousness which renders repression unnecessary. Indeed, repression has often been successful in stymieing these movements, in affecting their development, in making it difficult for them to succeed. But the fact that both repression and potential liberation come from the same place means that a struggle is going on between the forces of repression and those of popular control, a struggle that somebody is going to win. If it is the former, we can expect more of what we have now. If it is the latter, we can speculate on what kind of nonrepressive society could be built.

There is no way to predict whether the seeds of a nonrepressive society, which very much do exist, will bloom into something resembling a flower. A nonrepressive society is not "inevitable," something to just wait around for. But the desire of people not to be repressed, although restricted at the moment to a minority of the American population, is a very powerful desire. If it can be translated into reality, it could bring into being a truly liberal and democratic society, one that could become so by transcending the limitations of both traditional liberalism and democracy.

The important point is that a nonrepressive society need not be a utopia completely unrelated to the present society. To imagine a nonrepressive society, we do not have to consult our imagination; we can examine the world around us. What needs to be changed (at least at first) is not the institutions and the technologies that exist but the way in which they exist. The problem with television, for example, is not that the screen is small or that there is something "wrong" with the idea of broadcasting pictures. The trouble with television is simply that it serves the few and oppresses the many. If it were turned around, if television helped people understand the world instead of mystifying it for them, it would no longer be a force for repression but would have a potential for liberation. Therefore, all that needs to be done to obtain a picture of what a nonrepressive society would be like is to take all the repressive practices of America and change the nature of their beneficiaries. The resulting vision, far from being utopian, would indicate the enormous effect that a change in class society could produce.

Imagine, if you will, a society in which:

• television, instead of advertising in a repetitive manner, with the lowest denominator of intelligence, products that kept people slaves to consumerism, were to explain technology in a language that would demystify it for most people;

- prisons, as we know them, did not exist because the repressive dimensions of "crime"—drugs, poverty, psychological confusion—did not exist;
- the purpose of collective living arrangements, unlike the nuclear family of today, was to strengthen and liberate people, not to enable them to conform to self-defeating and unnatural sex roles;
- athletics contributed to health, not to vicarious identification, stereotyped sex roles, competitiveness, brutality, passivity;
- police forces, insofar as they existed, would serve the people, not inspire fear and blanket respect for authority;
- external wars, designed to repress the populations of other countries and to keep them from making the kinds of choices they wanted to make, did not take place because there was no need for them;
- there was no "science" of public relations because people would relate to each other in ways chosen by themselves, and not by some alien manipulator;
- domestic armies such as the National Guard, if they existed, would rebuild slum housing instead of shooting it full of holes, if slum housing existed;
- high schools and elementary schools were places where students wanted to be students and teachers, teachers because what went on there was interesting, exciting, and contributed to the development of all who came into contact with it;
- colleges and universities could freely pursue the search for truth without being impeded by political considerations, such as reinforcing the class structure, providing weaponry for foreign wars, and teaching people that what they know to be human cannot be permitted because it cannot be measured;
- taxpayers' money did not support clandestine semifascist "intelligence" operations into the affairs of other countries, and their own;
- the state, rather than continually siding with those who have the economic power in the society, would act as a genuine arbiter when there was conflict among groups in the society;
- generalized fears of others (McCarthyism, racism, anti-Semitism, male chauvinism) were eliminated by removing their social causes, especially the conscious manipulation of insecurities in order to keep people divided and thereby oppressed;
- the establishment of a propaganda apparatus for use in the internal affairs of other countries was dismantled and the money given for use in other areas, such as world poverty and massive social problems of that ilk;
- work was productive and resulted in feelings of wholeness and mutuality;
- information about the world—the "news"—was disseminated in such a way that people could make up their own minds about what was taking place, instead of having it presented in such subtle ways that they are not even aware that what they are viewing has already been distilled to prevent them from making those interpretations;
- religion was a truly spiritual experience, rather than one designed to keep

people ignorant, passive, and acting in ways contrary to their best interests;
- private foundations, whose fortunes were compiled through the exploitation of working people, were not permitted to benefit a small, unrepresentative ruling class, but were turned over to ordinary people to administer in their way;
- freedom of speech, and freedom of the press, instead of being a convenience only for those who can afford them and who will not "abuse" them, became a genuine reality in which a wide variety of opinions and true diversity existed and had an effect on people's lives;
- groups that sought to change the society would be free to try to build a movement, without having to worry about who in their midst was an agent of the state and without the expectation that the minute they became slightly successful, the means of state violence would be used against them in the name of "democracy";
- the function of entertainment was to entertain, not to lull and tranquilize;
- bureaucracy was no longer an end in itself but a means to accomplish other goals, such as universal health care and free transportation;
- technology freed people to improve their lives and their environment, instead of convincing them of their impotence.

Such a vision is within our grasp. It requires only one change: the replacement of a system based on private power and exploitation with a system based on participation and control, the replacement of an undemocratic, illiberal, and repressive capitalism with a democratic and liberating socialism. Of course, that one change is the rub, for it is not a simple matter to bring about. People have been struggling for such a change for sometime now, and it is doubtful whether they are any closer to it than they were a hundred years ago. Yet in one sense they are. Advanced industrial societies, though they have not, as some Marxists believed a few years ago, become postscarcity economies,[5] have at least produced in some people the vision of what a nonrepressive society can be like. Translating that vision into reality is a political struggle whose success cannot be predicted here. But the fact that people know what is wrong and what is needed to put it right indicates that there is a good chance of making that transation. If those who are engaged in the struggle are repressed, that is one of the problems of living in a society such as the United States. For each discouragement that comes from repression, however, there is the encouragement that if the vision were not so powerful, the need to repress would not be so compelling. A nonrepressive society can be built if enough people are moved to build it, and the very repressiveness of the existing society guarantees that there will always be people around to try.

notes

ONE: THE SOCIOLOGY OF REPRESSION

1. The classic example of this work is Carl J. Friedrich and Zbigniew Brzezinski, *Totalitarian Dictatorship and Autocracy* (New York: Praeger, 1963). It is a fascinating exercise to read the book now, substituting "America" for "Germany" to see what one comes to. For an effective critique of this kind of book, see Herbert J. Spiro and Benjamin Barber, "Totalitarianism as Counter-Ideology," *Politics and Society* 1 (November 1970): 3–21.

2. An example of this phenomenon is Tom Hayden, *Rebellion and Repression* (New York: Meridian Books, 1969). But each repressed group has put out its own materials, from the IWW to books on the Red scare and Herbert Aptheker's book on the McCarthy Period.

3. The best case studies are Robert K. Murray, *Red Scare* (New York: McGraw-Hill, 1964); William Preston, Jr., *Aliens and Dissenters* (Cambridge,

Mass.: Harvard University Press, 1963); Earl Latham, *The Communist Contro-versy in Washington* (Cambridge, Mass.: Harvard University Press, 1966); Audrie Gindner and Anne Goftis, *The Great Betrayal* (New York: Macmillan, 1969). A recent attempt to deal theoretically with repression was published after this book was written: Murray Levin, *Political Hysteria in America* (New York: Basic Books, 1971).

4. The concept of reproductive mechanisms is contained in Karl Marx, *Pre-Capitalist Economic Formations* (New York: International Publishers, 1965). For an example of how the term has been applied to repression, see Louis Althusser, "Ideology and Ideological State Apparatuses," in *Lenin and Philosophy* (London: New Left Books, 1971), pp. 121–73.

5. See Murray, *Red Scare*, pp. 18–56.

6. See chapter 2, p. 28.

7. See chapter 6, p. 155.

8. One who does define repression to include everything is Lefebvre: "Thus it is inexact to restrict an analysis of repression to economic conditions (one of the mistakes of economism) or to institutions and ideologies; both atti-tudes omit the important factor of everyday life, of the pressures and repres-sions at all levels, at all times and in every sphere of experience including sexual and emotional, private and family life, childhood, adolescence and maturity—in short, that which would seem to elude social repression because it is spon-taneous and 'natural.'" Henri Lefebvre, *Everyday Life in the Modern World* (New York: Harper Torchbooks, 1971), p. 145.

9. These points are made in Dave Meggyesy, *Out of Their League* (New York: Paperback Library, 1971). For a detailed analysis of the functions of sports in a capitalist society, see Pierre Laguillaumie, "Pour une critique fondementale du sport," *Partisans* 43 (July–September 1968): 27–44.

10. C. B. MacPherson, *The Political Theory of Possessive Individualism* (London: Oxford University Press, 1962).

11. Ibid., p. 3.

12. Thomas Hobbes, *Leviathan* (Baltimore: Penguin Books, 1968), p. 229.

13. Ibid., p. 235.

14. John Locke, "An Essay Concerning the True Origin, Extent, and End of Civil Government," in *Two Treatises on Government* (New York: New American Library, 1965), pp. 319–23.

15. Ibid., p. 460.

16. Ibid., p. 464.

17. Ibid., p. 467.

18. This same point has been made, in a more abstract fashion, by MacPherson: "No way out of the dilemma is to be found by rejecting those assumptions of possessive individualism while not rejecting market society, as so many theorists from John Stuart Mill to our own time have done on the ground that the assumptions are morally offensive." See *Possessive Individual-ism*, p. 275. For a comprehensive analysis of the ambiguities in Mill on these points, based on *Considerations on Representative Government*, see Richard

Lichtman, "The Facade of Equality in Liberal Democratic Theory," *Socialist Revolution* 1 (January–February 1970): 102–12.

19. John Stuart Mill, "On Liberty," in *Three Essays* (London: Oxford University Press, 1966), p. 92.

20. Ibid., pp. 8–9.

21. The most famous dissents of Holmes and Brandeis on free speech are Abrams v. U.S., 250 U.S. 616 (1919) and Gitlow v. U.S., 268 U.S. 652 (1925). Each of them, however, did write decisions either upholding state repression or concurring, on procedural grounds, in decisions of others which did. See Schenck v. U.S., 249 U.S. 47 (1919) and Whitney v. California, 274 U.S. 357 (1927).

22. The fact that civil liberties are occasionally recognized by the courts means that the state is not totally free to engage in repression. The existence of organizations such as the American Civil Liberties Union provides some protection to dissidents, and the belief on the part of some members of the ruling class that dissenters should have rights may inhibit the state from putting into practice repressive policies it has developed. However, there are two problems. One is that civil libertarians often care more about procedure than results. The argument is that the government is free to repress as much as it wants so long as it goes about it constitutionally. The other problem is that when it really wishes to take action against a group, the state generally can withstand any protests from civil libertarians, who may have right on their side, but who rarely have that much power.

23. This point is made well in Robert M. O'Neil, *The Price of Dependency* (New York: Dutton, 1970).

24. Arthur Schlesinger, Jr., *The Vital Center* (Boston: Houghton Mifflin, 1962), p. 211.

25. In his remarks to the 1968 American Sociological Association convention, Martin Nicolaus made this point brilliantly: "What if the machinery were reversed? What if the habits, problems, secrets and unconscious motivations of the wealthy and powerful were daily scrutinized by a thousand systematic researchers, were hourly pried into, analyzed and cross referenced, tabulated and published in a hundred inexpensive mass circulation journals and written so that even the fifteen-year-old high school drop-out could understand it and predict the actions of his landlord, manipulate and control him?"

26. Frederick Engels, *The Origins of the Family, Private Property, and the State* (New York: International Publishers, 1969), p. 155.

27. The best summary of the Marxist theory of the state is Ralph Miliband, "Marx and the State" in *Socialist Register 1965* (New York: Monthly Review Press, 1966).

28. V. I. Lenin, *State and Revolution* (New York: International Publishers, n.d.).

29. "A democratic republic is the best possible shell for capitalism, and, therefore, once capital has gained control over this very best shell . . . it establishes a power so securely, so firmly, that *no* change, whether of persons, of institutions, or of parties in the bourgeois-democratic republic can shake it."

Ibid., p. 24. After the revolution, Lenin pointed out that in Switzerland and the United States, the two countries often seen as the most democratic, ". . . nowhere is the suppression of the working class movement accompanied by such ruthless severity." V. I. Lenin, *The State* (New York: New Century Publishers, 1947), p. 23.

30. The best books about Gramsci are John M. Cammett, *Antonio Gramsci and the Origins of Italian Communism* (Stanford: Stanford University Press, 1967); and Giuseppe Fiori, *Antonio Gramsci: Life of a Revolutionary* (London: New Left Books, 1970). See the recently published *Prison Notebooks* (New York: International Publishers, 1972), and the older *Modern Prince* (New York: International Publishers, 1967).

31. Gwyn A. Williams, "Gramsci's Concept of Egomania," *Journal of the History of Ideas* 21 (October–December 1960): 587, quoted in Cammett, *Antonio Gramsci*, p. 204.

32. Ralph Miliband, *The State in Capitalist Society* (New York: Basic Books, 1969).

33. This point is made in Nicos Poulantzas, "The Problem of the Capitalist State," *New Left Review* 58 (November–December 1969): 69.

34. For example, the major book on the subject devotes only four pages to the question of force. See Nicos Poulantzas, *Pourvoir politique et classes sociales*, vol. 2 (Paris: Maspero, 1971), pp. 42–58.

35. See Herbert Marcuse, *Eros and Civilization* (New York: Vintage, 1955), and *One Dimensional Man* (Boston: Beacon Press, 1968).

36. The concept of preventive counterrevolution is developed in Herbert Marcuse, "The Movement in a New Era of Repression," *Berkeley Journal of Sociology* 16 (1971): 1–14.

TWO: THE BIAS OF THE DEMOCRATIC STATE

1. See Max Weber, "Politics as a Vocation," in *From Max Weber*, ed. Hans Gerth and C. Wright Mills (New York: Oxford University Press, 1958), p. 78.

2. Melvyn Dubofsky, *We Shall Be All* (Chicago: Quadrangle Books, 1969), p. 147.

3. The first quotation is from Major McClelland of the Cripple Creek detachment, and the second was made by his superior officer, General Sherman Bell, who commanded the troops. Both are quoted in ibid., p. 50.

4. Ibid., p. 202.

5. William Preston, Jr., *Aliens and Dissenters* (New York: Harper Torchbooks, 1966), p. 54.

6. Quoted in ibid., p. 101.

7. Quoted in ibid., p. 72.

8. Fong Yue Ting v. U.S., 149 U.S. 698 (1893); Japanese Immigrant Case 189 U.S. 86 (1903).

9. Sect. 19, Immigration Act of February 5, 1917, 39 U.S. Statutes 889. Quoted in Preston, *Aliens and Dissenters*, p. 83.

10. Dubofsky, *We Shall Be All*, p. 405.

11. This point that the IWW was willing to open its books is discussed in Philip Taft, "The Federal Trials of the I.W.W.," *Labor History* 3 (Winter 1962): 60; see also Preston, *Aliens and Dissenters*, p. 118.

12. Preston, *Aliens and Dissenters*, p. 119.

13. The complete charge is summarized in Taft, "Federal Trials."

14. Preston, *Aliens and Dissenters*, p. 100, is very clear on the pressure from lumber interests.

15. Dubofsky, *We Shall Be All*, p. 443.

16. Ibid., p. 414.

17. "Frankfurter taught President Wilson's mediators, including the Secretary of Labor, the refinements of industrial conciliation and the means of destroying the I.W.W." Ibid., p. 416.

18. Hans B. Thorelli, *The Federal Anti-Trust Policy* (Stockholm, 1954), p. 50.

19. Ibid., p. 53.

20. Munn v. Illinois, 94 U.S. 113 (1877).

21. Thorelli, *Federal Anti-Trust Policy*, p. 163.

22. Act of July 2, 1890, 26 U.S. Statutes 209, 51st Cong., 1st sess.

23. U.S. v. E. C. Knight Co., 156 U.S. 1 (1895).

24. These figures are cited in James Weinstein, *The Corporate Ideal in The Liberal State* (Boston: Beacon Press, 1968), p. 63.

25. Ibid.

26. Stanley I. Kutler, "Labor, the Clayton Act, and the Supreme Court," *Labor History* 3 (Winter 1962): 21.

27. Particularly in In Re Debs, 158 U.S. 564 (1895). This decision was handed down *on the same day* that the Court held, in the Knight case, that manufacturing was not commerce and therefore not subject to the Sherman Act.

28. Quoted in Weinstein, *Corporate Ideal*, p. 91. This is the best account of the origins of the FTC.

29. Figures taken from a chart in Richard J. Barber, *The American Corporation* (New York: Dutton, 1970), p. 23.

30. Adopted from ibid., p. 28.

31. Ibid., p. 20.

32. A good description of Roosevelt's attitude toward trusts is contained in Gabriel Kolko, *The Triumph of American Conservatism* (Chicago: Quadrangle Books, 1967), p. 57–138.

33. See how the doctrine develops to protect the trusts in the following cases: Standard Oil Co. v. U.S., 221 U.S. 1 (1911); U.S. v. American Tobacco Co., 221 U.S. 196 (1911); U.S. v. Winslow, 227 U.S. 202 (1913); and U.S. v. United States Steel Corp., 251 U.S. 417 (1920).

34. The most comprehensive account of the case, on which the following is based, is John G. Fuller, *The Gentlemen Conspirators* (New York: Grove Press, 1962).

35. Quoted in ibid., p. 65.

36. See almost any of the hearings of the Senate Antitrust Committee,

particularly those titled *Administered Prices.* The most popular book to emerge from that committee is Estes Kefauver, *In a Few Hands* (Baltimore: Penguin Books, 1965).

37. The IWW convictions are from Taft, "Federal Trials," p. 75; the GE/Westinghouse convictions from Fuller, *Gentlemen Conspirators*, p. 16.

38. Quoted in Fuller, *Gentlemen Conspirators*, p. 91. The individual is F. F. Loock, then president, general manager, and sales manager of the Allen-Bradley Company.

39. Thurman Arnold, *The Folklore of Capitalism* (New Haven: Yale University Press, 1937), pp. 212–16. Quoted in Murray Edelman, *The Symbolic Uses of Politics* (Urbana: University of Illinois Press, 1964), p. 40. Edelman's book is a brilliant attempt to turn Arnold's insight into a general theory about politics.

40. "Far from desiring to revolutionize all society for the revolutionary proletarians, the democratic petty bourgeois strive for a change in social conditions by means of which existing society will be made as tolerable as possible for them. . . . To accomplish this they need a democratic state structure. . . ." Karl Marx, "Address to the Central Committee of The Communist League," in *Selected Works,* ed. Karl Marx and Frederick Engels, vol. 1 (Moscow: Foreign Languages Publishing House, 1962), pp. 109–10. Quoted in Richard Lichtman, "The Facade of Equality in Liberal Democratic Theory," *Socialist Revolution* 1 (January–February 1970): 91.

41. Schechter v. U.S., 295 U.S. 495 (1935).

42. Quoted in Barton J. Bernstein, "The New Deal: The Conservative Achievements of Liberal Reform," in *Towards a New Past,* ed. Barton J. Bernstein (New York: Pantheon, 1963), p. 269.

43. Ibid., p. 274. J. David Greenstone, *Labor in American Politics* (New York: Knopf, 1969), p. 48; Murray Edelman, "Sensitivity to Labor," in *Labor and the New Deal,* ed. Milton Derber and Edwin Young (Madison: University of Wisconsin Press, 1957), p. 181.

44. 49 U.S. Statutes 449, Act of July 5, 1935.

45. *Handbook of Labor Statistics* (1968), p. 300.

46. Quoted in Ronald Radosh, "The Corporate Ideology of American Labor Leaders from Gompers to Hillman," in *For A New American,* ed. James Weinstein and David W. Eakins (New York: Vintage Books, 1970), p. 137.

47. Quoted in Sidney Lens, *The Crisis of American Labor* (New York: A. S. Barnes, 1961), pp. 93–94.

48. Radosh, "Corporate Ideology," p. 146.

49. Lens, *Crisis of American Labor,* pp. 183–88.

50. Quoted in ibid., p. 171.

51. Quoted in ibid., p. 184.

52. Arthur Schlesinger, Jr., *The Politics of Upheaval* (Boston: Houghton Mifflin, 1960).

53. Bernstein, "New Deal," p. 264.

54. For example, the Little Steel formula of July 1942 which put a low ceiling on how high an increase in wages labor could bargain for. See Lens,

Crisis of American Labor, p. 200. The most comprehensive treatment of the subject is Irving Bernstein, *The New Deal Collective Bargaining Policy* (Berkeley: University of California Press, 1950).

55. For example, the Kohler strike of the 1950s where NLRB proved impotent to act against the company even though it found it guilty of not bargaining in good faith. See Lens, *Crisis of American Labor,* p. 208.

56. When the steelworkers called a strike in April 1952, President Truman ordered his secretary of commerce to take possession of the steel strike mills for the duration of the strike. His actions were declared unconstitutional by the Supreme Court in Youngstown Sheet and Tube Co. v. Sawyer, 343 U.S. 579 (1952). It is extremely pertinent to note in this context that Congress considered giving the president such powers under Taft-Hartley but decided to accomplish the same end by giving the president the right to intervene against the unions instead. See Alfred H. Kelly and Winfred A. Harbison, *The American Constitution* (New York: Norton, 1955), p. 886.

57. *Handbook of Labor Statistics* (1968), p. 330.

58. *Manpower Report of the President* (1963), p. 323.

59. C. Wright Mills, *The New Men of Power* (New York: Harcourt Brace, 1948).

60. Ronald Radosh, *American Labor and United States Foreign Policy* (New York: Random House, 1970).

61. See Greenstone, *Labor in American Politics,* for a summary of such influence.

62. The address is reprinted in Albert P. Blaustein and Robert L. Zangrando, *Civil Rights and the American Negro: A Documentary History* (New York: Trident, 1968), p. 457.

63. Reprinted in Leon Friedman, *The Civil Rights Reader: Basic Documents of the Civil Rights Movement* (New York: Walker, 1968), pp. 64–65.

64. Lyndon Baines Johnson, "Address to the Nation, July 27, 1967," quoted as the epigraph to the *Report of the National Advisory Commission on Civil Disorders* (New York: Bantam, 1967), p. xv.

65. Theodore L. Cross, *Black Capitalism: Strategy for the Ghetto* (New York: Athencum, 1969), p. 5.

66. The origin of the term is not clear. The most detailed analysis of the politics of the legislation implies that Robert Kennedy saw the benefit of the idea and had to convince a reluctant Sargent Shriver about it. The idea seems to have come from staff members of the President's Committee on Juvenile Delinquency who had close contacts with Attorney General Kennedy. See John C. Donovan, *The Politics of Poverty* (New York: Pegasus, 1967), pp. 32–33.

67. Ralph M. Kramer, *Participation of the Poor* (Englewood Cliffs, N.J.: Prentice-Hall, 1969), p. 263.

68. The statistics given in the following few paragraphs have been calculated from a list of arrests and harassments circulated by the Black Panther Party in its newspaper, *Black Panther,* 21 February 1970, pp. 2–27. While it was impossible to verify all the arrests, a random check indicated that the list,

if anything was incomplete and erred on the side of being favorable to the government. For example, the Panther figures list Fred Hampton as having been arrested on various minor charges five times before his death, while non-Panther sources claim he was arrested as many as twenty-five times. See Christopher Chandler, "The Black Panther Killings," *New Republic* 161 (10 January 1970): 23.

69. *New York Times,* 19 May 1966, p. 1.

70. Quoted in Harry A. Marmion, *Selective Service: Conflict and Compromise* (New York: John Wiley, 1968), p. 19.

71. Ibid., p. 41.

72. The members of the Commission are listed as part of its report. See *In Pursuit of Equality: Who Serves When Not All Serve? Report of the National Advisory Commission on Selective Service* (Washington, D.C.: Government Printing Office, 1967).

73. Background information on the Clark panel is provided in its report. Civilian Advisory Panel on Military Manpower Procurement, *Report to The Committee on Armed Services, House of Representatives* (Washington, D.C.: Government Printing Office, 1967), pp. 28–30.

74. See Sol Tax, ed., *The Draft* (Chicago: University of Chicago Press, 1967), pp. 489–91. The whole book contains the papers given and transcriptions of some of the discussions.

75. Milton Friedman, "Why Not a Volunteer Army," and Walter Y. Oi, "The Costs and Implications of an All-Volunteer Force," in Tax, *The Draft,* pp. 200–7 and 221–51.

76. Marmion, *Selective Service,* p. 60.

77. Friedman, "Why Not a Volunteer Army," p. 202.

78. These figures are taken from a fact sheet on the volunteer army contained in *Congressional Quarterly Weekly Report* (*CQWR*), 3 April 1970, pp. 927–31.

79. *In Pursuit of Equality,* Summary.

80. The point is made in Marmion, *Selective Service,* pp. 76, 84–85.

81. See the astoundingly long list of educators who spoke against the bill in *Congressional Quarterly Almanac* (1968), pp. 783–85.

82. The document was reprinted in the *New York Times,* 14 May 1969, p. 20.

83. Quoted in *CQWR,* 3 April 1970, p. 931.

84. See *CQWR,* 6 January 1970, p. 12.

85. *CQWR,* 6 March 1970, p. 665; and *CQWR,* 3 April 1970, p. 931.

THREE: WHO BENEFITS FROM REPRESSION?

1. Daniel Bell, "Is There a Ruling Class in America?," in *The End of Ideology* (New York: Free Press, 1960), pp. 43–67; Robert A. Dahl, "A Critique of the Ruling Elite Model," *American Political Science Review* 52 (June 1958): 463–69; David B. Truman, *The Governmental Process* (New York: Knopf, 1951); John Kenneth Galbraith, *American Capitalism* (Boston:

Houghton Mifflin, 1956); Arnold Rose, *The Power Structure* (New York: Oxford University Press, 1967).

2. C. Wright Mills, *The Power Elite* (New York: Oxford University Press, 1956); G. William Domhoff, *Who Rules America?* (Englewood Cliffs, N.J.: Prentice-Hall, 1967); Paul Sweezy, "Power Elite or Ruling Class?," in *C. Wright Mills and the Power Elite*, ed. G. William Domhoff and Hoyt Ballard (Boston: Beacon Press, 1968), pp. 115–32. See also the essays by Robert Lynd and Herbert Aptheker in that volume.

3. Mills' *The Power Elite* is the most famous of this genre.

4. See, for example, Sweezy, "Power Elite or Ruling Class?"

5. Włodzimierz Wesolowski, "Ruling Class and Power Elite," *Polish Sociological Bulletin* 11 (January 1965): 22–37.

6. For examples of attempts to portray the consensus, see the Rockefeller Brothers Fund, *Prospects for America* (Garden City, N.Y.: Doubleday, 1961). This volume contains six separate studies whose titles and (more importantly) whose order of publication are significant to this discussion of consensus: the mid-century challenge to U.S. foreign policy; international security: the military aspect; foreign economic policy for the twentieth century; the challenge to America: its economic and social aspects, the pursuit of excellence: education and the future of America; the power of the democratic idea. Also relevant in this connection is the President's Commission on National Goals, *Goals of Americans* (Englewood Cliffs, N.J.: Prentice-Hall, 1960). This is concerned basically with economic and social policy. Other examples of consensus-shaping are the Godkin lectures, given each year at Harvard. A typical one is McGeorge Bundy, *The Strength of Government* (Cambridge, Mass.: Harvard University Press, 1968).

7. Neither Louis Hartz nor Daniel Boorstin concerns himself with the beneficiaries of the traditions he so much glorifies. See Louis Hartz, *The Liberal Tradition in America* (New York: Harcourt Brace, 1955); and Daniel Boorstin, *The Genius of American Politics* (Chicago: University of Chicago Press, 1953).

8. James Weinstein, *The Corporate Ideal in the Welfare State* (Boston: Beacon Press, 1968).

9. Ferdinand Lundberg, *America's Sixty Families* (New York: Halcyon House, 1937). For a more recent and just as simplistic account by the same writer see *The Rich and the Super Rich* (New York: Lyle Stuart, 1968).

10. E. Digby Baltzell, *An American Business Aristocracy* (New York: Collier Books, 1962); E. Digby Baltzell, *The Protestant Establishment* (New York: Random House, 1964); Stephen Birmingham, *The Right People* (Boston: Little, Brown, 1968). There are, of course, many other books on the subject too numerous to mention.

11. Stephen Hess, *America's Political Dynasties* (Garden City, N.Y.: Doubleday, 1966), contains information on some such last names.

12. On McCloy, see Domhoff, *Who Rules America?*, pp. 67, 76–79; on Bundy see Patrick Anderson, *The President's Men* (Garden City, N.Y.: Doubleday, 1968), pp. 260–62.

13. Deborah Leavy, "Where the Ruling Class Lives: A Study of Centre Island, N.Y." (unpublished paper, Old Westbury College, State University of New York, n.d.).

14. For material on the CED, see Domhoff, *Who Rules America?*, pp. 74–75, and G. William Domhoff, "Who Made American Foreign Policy, 1945–1963?," in *Corporations and the Cold War*, ed, David Horowitz (New York: Monthly Review Press, 1969), pp. 36–37.

15. These organizations are discussed in Domhoff, *Who Rules America?*, pp. 64–70 and 75–76, and "Who Made American Foreign Policy," pp. 37–38.

16. Richard J. Barber, *The American Corporation* (New York: Dutton, 1970), p. 259.

17. Harry Magdoff, *The Age of Imperalism* (New York: Monthly Review Press, 1969), p. 74.

18. Ibid., p. 56.

19. Ibid., pp. 203–6, contains a list of those treaties.

20. Ibid., p. 42.

21. See Domhoff, "Who Made American Foreign Policy," pp. 28–36.

22. Gabriel Kolko, *The Roots of American Foreign Policy* (Boston: Beacon Press, 1969), pp. 17–23.

23. David T. Stanley, Dean E. Mann, Jameson W. Doig, *Men Who Govern* (Washington, D.C.: Brookings Institution, 1967), p. 36.

24. Fred Goff and Michael Locker, "The Violence of Domination: U.S. Power and the Dominican Republic," mimeographed (North American Congress on Latin America, n.d.). Quoted in James Petras, "Patterns of Intervention: American Business and U.S. Foreign Policy in Latin America," in Alan Wolfe and Marvin Surkin, *An End to Political Science* (New York: Basic Books, 1970), p. 202.

25. These figures were taken from Domhoff, *Who Rules America?*, pp. 73–76, and "Who Made American Foreign Policy," pp. 28–38.

26. Baltzell, *Protestant Establishment*, p. 382.

27. Amaury de Riencourt, *The Coming Caesars* (New York: Capricorn Books, 1957), p. 330. This is a standard argument to the point that the American president is too powerful.

28. Andrew Hacker, "The 'Elected' and the 'Anointed,'" *American Political Science Review* 55 (September 1961): 539–49.

29. Donald R. Matthews, *U.S. Senators and Their World* (New York: Vintage Books, 1960), p. 44.

30. William J. Keefe and Morris S. Ogul, *The American Legislative Process* (Englewood Cliffs, N.J.: Prentice-Hall, 1964), p. 122.

31. In order, see Joseph Schmidhauser, *The Supreme Court* (New York: Holt, Rinehart, and Winston, 1960), pp. 30–62; Stanley, Mann, and Doig, *Men Who Govern*, pp. 14–16 and *passim;* Lester Milbrath, *The Washington Lobbyists* (Chicago: Rand McNally, 1963), pp. 90–97; and Morris Janowitz, *The Professional Soldier* (New York: Free Press, 1964), pp. 79–103. For similar material on the backgrounds of corporation executives (sex, religion,

income, etc.), see Robert S. Diamond, "A Selfportrait of the Chief Executive," *Fortune* (May 1970): 180.

32. From various points of view, but all with conservative implications, see James Burnham, *The Managerial Revolution* (New York: John Day, 1941); M. Djilas, *The New Class* (New York: Praeger, 1957); and Adolf Berle and Gardiner C. Means, *The Modern Corporation and Private Property* (New York: Macmillan, 1933).

33. Ralph Miliband, *The State in Capitalist Society* (New York: Basic Books, 1969), pp. 28–39.

34. Adolf Berle, Jr., *The 20th Century Capitalist Revolution* (New York: Harcourt Brace, 1954), pp. 166–67.

35. See Grant McConnell, *Private Power and American Democracy* (New York: Knopf, 1966); Martha Derthick, *The National Guard in Politics* (Cambridge, Mass.: Harvard University Press, 1965); Samuel P. Huntington, "Inter-Service Competition and the Political Roles of the Armed Services," *American Political Science Review* 55 (March 1961): 40–52; Michael D. Reagan, *The Managed Economy* (New York: Oxford University Press, 1963).

36. Arthur Vidich and Joseph Bensman, *Small Town in Mass Society* (Garden City, N.Y.: Doubleday Anchor, 1968).

37. Robert and Helen Lynd, *Middletown in Transition* (New York: Harcourt, Brace, 1937); and Floyd Hunter, *Community Power Structure* (Chapel Hill: University of North Carolina Press, 1953). Hunter's difficulty in dealing with a national ruling class becomes obvious in his *Top Leadership, U.S.A.* (Chapel Hill: University of North Carolina Press, 1959).

38. Nelson Polsby, *Community Power and Political Theory* (New Haven: Yale University Press, 1963). If the Lynds and Hunter were misdirected, Polsby is totally wrong.

39. See the examples given in Robert Engler, *The Politics of Oil* (Chicago: University of Chicago Press, 1967), pp. 231–47.

40. John H. Bunzel, *The American Small Businessman* (New York: Knopf, 1969), p. 1037.

41. J. David Greenstone, *Labor in American Politics* (New York: Knopf, 1969), pp. 110, 121.

42. Arthur F. Neiderhoffer, *Behind The Shield* (Garden City, N.Y.: Doubleday Anchor, 1969), pp. 95–160.

43. Harmon Zeigler, *The Political Life of American Teachers* (Englewood Cliffs, N.J.: Prentice-Hall, 1967), pp. 49, 100.

44. Richard E. Dawson and James A. Robinson, "Inter-Party Competition, Economic Variables, and Welfare Policies in the American States," *Journal of Politics* 25 (May 1963): 289.

45. This literature has by now reached enormous proportions. The following are representative examples: Thomas Dye, *Politics, Economics and the Public* (Chicago: Rand McNally, 1966); Ira Sharkansky, *Policy Analysis in Political Science* (Chicago: Markham, 1970); Richard I. Hofferbert, "The Relationship Between Public Policy and Some Structural and Environmental Variables in the American States," *American Political Science Review* 60

(March 1966): 73–82; and James W. Clarke, "Environment, Process, and Policy," *American Political Science Review* 63 (December 1969): 1172–82.

46. Guenther Schaefer and Stuart H. Rakoff, "Politics, Policy and Political Science," *Politics and Society* 1 (November 1970): 51–77.

47. For a discussion of this proposition, see McConnell, *Private Power and American Democracy*, pp. 185–90.

48. From a different political perspective, this is discussed in Edward Shils, *The Torment of Secrecy* (New York: Free Press, 1956), pp. 105–49.

49. The belief that it was a lower-class phenomenon is contained in Daniel Bell, ed., *The Radical Right* (Garden City, N.Y.: Doubleday Anchor, 1964). For a most effective critique and counter explanation, consult Michael Paul Rogin, *The Intellectuals and McCarthy* (Cambridge, Mass.: Massachusetts Institute of Technology Press, 1967).

50. John C. Wahlke, Heinz Eulau, William Buchanan and Leroy C. Ferguson, *The Legislative System* (New York: John Wiley, 1962), pp. 112, 129, 82.

51. The point that members of groups play a role in the governance of the entire society through their membership is made in Truman, *Governmental Process*, p. 155. In his last chapter he extends that generalization to all groups, organized or not.

52. Seymour Martin Lipset, *Political Man* (Garden City, N.Y.: Doubleday Anchor, 1963), pp. 87–126.

53. Lewis Lipsitz, "Work Life and Political Attitudes: A Study of Manual Workers," *American Political Science Review* 58 (December 1964): 955.

54. Ibid., p. 958.

55. Eli Chinoy, *Automobile Workers and the American Dream* (Boston: Beacon Press, 1965).

56. Harold M. Baron et al., "Black Powerlessness in Chicago," *Transaction* 6 (November 1968): 27–33.

57. Ibid., p. 29.

58. William H. Grier and Price M. Cobbs, *Black Rage* (New York: Bantam Books, 1968); Kenneth Clark, *Dark Ghetto* (New York: Harper Torchbooks, 1967), pp. 154–98.

59. Wilson Record, *The Negro and the Communist Party* (Chapel Hill: University of North Carolina Press, 1959), and *Race and Radicalism* (Ithaca: Cornell University Press, 1964).

60. Stanley, Mann and Doig, *Men Who Govern*, p. 2.

61. Cited in Marlene Dixon, "Why Women's Liberation," *Ramparts* 8 (December 1969): 57–63.

62. Ibid., p. 62.

63. This seems to be the conclusion that emerges out of an interesting argument on the nature of women under capitalism. One side holds that women have essentially become irrelevant to the needs of modern capitalism, hence they are kept in the home as housewives. The other sees women's oppression as based on their integration into capitalism, for it is women who

are added to the labor force to fill menial and temporary positions when they cannot be filled elsewhere. The former view is elaborated in Margaret Benston, "The Political Economy of Women's Liberation," *Monthly Review* 21 (September 1961): 13–25; the latter in Mickey and John Rowntree, "More on the Political Economy of Women's Liberation," *Monthly Review* 21 (January 1970): 26–32.

64. See Kathy McAfee and Myrna Wood, "Bread and Roses," *Leviathan* 1 (June 1969).

65. The four concepts are borrowed from and discussed in Juliet Mitchell, "Women: The Longest Revolution," *New Left Review* (November–December 1966) and *Woman's Estate* (New York: Pantheon, 1972).

66. This attitude is analyzed in John Higham, *Strangers in the Land* (New Brunswick, N.J.: Rutgers University Press, 1955).

FOUR: VIOLENT REPRESSION

1. See Hugh Davis Graham and Ted Robert Gurr, *Violence in America: Historical and Comparative Perspectives* (New York: Signet Books, 1961). One of the best studies of state violence is Barrington Moore, *The Social Origins of Dictatorship and Democracy* (Boston: Beacon Press, 1966).

2. This point is made in ways very similar to this presentation in Stanley Aronowitz, "Law, The Breakdown of Order, and Revolution," in *Law Against the People*, ed. Robert Lefcourt (New York: Random House, 1971), pp. 150–82.

3. *New York Times*, 5 March 1966, p. 1.

4. Paul Chevigny, *Police Power* (New York: Pantheon, 1969), pp. 208–9.

5. U.S. v. Schwimmer, 279 U.S. 644 (1929); U.S. v. MacIntosh, 238 U.S. 605 (1931). Both were overruled in Girouard v. U.S., 328 U.S. 61 (1946).

6. William Preston, Jr., *Aliens and Dissenters* (Cambridge, Mass.: Harvard University Press, 1963).

7. Political notations ("subversive" or "anarchistic") increased as the official reason cited for deportations from 3 percent in 1950 to 33 percent seven years later. See Anthony T. Bouscaren, *The Security Aspects of Deportation Work* (Milwaukee: Marquette University Press, 1959), p. 91. Cited in Otto Kirchheimer, *Political Justice* (Princeton: Princeton University Press, 1961), p. 360.

8. Philip Taft and Philip Ross, "American Labor Violence," in Graham and Gurr, *Violence in America*, pp. 318–20.

9. The evidence for the police riot is, of course, in the government's own investigation. See the National Commission on the Causes and Prevention of Violence, "Walker Report," *Rights in Conflict* (New York: Signet, 1968). Although all the policemen were exonerated, five of the seven dissidents were convicted with no evidence presented of actual crimes. Here is the bias of the

democratic state expressed in miniature to such a perfect degree that most have missed its meaning.

10. "Without this court decision [Dennis], the later, more far-reaching security legislation blocking off communist inspired activity, and in particular the crowning enactment of 1954, would have been difficult to pass." Kirchheimer, *Political Justice*, p. 130.

11. Robert K. Carr, *The House Committee on Un-American Activities* (Ithaca: Cornell University Press, 1952). Contempt of Congress citations under HUAC were handed down as late as 1968 (against the KKK).

12. This point is made in Robert M. O'Neil, *The Price of Dependency* (New York: Dutton, 1970).

13. The Goldsmith phrase is quoted in E. P. Thompson, *The Making of the English Working Class* (New York: Pantheon, 1963), p. 60; Anatole France's statement is in *The Red Lily* (New York: Modern Library, n.d.).

14. Judges 16: 9–24.

15. Richard C. Donnelly, "Judicial Control of Informants, Spies, Stool Pigeons, and Agent Provocateurs," *Yale Law Journal* 60 (November 1951): 1091.

16. This section is based on James D. Horan, *The Pinkertons* (New York: Crown, 1967), pp. 445–79.

17. Quoted in ibid., p. 461.

18. Taft and Ross, "American Labor Violence," p. 321, 332–34.

19. U.S. Senate, *Hearings Before a Subcommittee of the Committee on Education and Labor*, 75th Cong., 3rd sess.

20. See the list included in a book summarizing the hearings: Leo Huberman, *The Labor Spy Racket* (New York: Modern Age Books, 1937), pp. 165–69. Also dealing with the findings of the LaFollette Committee is Clinch Calkins, *Spy Overhead: The Story of Industrial Espionage* (New York: Harcourt Brace, 1937). An engrossing "inside" picture of the problem, which contains much material linking the state to industrial espionage, is GT-99, *Labor Spy* (Indianapolis: Bobbs-Merrill, 1937).

21. Huberman, *Labor Spy Racket*, pp. 178–79.

22. This paragraph is based upon the Bureau's own "official" history. See Don Whitehead, *The FBI Story* (New York: Random House, 1956), pp. 34–39.

23. See the full story in Theodore Draper, *The Roots of American Communism* (New York: Viking, 1957), pp. 366–75.

24. Donald O. Schultz and Loran A. Norton, *Police Operational Intelligence* (Springfield, Ill.: Charles C Thomas, 1968), p. 77.

25. Ibid., p. 78.

26. Ibid., p. 26. Emphasis added.

27. Ibid., p. 91.

28. J. Edgar Hoover, in the *Law Enforcement Bulletin* (June 1955). Quoted in Malachi L. Harney and John C. Cross, *The Informer In Law Enforcement* (Springfield, Ill.: Charles C Thomas, 1968), p. 19. Emphasis added.

29. William F. Tompkins, in the *Law Enforcement Bulletin* (June 1955). Quoted in ibid., p. 70. Emphasis in original.

30. Donnelly, "Judicial Control of Informants," pp. 1124–25.

31. Tom Hayden, "The Trial," *Ramparts* 9 (July 1970): 19.

32. See Alan F. Westin, *Privacy and Freedom* (New York: Atheneum, 1967). Also informative is Samuel Dash, *The Eavesdroppers* (New Brunswick, N.J.: Rutgers University Press, 1959).

33. Hoffa v. U.S., 385 U.S. 311 (1966).

34. The best summary of all the revelations about covert agencies in Morton Halperin et al., *The Lawless State* (New York: Penguin, 1976). The material cited here comes from this book.

35. Draper, *Roots of American Communism*, p. 368.

36. *Annual Report of the Attorney General*, 1964, p. 373. Mr. Hoover's annual remarks on Communist party repression are contained in the section entitled "Protecting Democracy."

37. Kirchheimer, *Political Justice*, p. 237.

38. Thomas Erskine May, *Constitutional History of England*, vol. 2 (London: Longmans, Green, 1863), p. 275. Quoted in Donnelly, "Judicial Control of Informants," p. 1131.

39. Dumbrowski v. Pfister, 380 U.S. 479 (1965).

40. In Gary, Indiana, in 1920. See Taft and Ross, "American Labor Violence," p. 321.

41. Robert S. Rankin, *When Civil Law Fails* (Durham: Duke University Press, 1939), p. 85. This paragraph is based on Rankin's account.

42. Quoted in ibid., p. 87.

43. Ibid., p. 105.

44. Graham and Gurr, *Violence in America*, p. 750.

45. Martha Derthick, *The National Guard in Politics* (Cambridge, Mass.: Harvard University Press, 1965), p. 51. When he sought a place of influence to meet businessmen and leaders of his state, the anonymous labor spy cited earlier turned immediately to the National Guard. His explanation confirms Derthick's point: "It is cheaper for an employer to receive protection from a few companies of National Guardsmen than for him to hire several hundred private guards, which he would have to pay and maintain out of his own pocket. Many Chambers of Commerce make direct cash contributions to Guard units in their cities and the reason for their liberality is obvious." GT-99, *Labor Spy*, p. 197.

46. Derthick, *National Guard in Politics*, p. 52.

47. Bennett M. Rich and Philip M. Burch, Jr., "The Changing Role of the National Guard," *American Political Science Review* 50 (September 1956): 702.

48. Robert S. Rankin and Winfried R. Dallmayr, *Freedom and Emergency Powers in the Cold War* (New York: Appleton-Century-Crofts, 1964), p. 146. Emphasis added. Another discussion of the use of "emergency powers" is J. Malcolm Smith and Cornelius P. Cotter, *Powers of the President During Crises* (Washington, D.C.: Public Affairs Press, 1960).

49. See Preston, *Aliens and Dissenters;* Robert Murray, *Red Scare* (New York: McGraw-Hill, 1964); and Murray Levin, *Political Hysteria in America* (New York: Basic Books, 1971).

50. Arthur Waskow, *From Race Riot to Sit-In* (Garden City, N.Y.: Doubleday Anchor, 1967), p. 1.

51. Allen D. Grimshaw, "Actions of Police and the Military in American Race Riots," *Phylon* 24 (Fall 1963): 283.

52. Waskow, *From Race Riot to Sit-In,* p. 11.

53. Eldridge Foster Dowell, *A History of Criminal Syndicalist Legislation in the United States* (Baltimore: Johns Hopkins University Press, 1939), pp. 147, 150–51.

54. See the interesting comments on this point by Earl Browder in "The American Communist Party in the Thirties," in *As We Saw the Thirties,* ed. Rita James Simon (Urbana: University of Illinois Press, 1967), p. 234.

55. These figures are from Audrie Gindner and Anne Goftis, *The Great Betrayal: The Evacuation of Japanese Americans During World War II* (New York: Macmillan, 1969), pp. 96–97. For more on the subject, see Jacobus ten Broek, Edward N. Barnhart, and Floyd W. Matson, *Prejudice, War, and the Constitution* (Berkeley: University of California Press, 1966); Morton Grodzins, *Americans Betrayed* (Chicago: University of Chicago Press, 1959); and Allan R. Bosworth, *America's Concentration Camps* (New York: Norton, 1967).

56. Gindner and Goftis, *Great Betrayal,* p. 433.

57. Athan Theoharis, "The Rhetoric of Politics: Foreign Policy, Internal Security and Domestic Politics in the Truman Era, 1945–50," in *Politics and Policies of the Truman Administration,* ed. Barton J. Bernstein (Chicago: Quadrangle Books, 1970), pp. 196–241. See also Theoharis's "The Evolution of the Loyalty Program" in ibid., pp. 242–68, and *Seeds of Repression* (Chicago: Quadrangle Books, 1971); plus Alan D. Harper, *The Politics of Loyalty* (Westwood, Conn.: Greenwood, 1969).

58. For a discussion of the origin of the "militia clause," its use and its problems, see Frederick B. Weiner, "The Militia Clause of the Constitution," *Harvard Law Review* 54 (December 1940): 181–220.

59. The current law is contained in *U.S. Code,* vol. 2 (1964 ed.), p. 1121. It is sec. 331 of Title 10.

60. These seventy-seven incidents are systematically discussed in a fascinating document, *Federal Aid in Domestic Disturbances,* Senate Document No. 263, 67th Cong., 2nd sess. (Washington, D.C.: Government Printing Office, 1922). A Chinese outrage was an attack on Chinese mineworkers by whites, often stimulated by employers. See also Martin S. Reichley, "Federal Military Intervention in Civil Disturbances" (Ph.D. dissertation, Georgetown University, 1939).

61. Dennis v. U.S., 341 U.S. 494 (1951). During his long career, Frankfurter upheld each of the following repressive actions of the state: a local ordinance against sound trucks, the arrest of a speaker who *may* have caused disorder, a law which restrained the right to picket, the registration

powers of the Subversive Activities Control Board, the arrest of a book-seller charged with selling "obscene" material, and the Illinois law prohibiting "group libel." In order, the cases are: Kovacs v. Cooper, 336 U.S. 77 (1949); Feiner v. New York, 340 U.S. 315 (1951); International Brotherhood of Teamsters v. Vought, 335 U.S. 284 (1957); Communist Party v. Subversive Activities Control Board, 367 U.S. 1 (1961); Kingsley Books v. Brown, 354 U.S. 436 (1957); Beauharnais v. Illinois, 343 U.S. 250 (1952). Of course, Frankfurter also struck down some laws as unconstitutional. The only point being made concerns the ones he upheld.

62. It is often forgotten that Frankfurter's most eloquent defense of civil liberty was not over a political matter: "It is conduct which shocks the conscience. . . . This course of proceeding by agents of government to obtain evidence is bound to offend even hardened sensibilities. They are methods too close to the rack and screw to permit of constitutional differentiation." Rochin v. California, 342 U.S. 165 (1952). Perhaps I am not hardened enough, but there seems to me to be nothing more shocking in this case than in many other state actions. Here is a case in which, since no politics were involved, Frankfurter felt the state was "safe." Then and only then could civil liberty be eloquently defended.

63. On the relationship between capitalism and liberalism, see C. B. MacPherson, *The Real World of Democracy* (London: Oxford University Press, 1966).

FIVE: PRIVATE IDEOLOGICAL REPRESSION

1. Ralph Miliband, *The State in Capitalist Society* (New York: Basic Books, 1969), pp. 179–264.

2. The most important attempt to deal with these concerns is Louis Althusser, "Ideology and the Ideological Apparatus of the State," in *Lenin and Philosophy* (London: New Left Books, 1971).

3. See Henri Lefebvre, *Everyday Life in the Modern World* (New York: Harper Torchbooks, 1971).

4. See Wilhelm Reich, *The Mass Psychology of Fascism* (New York: Farrar, Straus, and Giroux, 1970); David Cooper, *The Death of the Family* (New York: Pantheon, 1970); and the writings of R. D. Laing, particularly, *The Politics of Family* (New York: Random House, 1971).

5. Edward L. Bernays, *Biography of an Idea: Memoirs of Public Relations Counsel Edward L. Bernays* (New York: Simon & Schuster, 1965), p. 191. This account is taken from this book.

6. Ibid., p. 192.

7. Ibid., p. 193. Emphasis added.

8. Ibid., p. 466.

9. Ibid., p. 468.

10. Edward L. Bernays, "Manipulating Public Opinion," *American Journal of Sociology* 33 (May 1928): 959. Although this quotation is over forty years old, it not only reflects Bernays' thought at a crucial period in the de-

velopment of capitalism, it also bears on the fact that Bernays' thought has changed little over time. In his recently published autobiography, Bernays' only regret is that he used the word "manipulating" too easily, not because he didn't mean it, but because it was bad public relations to use it. See *Biography of an Idea*, p. 294.

11. Edward L. Bernays, *Propaganda* (New York: Liveright, 1928), p. 159. The publisher of this book was one of his clients.

12. Ibid., p. 31.

13. Ibid., p. 72.

14. Bernays, *Biography of an Idea*, p. 379.

15. Ibid., pp. 299–460.

16. Bernays, "Manipulating Public Opinion," p. 971.

17. Bernays, *Propaganda*, p. 69.

18. Bernays, "Manipulating Public Opinion," p. 960.

19. See Edward L. Bernays, ed., *The Engineering of Consent* (Norman: University of Oklahoma Press, 1955).

20. Bernays, *Propaganda*, p. 158.

21. An example of that literature is Bernard Berelson, Paul Lazarsfeld, and William McPhee, *Voting* (Chicago: University of Chicago Press, 1954), whose chapter 14 makes some conclusions about democratic theory based on the "irrationality" of the masses.

22. See Sidney Hyman, *The Many Lives of William Benton* (Chicago: University of Chicago Press, 1969).

23. All references to Mr. Kelley in the next few pages are based upon Richard Rogin, "Joe Kelly Has Reached His Boiling Point," *New York Times Magazine*, 28 June 1970, p. 12.

24. David Riesman, *The Lonely Crowd* (New Haven: Yale University Press, 1950).

25. See William Kornhauser, *The Politics of Mass Society* (New York: Free Press, 1959). One of the interesting things about the notion was that it transcended Left and Right divisions, being attractive to both conservatives and radicals. See, for example, Hannah Arendt, *The Origins of Totalitarianism* (New York: Harcourt Brace, 1966), and C. Wright Mills, *The Power Elite* (New York: Oxford University Press, 1956). Here in one of the few areas where there really was an end of ideology, those who proclaimed ideology's end found themselves denying the importance of this very agreement. See Daniel Bell, *The End of Ideology* (New York: Free Press, 1960), pp. 21–36.

26. William H. Whyte, *The Organization Man* (New York: Simon & Shuster, 1956).

27. Commenting on democratic man, Tocqueville noted: "His reverses teach him that none have discovered absolute good; his success stimulates him to the never ending pursuit of it. Thus, forever seeking, forever falling to rise again, often disappointed, but not discouraged, he tends increasingly towards that unmeasured greatness so indistinctly visible at the end of the long track which humanity has yet to tread." Alexis de Tocqueville, *Democracy in America*, vol. 2 (Bradley ed.; New York: Knopf, 1966), p. 34.

28. William Hinton, *Fanshen* (New York: Vintage Books, 1968), p. 27.

29. Rogin, "Joe Kelly," p. 16.

30. Richard Hofstadter, *Anti-Intellectualism in American Life* (New York: Knopf, 1963).

31. T. W. Adorno et al., *The Authoritarian Personality* (New York: Harper, 1950). The major critical works are Richard Christie and Marie Jahoda, *Studies in the Scope and Method of "The Authoritarian Personality"* (New York: Free Press, 1954), and Milton Rokeach, *The Open and Closed Mind* (New York: Basic Books, 1960). Another popular "authoritarian personality" thesis is contained in Erich Fromm, *Escape From Freedom* (New York: Farrar & Rinehart, 1941). For a critique, see John Schaar, *Escape From Authority* (New York: Basic Books, 1961).

32. Rosser Reeves, *Reality in Advertisting* (New York: Knopf, 1968), p. 121.

33. Jules Henry, *Culture Against Man* (New York: Random House, 1963). Any examination of the themes of contemporary advertising must begin with this book. For another good discussion based on Reeves, see Paul Baran and Paul Sweezy, *Monopoly Capital* (New York: Monthly Review Press, 1966).

34. Pierre Martineau, *Motivation in Advertising: Motives That Make People Buy* (New York: McGraw-Hill, 1957), p. 192. Emphasis added.

35. David Ogilvy, *Confessions of an Advertising Man* (New York: Dell, 1963), pp. 160–65.

36. Ibid., p. 119.

37. In one case black glass was used instead of wood so that the polish being advertised would appear better; in another fresh liver was used in a cat food advertisement ". . . because the cat refused to oblige by eating the tinned product." J. A. C. Brown, *Techniques of Persuasion* (Baltimore: Penguin Books, 1963), p. 172.

38. A survey taken in 1958 revealed that 50 percent of the female (only women, naturally, were surveyed) respondents thought that advertising meant exaggeration and 86 percent thought it dishonest. In Britain, another survey showed that 89 percent disbelieved that celebrities who touted products really like them. Cited in ibid., p. 190. A more recent survey found that one of the major reasons people cited for their dislike of commercials was that they were misleading or dishonest. Gary A. Steiner, *The People Look at Television* (New York: Knopf, 1963), p. 209. This same study found that the overall effect of television commercials, outside of the question of content, was to reinforce a cynical fatalism. Respondents often said things like this: "Whoever sponsors the program would have something to say about it, I would think—it's their nickel that's paying the show." Or, "If I were the sponsor, I'd decide what program should be on." See ibid., p. 222.

39. Nicholas Johnson, *How to Talk Back to Your Television Set* (Boston: Atlantic–Little, Brown, 1970), p. 50.

40. Triangle Publications owned the *Philadelphia Inquirer* and the *Daily News*, the local ABC-TV affiliate, and the nation's largest circulation

magazine, *TV Guide*. The company is directed by Walter Annenberg, currently U.S. ambassador to the Court of St. James, and the man who provided name and money for Philadelphia's graduate programs in communications (at Temple and the University of Pennsylvania).

41. Johnson, *How to Talk Back*, p. 65.

42. Harry J. Skornia, *Television and Society* (New York: McGraw-Hill, 1965), pp. 28–29.

43. Paul F. Lazarsfeld and Robert K. Merton, "Mass Communication, Popular Taste, and Organized Social Action" in *Mass Culture*, ed. Bernard Rosenberg and David Manning White (New York: Free Press, 1957), p. 465.

44. All quotations are from Rudolf Arnheim, "The World of the Daytime Serial" in *Radio Research, 1942–43*, ed. Paul F. Lazarsfeld and Frank N. Stanton (New York: Duell, Sloan & Pearce, 1944), p. 78.

45. *Television Magazine* (July 1967): 37. Cited in Herbert I. Schiller, *Mass Communications and American Empire* (New York: Augustus M. Kelley, 1969), p. 98.

46. Hilde Himmelweit, A. N. Oppenheim and Pamela Vance, *Television and the Child* (London: Oxford University Press, 1958), p. 258.

47. Ibid., p. 384.

48. From a letter written by Frank Stanton, reprinted in Fred W. Friendly, *Due to Circumstances Beyond Our Control* (New York: Random House, 1967), p. 209.

49. Clifton Daniel, "Responsibilities of the Reporter and Editor," in *Reporting the News*, ed. Louis M. Lyons (Cambridge, Mass.: Belknap Press of Harvard University Press, 1965), p. 121.

50. Henry Shapiro, "Interpreting the Soviet," in ibid., p. 315.

51. Daniel, "Responsibilities of the Reporter," p. 120.

52. CBS News, *Television News Reporting* (New York: McGraw-Hill, 1958), p. 90.

53. Ibid., p. 93.

54. This discussion is based on William Rodgers, *Think* (New York: Stein & Day, 1969), pp. 79–104.

55. Ibid., p. 110.

56. Karl Marx, *Economic and Philosophical Manuscripts of 1844* (New York: International Publishers, 1964).

57. See especially Daniel Bell, *Work and Its Discontents* (Boston: Beacon Press, 1956), and Hannah Arendt, *The Human Condition* (Chicago: University of Chicago Press, 1958).

58. Robert Blauner, *Alienation and Freedom* (Chicago: University of Chicago Press, 1964).

59. Melvin Seeman, "On the Personal Consequences of Alienation in Work," *American Sociological Reviews* 32 (April 1967): 273–85.

60. W. Lloyd Warner and J. O. Low, *The Social Life of the Modern Factory* (New Haven: Yale University Press, 1947), pp. 173–76.

61. See Mirra Komarovsky, *Blue Collar Marriage* (New York: Vintage Books, 1967).

62. C. Wright Mills, *White Collar* (New York: Oxford University Press, 1951).

63. Robert Presthus, *The Organizational Society* (New York: Vintage Books, 1962).

64. One of the most fascinating general examples of the relationship between bureaucracy and parochialism is the story of Admiral Byrd's pilot whose request for American citizenship was denied because he had not been in the country long enough. The reason, of course, was that he was discovering the South Pole for the United States. See Robert K. Merton, "Bureaucratic Structure and Personality," in Robert K. Merton et al., *Reader in Bureaucracy* (New York: Free Press, 1952), p. 366.

65. Harry Braverman, *Labor and Monopoly Capital* (New York: Monthly Review Press, 1974).

SIX: PUBLIC IDEOLOGICAL REPRESSION

1. Committee on Public Information, *National Service Handbook* (Washington, D.C.: Government Printing Office, 1917), p. 14.

2. Edward L. Bernays, *Biography of an Idea* (New York: Simon & Schuster, 1965), p. 150.

3. James R. Mock and Cedric Lawson, *Words That Won the War: The Story of the Committee on Public Information, 1917–19* (Princeton: Princeton University Press, 1939), p. 191. See also Ronald Radosh, *American Labor and United States Foreign Policy* (New York: Vintage Books, 1970), pp. 59–71.

4. Mock and Lawson, *Words That Won the War*, pp. 190–91.

5. Ibid., p. 193.

6. Ibid., pp. 189–90.

7. This idea has been discussed at length in E. H. Carr, *The Twenty Years Crisis* (London: Macmillan, 1961), pp. 80–85.

8. Mock and Lawson, *Words That Won the War*, p. 213.

9. Ibid., p. 215.

10. George Creel, *How We Advertised America* (New York: Harper, 1920), p. 184.

11. Ibid., pp. 192–94; Mock and Lawson, *Words That Won the War*, p. 219.

12. Creel, *How We Advertised America*, p. 194.

13. Ibid., pp. 192–93.

14. See the bitterness with which Creel writes about the decision of Congress to terminate his position in the preface to ibid., p. ix.

15. Francis E. Rourke, *Secrecy and Publicity* (Baltimore: Johns Hopkins University Press, 1961), p. 187.

16. This was popularly called the Harkness Committee. See Final Report of the Subcommittee on Publicity and Propaganda, *Twenty-third Intermediate Report of the Committee on Expenditures in the Executive Departments*, 80th Cong., 2nd sess., House Report No. 2474 (Washington, D.C.: Government Printing Office, 1949).

17. These figures are taken from a summary of the Harkness Committee Report in the *Congressional Record*, vol. 96, part 17, p. A6861. 81st Cong., 2nd sess.

18. *Twenty-third Intermediate Report*, p. 2.

19. From a summary of the Hoover Commission Report in *Congressional Record*, vol. 96, part 17, p. A6861. 81st Cong., 2nd sess. See the discussion in Rourke, *Secrecy and Publicity*, pp. 188–89.

20. *The Budget of the United States (Fiscal Year 1971)* (Washington, D.C.: Government Printing Office, 1970), appendix, pp. 213, 274, 641.

21. Rourke, *Secrecy and Publicity*, pp. 209–21.

22. Benjamin Floyd Pittenger, *Indoctrination for American Democracy* (New York: Macmillan, 1941), p. 1.

23. Michael B. Katz, *The Irony of Early School Reform* (Cambridge, Mass.: Harvard University Press, 1968), p. 92. See also David K. Cohen and Marvin Lazerson, "Education and the Corporate Order," *Socialist Revolution* 2 (March–April 1972): 47–72, and Colin Greer, *The Great School Legend* (New York: Basic Books, 1972).

24. See Merle Curti, *The Social Ideas of American Educators* (Paterson, N.J.: Littlefield, Adams, 1961), pp. 101–68.

25. National Education Association, Educational Policies Committee, *Policies for Education in American Democracy* (Washington, D.C.: National Education Association, 1946), p. 251.

26. This law is reprinted in Annette Zelman, *Teaching "About Communism" in American Public Schools* (New York: Humanities Press, 1965), p. 43.

27. The laws and rules of every state in the United States on this subject are summarized in ibid.

28. American Bar Association, Special Committee on Education in the Contrast Between Liberty Under Law and Communism, National Education Association, Educational Policies Committee and the American Association of School Administrators, *American Education and International Tensions* (Washington, D.C.: National Education Association, 1949). The resolutions of the other groups mentioned are reprinted in Zelman, and in a guide book to teachers on how to deal with the "Communist problem." See Richard I. Miller, *Teaching About Communism* (New York: McGraw-Hill, 1966), pp. 276–92.

29. American Federation of Teachers, Commission on Educational Reconstruction, "Teachers and Communism." Reprinted in *American Teacher* 33 (December 1948): 3.

30. The most important of these calls are James B. Conant's works, especially *The American High School Today* (New York: McGraw-Hill, 1959). Also important is John W. Gardner, *Excellence* (New York: Harper, 1961). The Carnegie Commission's study of higher education, directed by Clark Kerr, gives an idea of ruling-class concern with what is to be done with the universities. For a critique, see Alan Wolfe, "Reform Without Reform," *Social Policy* 2 (May–June 1971): 18–27. The best recent ruling-class approach to reform is Charles Silberman, *Crisis in the Classroom* (New York: Vintage Books, 1971).

31. These figures are mentioned in James D. Koerner, *Who Controls American Education?* (Boston: Beacon Press, 1968), pp. 5, 10.

32. Among the many books are Edgar Z. Friedenberg, *Coming of Age in America* (New York: Random House, 1965); David Rogers, *110 Livingston Street* (New York: Random House, 1968); Paul Goodman, *Compulsory Miseducation* (New York: Horizon, 1964); John Holt, *How Children Fail* (New York: Pitman, 1964); Herbert Kohl, *Thirty-six Children* (New York: New American Library, 1967); Jonathan Kozol, *Death at an Early Age* (Boston: Houghton Mifflin, 1967); and Beatrice and Ronald Gross, *Radical School Reform* (New York: Simon & Schuster, 1970).

33. Paul Lauter and Florence Howe, "How the School System is Rigged for Failure," *New York Review of Books* 14 (18 June 1970): 14–21.

34. Thus, for example, the *Wall Street Journal* wrote a stinging editorial, outraged at the inanity of a television commercial for Winston cigarettes, the one which asks whether you want good grammar or good taste. The *Journal* points out that you could have both (or neither). See the *Wall Street Journal*, 6 July 1970, p. 8.

35. This is the message of Carl I. Howland, Irving L. Janis, and Harold H. Kelley, *Communication and Persuasion* (New Haven: Yale University Press, 1953).

36. David Fellman, *The Constitutional Right of Association* (Chicago: University of Chicago Press, 1963), p. 104.

37. See the themes which run through Sigmund Neumann, *Permanent Revolution* (New York: Praeger, 1965).

38. Roberto Michels, *Political Parties* (Glencoe, Ill.: Free Press, 1949).

39. The whole story of the anti-Communist purge is not yet known, but there is an excellent treatment of what is known in Radosh, *American Labor*, pp. 435–40.

40. See Rodney Stark and Charles Y. Glock, *American Piety: The Nature of Religious Commitment* (Berkeley and Los Angeles: University of California Press, 1968), p. 28.

41. Samuel Stouffer, *Communism, Conformity and Civil Liberties* (Garden City, N.Y.: Doubleday, 1955), p. 205.

42. Lloyd A. Free and Hadley Cantril, *The Political Beliefs of Americans* (New Brunswick, N.J.: Rutgers University Press, 1967), pp. 216–35.

43. Herbert M. Hyman, *Political Socialization* (New York: Free Press, 1959), p. 72.

44. For example, see Richard Flacks, "The Liberated Generation: Roots of Student Protest," *Journal of Social Issues* 23 (July 1967): 52–75.

45. See the host of studies cited and summarized in Hyman, *Political Socialization*, pp. 70–71.

46. M. Kent Jennings and Richard G. Niemi, "The Transmission of Political Values From Parent to Child," *American Political Science Review* 62 (March 1968): 169–70, and the literature cited therein.

47. Robert D. Hess and Judith V. Torney, *The Development of Basic Attitudes and Values Toward Government and Citizenship During the Ele-*

mentary School Years, Part I (Cooperative Research Project No. 1078, U.S. Office of Education, 1965), pp. 192, 200. Cited in ibid.

48. This paragraph is based on Mirra Komarovsky, *Blue Collar Marriage* (New York: Vintage Books, 1967), pp. 186, 233, 236.

49. At least since 1884. See Frederick Engels, *The Origins of the Family, Private Property and the State* (New York: International Publishers, 1942).

50. There is evidence for this view in Philippe Aries, *Centuries of Childhood* (New York: Vintage Books, 1965).

51. Hans Magnus Enzensberger, "Constituents of a Theory of the Media," *New Left Review* 64 (November–December 1970): 16.

52. For a longer discussion of these issues, see Alan Wolfe, *The Limits of Legitmacy* (New York: Free Press, 1977).

SEVEN: EXPORTING REPRESSION

1. Andre Gunder Frank, *Capitalism and Underdevelopment in Latin America* (New York: Monthly Review Press, 1969).

2. See Graham Adams, Jr., *The Age of Industrial Violence* (New York: Columbia University Press, 1966), pp. 146–75.

3. U.S. Congress, *Report of the Committee on Foreign Relations,* 80th Cong. 2nd sess., Report No. 855, part 2, Appendix, pp. 199–210. Cited in Robert T. Holt and Robert W. van de Velde, *Strategic Psychological Operations and American Foreign Policy* (Chicago: University of Chicago Press, 1960), p. 169. The following paragraphs are based on this account.

4. Thus, Holt and van de Velde, defenders of the American activities in Italy, admit that the Soviet Union played no significant role in these events, but they attribute this to a strategic desire to appear uninvolved. See ibid., pp. 200–1.

5. See 22, *U.S. Code Annotated,* par. 1431, p. 5.

6. One of the bureaucrats attacked by McCarthy—the assistant to IIA's director Robert L. Johnson—has written an account of the last two days before the creation of USIS. See Martin Merson, *The Private Diary of a Public Servant* (New York: Macmillan, 1955).

7. The composition of the committee is discussed in Oren Stephens, *Facts to a Candid World* (Stanford: Stanford University Press, 1955), p. 42.

8. Ronald I. Rubin, *The Objectives of the U.S. Information Agency* (New York: Praeger, 1968), p. 51; USIA, *Thirty-second Semi-Annual Report to Congress* (January–June 1969), p. 14.

9. See Stephens, *Facts to a Candid World,* and Wilson P. Dizard, *The Strategy of Truth: The Story of the U.S. Information Service* (Washington, D.C.: Public Affairs Press, 1961).

10. Dizard, *Strategy of Truth,* pp. 191–92.

11. Murray Dyer, *The Weapon on the Wall: Rethinking Psychological Warfare* (Baltimore: Johns Hopkins University Press, 1959), p. 166.

12. Figures are from Dizard, *Strategy of Truth,* pp. 88–90.

13. Quoted in ibid., p. 92. The film magnate cited is Herman Cohen.

14. Dizard, *Strategy of Truth,* p. 93.

15. Ibid., p. 96.

16. David McClelland, *The Achieving Society* (Princeton, N.J.: Van Nostrand, 1961).

17. Dizard, *Strategy of Truth,* p. 192.

18. Ibid., p. 97.

19. Harry J. Skornia, *Television and Society* (New York: McGraw-Hill, 1965), pp. 184–85.

20. For the full story of one of these "pirate" ship invasions and the effect it had on the politics of another country, see H. H. Wilson, *Pressure Group: The Campaign for Commercial Television* (London: Secker & Warburg, 1961).

21. Oscar Lewis, *Five Families* (New York: Basic Books, 1959), p. 8.

22. Skornia, *Television and Society,* p. 187.

23. Columbia Broadcasting Company, *Annual Report,* 1966, pp. 2, 19. *NEC Year-End Report,* 1965, p. 28. Cited in Herbert I. Schiller, *Mass Communications and American Empire* (New York: Augustus M. Kelley, 1969). This book is the most comprehensive survey to date of the international relations of American communications corporations.

24. For an account of these transformations, see Jerry Turnstall, *The Media Are American* (New York: Columbia University Press, 1977).

25. See Schiller, *Mass Communications,* pp. 115–19.

26. Skornia, *Television and Society,* p. 109.

27. *Wall Street Journal,* 15 March 1966. Cited in Schiller, *Mass Communications,* p. 74.

28. On COMSAT, see James Weeks, "Comsat: The Technology for Ruling Global Communications," in *An End to Political Science,* ed. Marvin Surkin and Alan Wolfe (New York: Basic Books, 1970), pp. 215–40. Also relevant in Schiller, *Mass Communications,* pp. 70–78.

29. G. William Domhoff, *Who Rules America?* (Englewood Cliffs, N.J.: Prentice-Hall, 1967), pp. 64–71.

30. For a list of the directors of the Ford Foundation, see any of its publications, particularly its Annual Report. At the time this was written, the newspaper publishers were Mark Ethridge and John Cowles; the *Time* executive, Roy Larson; the college presidents, Lawrence M. Gould (Carleton) and Julius A. Stratton (M.I.T.).

31. In response to a congressional charge that the leading foundations were characterized by interlocking directors, the then President of the Rockefeller Foundation Dean Rusk (himself to become involved in repression through a wide range of different institutions) admitted that "Some of our trustees also serve as trustees of other institutions and organizations, including other foundations." However, Rusk noted, "the principal occasions for consultation among Foundations . . . arise from the desire on the part of each to use its funds to the best advantage." This is exactly the point. See *Statement of the Rockefeller Foundation and the General Education Board, Before the*

Special Committee to Investigate Tax Exempt Foundations (House of Representatives, 83rd Cong.), pp. 68–69.

32. Ford Foundation, "The Ford Foundation in the 1960's" (Statement of the Board of Trustees on Policies, Programs, and Operations, July 1962), p. 2.

33. Since the testimony of Dean Rusk quoted above was delivered near the end of the McCathy period, it is particularly revealing about political bias. Rusk tries hard to show—convincingly—that his foundation is strongly anti-Communist and only supports "those patriotic institutions which recognize their obligation to serve the public interest." "Ford Foundation in the 1960s," p. 41.

34. See the pamphlet, "The Ford Foundation and Foundation Supported Activities in India" (January 1955), p. 9.

35. Ibid., pp. 28–94. This is a selected list.

36. This paragraph is based on Ford Foundation pamphlets, "The Ford Foundation and Pakistan" (1959) and "Design for Pakistan" (February 1965). For a discussion on the rationale behind the project, see David Bell, "Allocating Development Resources: Some Observations Based on Pakistan Experience," *Public Policy* 9 (1959).

37. John McDermott, "Knowledge is Power," *The Nation* 208 (April 14, 1969): 458–62.

38. "Design for Pakistan," p. 34.

39. Rockefeller Foundation, Quarterly Report No. 4 (1969), pp. 47–52. For the official history of the Rockefeller Foundation, which contains some interesting information if one can read through the obsequious prose, see Raymond B. Fosdick, *The Story of the Rockefeller Foundation* (New York: Harper, 1952).

40. David Horowitz, "Social Science or Ideology," *Berkeley Journal of Sociology* 15 (1970): 6.

41. Idem.

42. Thus, Domhoff inadvertently points out that these minor foundations have fewer ruling-class connections. (He was trying to prove the opposite.) See *Who Rules America?*, pp. 70–71.

43. The institute mentioned is the Institute of Hispanic-American Studies at Stanford University. For the story of its demise and for an informative treatment of all the research institutes of the post-war period, see David Horowitz, "Billion Dollar Brains," *Ramparts* (July 1969).

44. For material on the international activities of American business corporations, see some of the trade publications: *Far Eastern Economic Review, Southern Africa Financial Mail, Business Latin America, Oil and Gas Journal,* etc. Books from a critical perspective include Robert Engler, *The Politics of Oil* (Chicago: University of Chicago Press, 1961); Michael Tanzer, *The Political Economy of International Oil and the Underdeveloped Countries* (Boston: Beacon Press, 1968) and David Horowitz, ed., *Corporations and the Cold War* (New York: Monthly Review Press, 1969).

45. Quoted in Richard J. Barber, *The American Corporation* (New York: Dutton, 1970), p. 265.

46. See Hans Morgenthau, *Politics Among Nations* (New York: Knopf, 1962), p. 278 and the literature cited there.

47. William Appleman Williams, *The Tragedy of American Diplomacy* (New York: Delta Books, 1962), p. 95.

48. Dean Acheson, *Present at the Creation* (New York: Norton, 1969), p. 405. Emphasis added.

49. The fullest story is in Ronald Radosh, *American Labor and United States Foreign Policy* (New York: Vintage Books, 1970); and George Morris, *The CIA and American Labor* (New York: International Publishers, 1967).

50. Harry Howe Ransom, *Central Intelligence and National Security* (Cambridge, Mass.: Harvard University Press, 1958), p. 78.

51. Harry Howe Ransom, *Can American Democracy Survive Cold War?* (Garden City, N.Y.: Doubleday, 1963), p. 141.

52. Ibid., pp. 142–43.

53. See especially David Wise and Thomas B. Ross, *The Invisible Government* (New York: Random House, 1964), pp. 165–83, 9–73; and David Horowitz, *The Free World Colossus* (New York: Hill & Wang, 1967).

54. Roger Hilsman, *To Move a Nation* (New York: Delta Books, 1967), pp. 63–64. Hilsman does go on to account for the CIA's influence by mentioning such things as people, money, information, and secrecy. Yet nowhere, of course, does he talk about the relationship between the CIA and the corporate structure.

55. Ibid., p. 85.

56. For the role of those gentlemen in intelligence activities, see Wise and Ross, *Invisible Government*, pp. 114–17 and 238.

57. An authoritative list of all the times American troops have been used abroad is contained in the *Congressional Record*, vol. 115 part 3 (23 June 1969), pp. 16840–43, 91st Cong., 1st sess. This account is relied on substantially in the following paragraphs. It is interesting to note that this material was placed in the *Record* by Senator Dirksen (R-Ill.), who was obviously trying to prove that Vietnam was nothing new. He was obviously correct.

58. For a good account, see Walter Lafeber, *The New Empire* (Ithaca: Cornell University Press, 1963).

59. W. W. Rostow, "Guerrilla Warfare in Underdeveloped Areas," in *The Vietnam Reader*, eds. Marcus G. Raskin and Bernard B. Fall (New York: Vintage Books, 1967), pp. 108–16.

60. Ibid., p. 116.

61. Robert Scheer and Warren Hinckle, "The Vietnam Lobby," in ibid., pp. 66–81.

62. Quoted in Joe Stork, "World Cop," *Hard Times* 85 (10–17 August 1970): 1.

63. Quoted in ibid., p. 2.

64. Ibid., p. 2.

65. Ibid., p. 3.

66. As compiled by the secretary of state to the U.S. Senate Committee on Armed Services, *World Wide Military Commitments* (Hearings before the Preparedness Investigating Subcommittee of the Committee on Armed Services, U.S. Senate, 89th Cong., 2nd sess.), 25 and 30 August 1966, part 1, pp. 31–32. Cited in Harry Magdoff, *The Age of Imperialism* (New York: Monthly Review Press, 1969), pp. 206–7.

67. Townsend Hoopes, *The Limits of Intervention* (New York: David McKay, 1969), p. 149.

EIGHT: REPRESSION AND THE LIBERAL STATE

1. Quoted in Milton R. Konvitz, *Expanding Liberties* (New York: Viking, 1967), p. xiii.

2. Ibid.

3. Tom Hayden, *Trial* (New York: Holt, Rinehart and Winston, 1970), pp. 4, 9.

4. See Norman Pollock, *The Populist Response to Industrial America* (Cambridge, Mass.: Harvard University Press, 1962) for the argument that the Populist Party was socialist.

5. The first state "constable" was created in 1865 in Massachusetts for the purpose of helping the governor enforce the laws. But most police historians recognize the 1905 state police force of Pennsylvania as the first modern state police agency. Its chief purpose was to maintain the peace and to protect lives and property. So successful was the force in proving how state governments could do this kind of work for the corporations that the idea rapidly spread after 1905. For a somewhat incomplete background, see Bruce Smith, *The State Police* (Montclair, N.J.: Patterson Smith Publishing Company, for the National Institution of Public Administration, 1969), pp. 37–39.

6. Pullman felt that his town would stimulate his workers to hold the "right" values, thereby making them accept the legitimacy of his power, a classic case of ideological repression. See Stanley Buder, *Pullman: An Experiment of Industrial Order and Community Planning, 1880–1930* (New York: Oxford University Press, 1967), pp. 28–45.

7. Melvyn Dubofsky, *We Shall Be All* (Chicago: Quadrangle Books, 1969), p. 916.

8. For an example of Creel's thinking, see his *How We Advertised America* (New York: Harper, 1920).

9. John P. Diggins, "Flirtation with Fascism: American Pragmatic Liberals and Mussolini's Italy," *American Historical Review* 71 (January 1966): 487–506, and *Mussolini and Fascism* (Princeton: Princeton University Press, 1972).

10. James Weinstein, *The Corporate Ideal in the Liberal State* (Boston: Beacon Press, 1968).

11. Christopher Lasch, *The Agony of the American Left* (New York: Vintage Books, 1969), p. 35; James Weinstein, *The Decline of American Socialism* (New York: Monthly Review Press, 1967).

12. Dubofsky, *We Shall Be All.*

13. See Theodore Draper, *The Roots of American Communism* (New York: Viking, 1957); and Robert K. Murray, *Red Scare* (Minneapolis: University of Minnesota Press, 1955).

14. On Hoover's appointment (from a favorable point of view), see Don Whitehead, *The F.B.I. Story* (New York: Random House, 1956).

15. William Preston, Jr., *Aliens and Dissenters* (New York: Harper Torchbooks, 1966), p. 83.

16. Murray, *Red Scare.*

17. On the use of the Selective Service Act as a political weapon, plus material on the Debs case, see H. C. Peterson and Gilbert C. Fite, *Opponents of War, 1917–18* (Seattle: University of Washington Press, 1968).

18. William M. Tuttle, Jr., *Race Riot* (New York: Atheneum, 1970); Arthur Waskow, *From Race to Riot to Sit-In* (Garden City, N.Y.: Doubleday Anchor, 1967).

19. William Appleman Williams, *American-Russian Relations, 1781–1947* (New York: Rinehart, 1952).

20. The story is contained in Draper, *Roots of American Communism,* pp. 366–75.

21. Ronald Radosh, *American Labor and United States Foreign Policy* (New York: Vintage Books, 1970).

22. Martha Derthick, *The National Guard in Politics* (Cambridge, Mass.: Harvard University Press, 1965).

23. Schneck v. U.S., 249 U.S. 47 (1919).

24. See Dubofsky, *We Shall Be All.*

25. Richard Harris, *Justice* (New York: Dutton, 1969).

26. See Jessica Mitford, *The Trial of Dr. Spock* (New York: Vintage Books, 1970).

27. This point has been brilliantly made by Gary Wills, *Nixon Agonistes* (New York: New American Library, 1971), pp. 308–27.

28. Quoted in Alan Dershowitz, " 'Stretch Points' of Liberty," *The Nation* 212 (15 March 1971): 329.

29. Hayden, *Trial,* p. 11.

30. Herbert Marcuse, "The Struggle Against Liberalism in the Totalitarian View of the State," in *Negations* (Boston: Beacon Press, 1968), pp. 3–42.

31. Ibid., pp. 9, 19.

32. On the importance of the lack of a liberal theory in Germany, see Franz Neumann, *Behemoth* (New York: Harper Torchbooks, 1966), p. 4.

33. Göran Therborn, "A critique of the Frankfurt School," *New Left Review* 63 (September–October 1970): 65–96.

34. Sinclair Lewis, *It Can't Happen Here* (New York: Collier, 1935); Arthur Schlesinger, Jr., *The Politics of Upheaval* (Boston: Houghton Mifflin, 1957).

35. For an effective critique of this notion, see Philip Green, "Can It

Happen Here? Is It Already Happening?," *New York Times Magazine,* 20 September 1970, pp. 30 ff.

36. Bertram Gross, "Friendly Fascism: A Model for America," *Social Policy* 1 (November–December 1970): 44–53.

37. Thirteenth Plenary Session of the Executive Committee of the Communist International, December 1932, cited in Ernst Nolte, *Three Faces of Fascism* (New York: Holt, Rinehart and Winston, 1966), p. 465.

38. The conservative approach to fascism is best contained in Hannah Arendt, *The Origins of Totalitarianism* (Cleveland: Meridian Books, 1958); and J. L. Talmon, *The Origins of Totalitarian Democracy* (New York: Praeger, 1961).

39. See J. Salwyn Shapiro, *Liberalism and the Challenge of Fascism* (New York: McGraw-Hill, 1949).

40. Nolte, *Three Faces of Fascism,* p. 21.

41. Dante L. Germino, *The Italian Fascist Party in Power* (Minneapolis: University of Minnesota Press, 1959), p. 9.

42. Arendt, *Origins of Totalitarianism.*

43. Neumann, *Behemoth.* The best alternative argument is offered in David Schoenbaum, *Hitler's Social Revolution* (Garden City, N.Y.: Doubleday, 1966).

44. As quoted in Carl Cohen, *Communism, Fascism, and Democracy* (New York: Random House, 1962), p. 332.

45. Neumann, *Behemoth,* p. 462.

46. See Diggins, "Flirtation with Fascism."

47. For a discussion of the relationship between romanticism and political conservatism, see Judith Shklar, *After Utopia* (Princeton: Princeton University Press, 1969), pp. 26–64.

48. The concept of a police state is defined conceptually and historically by Brian Chapman, *Police State* (London: Pall Mall Press, 1970).

49. See, for example, Stanley Aronowitz, "Law, the Breakdown of Order, and Revolution," in *Law Against the People,* ed. Robert Lefcourt (New York: Random House, 1971), pp. 150–82.

50. Quoted in Georg Lukacs, *History and Class Consciousness* (London: Merlin, 1971), p. 96. This quotation was also cited in another work which was helpful in formulating the material in this section, the forthcoming book by Isaac Balbus on the American system of criminal justice, *The Dialectics of Legal Repression* (New York: Russell Sage Foundation, 1973).

51. Andrew Hacker, "Liberal Democracy and Social Control," *American Political Science Review* (December 1957): 1013–14.

52. Ibid., p. 1010.

NINE: BUILDING A NONREPRESSIVE SOCIETY

1. C. B. MacPherson, *The Real World of Democracy* (London: Oxford University Press, 1966), pp. 10–11.

2. Quoted in Gary Wills, *Nixon Agonistes* (New York: New American Library, 1971), p. 318.

3. This idea is explicit in one of the more provocative attempts to deal with the origins of a nonrepressive society, Andre Gorz, *Strategy for Labor* (Boston: Beacon Press, 1967).

4. For one example, see Barry Commoner, *The Poverty of Progress* (New York: Knopf, 1976).

5. See Andre Gorz and Herbert Marcuse, *An Essay on Liberation* (Boston: Beacon Press, 1969).

index